THE FRONTIER OF LOYALTY

OTHER BOOKS BY YOSSI SHAIN

Kinship and Diasporas in International Relations

Marketing the American Creed Abroad: Diasporas in the U.S. and Their Homelands

Between States: Interim Governments and Democratic Transitions (with Juan J. Linz)

Democracy: The Challenges Ahead (edited with Aharon Klieman)

Governments-in-Exile in Contemporary World Politics

PRAISE FOR *The Frontier of Loyalty*

"Its strength lies in the range of examples drawn from history and contemporary politics and in its attempt to be analytical as well as descriptive. The cases of Juan Perón, Ayatollah Khomeini, the African National Congress, the Dalai Lama, and East European exiles now returning to their native countries all point to the crucial interaction between exiles and political regimes. . . . the narrative is engrossing, and the subject neglected in the field of international relations."

—JAMES G. KELLAS, University of Glasgow, in *International Affairs*

THE FRONTIER
OF LOYALTY

Political Exiles in the Age
of the Nation-State

YOSSI SHAIN

With a New Preface

 THE UNIVERSITY OF MICHIGAN PRESS
Ann Arbor

Copyright © 1989, 2005 by Yossi Shain
Published by the University of Michigan Press 2005
First published by Wesleyan University Press 1989
All rights reserved
Published in the United States of America by
The University of Michigan Press
Printed and bound by CPI Group (UK) Ltd, Croydon, CR0 4YY

2008   2007   2006   2005   4   3   2   1

ISBN 0-472-03042-6
Library of Congress Cataloging-in-Publication Data applied for

The introduction appeared originally, in somewhat different form,
in *International Migration* 25, no. 4 (December 1988).

ISBN13 978-0-472-02612-8 (electronic)

To My Parents,
Hannah and David Shain

Contents

Acknowledgments xi
Preface to the Reprint Edition xiii

INTRODUCTION 1
The Political Exile and the Evolution of National Loyalty 1
Who Is an Exile? 7
The Political Exile as a Political Activist 13

CHAPTER ONE: *Who Represents the Nation's Will?* 18
Loyalty and Disloyalty in the Nation-State 20
Political Exiles: National Loyalists or Traitors? 23

CHAPTER TWO: *Exile Organizations: Competing Claims to Represent the National Interest from Abroad* 27
Governmental and Nongovernmental Claims 27
The Role of Origin 30
The Validation of Claims to Power 31
The Hope of Return and International Recognition 33

CHAPTER THREE: *The Politics of Schism* 38
Autonomy and Identity 39
Exile Coalitions 41
Ideological Purity 43
The Insider-Outsider Dilemma 45
Foreign Intervention 46

CHAPTER FOUR: *Political Exiles and the Diaspora* 50
National Diaspora 51

The Incentives for Mobilization   56
The Case of the Russian Diaspora   62
The Case of the Spanish Republicans   70

CHAPTER FIVE: Political Exiles and the
    Domestic Opposition   77

Pre-exile Organizations and Loyalty at Home   77
The Internal-External Legitimacy Nexus   79
Exiles and Hegemonic Home Regimes   83
Mixed Regime or Pluralistic Hegemony   86
Collaboration with the Opposition or Infiltration   88
Exile-Insider Relations over Time   92
Italian Exiles Who Failed to Reach the Promised Land   94
Pragmatism in Exile Politics   97

CHAPTER SIX: Recognition in the International
    Community   110

Patterns of International Recognition   110
Governments-in-Exile   113
National Exile Committees   116
Rationales for Support by Other Nations   118
Relations with the Host State   119
Exile Diplomacy: the Politics of Image   124
International Organizations and the Global Mythology   127

CHAPTER SEVEN: My Country Right or Wrong:
    The Exile War Trap   130

The Government's Defeat Is the Nation's Victory   134
In Defense of a Home People, Not a Home Regime   139

CHAPTER EIGHT: Counterexile Strategies by
    the Home Regime   145

Denationalization and Statelessness   147
Divisions and Splinters within Exile Organizations   153
Diplomatic Pressures on the Host Government   155

Assassinations and Kidnappings of Key Leaders 157
Likelihood of the Use of Antiexile Measures 161

CONCLUSION 163

The Moving Frontier of National Loyalty 163

Notes 169
Index 201

Acknowledgments

This book originated as a doctoral dissertation at Yale University. I wish to thank teachers, colleagues, and friends who supported my efforts from beginning to end. My greatest debt is to Juan Linz, who generously granted his time and shared his ideas from the moment the subject was conceived. As teacher and mentor Linz sharpened my analytical instincts, broadened my historical perspective, and helped me overcome my initial hesitations. Juan and Rocío Linz graciously opened their home to me and showed me what it means for a teacher to be responsible for a student.

I have benefited immeasurably from Joseph Hamburger's deep knowledge of philosophy and history and have grown personally because of his ability to recognize and address his students' most subtle emotions.

I am also grateful to Yale professors Robert Dahl, Leon Lipson, David Mayhew, Rogers Smith, and Steven Smith, who made significant contributions to the shaping of my thought.

Garth Lepere spent many long hours helping me to clarify conceptual and stylistic problems. With him I experienced the deep connection between friendship and intellectual discovery.

My friends Rebecca Kook and Gideon Doron shared with me their profound insight into the question of legitimacy.

Rabbi James and Elana Ponet, David Weiner, and Joyce Romanow, all inspiring soulmates, have been for me a second family from the day I first arrived in New Haven.

Richard Bardenstein, Peter Berkowitz, Dana Green, and Adam Vital suffered the agonies of my linguistic handicaps and led me to whatever literary grace I have achieved.

Hubert O'Gorman played an integral part in bringing the manuscript to the attention of Wesleyan University Press. Jeannette Hopkins, director of the Wesleyan Press, magically conducted the transformation of a doctoral dissertation into a book. Her sharp mind, professionalism, and spirited commitment contributed immensely to the evolution of this work. My thanks also go to the staff of the Wesleyan Press, Peter J. Potter, Margaret Klumpp, and Eliza Childs, for their continued support. Matthew Allen typed the manuscript with great skill.

With the completion of this book, I find myself not only intellectually enriched, but personally transformed. For in the last few years I not only met teachers, colleagues, and friends, but I found my life companion, Nancy.

Preface

The Frontiers of Loyalty: Do They Really Change?

In December 1914, Tomaš Masaryk, the future first president of Czechoslovakia, departed Austria-Hungary for Switzerland, convinced that Czech self-determination under the Habsburgs' rule was impossible. First from England and then from the United States, Masaryk agitated for Czechoslovakia's independence while forming ties with Czech and Slovak communities in the United States that forcefully lobbied the White House and Congress for national liberation. Masaryk seized upon the American entry into World War I to persuade his friend Woodrow Wilson to award his people an independent, democratic state. Czechoslovakia, in many ways, was the creation of exiles and diaspora members who signed the famous Pittsburgh Agreement of May 1918 as the founding document of their country. Historian Aviel Roshwald wrote that Masaryk is "the most striking example of how war-time exile in the Allied countries could propel a hitherto respected but relatively powerless figure into the seat of power" in his homeland.[1]

Almost a century later, even though Iraq's territorial integrity and the right of its people to govern themselves are taken for granted today, the future role of Iraqi exiles and diaspora members in the post–Saddam Hussein era must withstand a withering test of loyalty among Iraqis and Arabs, many of whom charge Americans with harboring imperial intentions. In the debate over who ought to speak on behalf of the Iraqi people and who ought to govern post-Saddam Iraq, returning expatriates hope to be at the forefront of nation building. Yet with the pervasive instability in the aftermath of Saddam's fall, shifting domestic alliances, clashes between sectarian groups, and rivalries among contenders to power, both insiders and outsiders have demanded a revision of thinking and repositioning of both the returnees and their American patrons. Thus as we contemplate the future of Iraq and the prospects of democracy in the Middle East, we must wonder whether returned Iraqi exiles, like Prime Minister Iyyad Allawi, President Ghazi al-Yawir, and Ahmad Chalabi (who served as head of the American-backed Iraqi National Congress [INC] in exile), are harbingers of newfound political orientations that may help salvage their people and state.

Indeed, throughout history, political exiles have challenged traditional boundaries of authority and loyalty. As external opponents to the regimes of their native homelands, political exiles have always served as ready instruments for host governments wishing to intervene in the affairs of their enemies. Because of the difficulty of their situation, having to depict their struggle from abroad to unseat a native home regime as a patriotic mission, political exiles tend to test the limits of and reshape concepts such as loyalty, obligation, and "the national interest."

The Frontier of Loyalty was written during 1986–88 and was first published in April 1989, shortly before the world order dramatically turned a corner. The book probed the subject of exile political activism in an attempt to move away from and expand upon the dominant tendency of political scientists at the time to endorse a rigid demarcation between national and international politics. It identified two main concerns that affect all exile political activists and shape their behavior: "national loyalty" and "recognition." "National loyalty" refers to more than just the behavioral or verbal expression of allegiance. Who is a national loyalist is a critical question political exiles always confront when defining varieties of "loyal" behavior to the nation. Moreover, the fact that even the most repressive regimes enjoy the advantages of defining group membership and national identity and have at their disposal the material and symbolic resources of their state with which they can reward their "loyalists" or punish their detractors (including those residing abroad) highlights the ongoing challenges of exiles to assert their political legitimacy and extract support from kin in the diaspora and conationals in the homeland.

The term "recognition" was intended to highlight the international dimension of exile political activism. The book argued that the embrace of sovereignty as the primary constitutive rule of international relations gives advantages to those who dominate nation-states in translating their de facto control into de jure acceptance in the international arena, as well as revealing how vulnerable exiled opponents are to the vagaries of the international system. Yet, the book also demonstrated the limitations of coercive regimes in facing external opponents who operate in the relatively free environment of democratic host states with much better forms of communication and international recognition.

Of course, both the international system and the scholarly literature have evolved substantially since the original publication of *The Frontier of Loyalty,* with much greater emphasis on globalization, transnational influences, and the myriad of links between diasporas and homelands. By the beginning of the 1990s, the argument that nationalism was the sole surviving claimant on primary loyalties had begun to erode. With the end of the Cold War, as economic and cultural factors seemed to escape the mastery of the state and the realm of politics, many rushed to question the durability of the nation-state as the supreme contender for loyalty and belonging. Adam Smith's famous dictum that "the proprietor of stock is properly a citizen of the world and is not necessarily attached to any particular country" seemed to govern the new world order in which markets overwhelmed national boundaries.[2] With the structural shifts in the global economy, the digital revolution, the decline of ideologies, and the perceived triumph of democratic governments worldwide, there was a sense that exile politics as a distinctive arena of activity was also becoming out of date. Indeed, "political activity in exile and democracy can be regarded as opposites canceling each other,"[3] and in the 1990s political exiles were some of the most prominent harbingers of regime change. Moreover, while nationalism and exiles can be seen as "opposites informing and constituting each other,"[4] a world without homelands almost by definition negates exile politics that are predicated on the existence of the wounds of separation and the struggle for return.

Nevertheless, in recent years scholars have begun to realize that the relevance of migrant communities is rising in other ways. With new records of people fleeing their countries to escape violence and persecution, or in search of employment and better lives, a sense of a global migration crisis has triggered real fears and xenophobic reactions about the economic well-being of countries, their cultural national identity, and their political stability.[5] At the same time, consistent with the thesis of a world without homelands, normalized-economic diasporas whose lives transcend national boundaries (rather than political exiles of fixed loyalty and troubled existence) have become celebrated epitomes of "transnationalism": bearers of "multiple identities and citizenship" as well as representatives of a new era of "deterritorialization." Over the 1990s the shift from exile politics to diaspora/ethnic politics became apparent in the international system, reflecting a growing acceptance by liberal democracies (and the United States in particular) of the need to accommodate more diverse polities and to allow a greater voice to ethnic identities even in their foreign policy.

In March 2000, when Marie Jana Korbelova returned to her birth city, Prague, this time as Madeleine Albright, U.S. secretary of state, Czech president Václav Havel declared, "I would personally consider it excellent [if Madeleine Albright could succeed me as president of the Czech Republic] because into this rather staid provincial environment this would bring an international spirit, someone who knows the world well, understands it, and would be able to act." In the Czech Republic, the president must be a Czech citizen over forty years of age. Albright, a naturalized U.S. citizen, qualifies for Czech citizenship under the law that enables those who fled the communist regime after 1948 to reclaim citizenship. Albright smiled and said, "I am not a candidate and will not be a candidate. . . . My heart is in two places, and America is where I belong."

Havel's extraordinary invitation was just one sign of a changing configuration of national and ethnic loyalties and of the broadening vision that transnational allegiance to both an ancestral homeland and to the United States could exist without conflict. To be sure, liberal democracies now recognize the fact that people may remain dedicated emotionally and politically to the life and well-being of their kin communities in other parts of the world and retain lasting ties to ancestral homelands. Such affinities largely are interpreted as part of the global hybridism of culture and the economy and no longer inflame nativist fears and charges of dual loyalty. Certainly, in the United States, old fears—that Americans with emotional ties to their ancestral homelands cannot be fully loyal to the United States—are declining though not entirely disappearing, as Samuel Huntington exhibits in his controversial book *Who Are We? The Challenges to America's National Identity*, regarding the alleged inability or unwillingness of Latinos in America to assimilate. Huntington, like Morris Janowitz before him, has depicted Mexican-Americans as colonizers who are resisting acculturation inside the United States, undermining America's Anglo-Saxon heritage and plotting irredentism that ultimately may result in "the demographic *reconquista* of area Americans took from Mexico by force in the 1830s and 1840s." In reality, people once disparagingly called "hyphenated Americans" feel increasingly free to organize and lobby on behalf of the "old country" as long as they embrace their homeland in a way that is not threatening to their identity within the parameters of American pluralism. Within America's foreign policy establishment, one finds increasing acceptance of the legitimacy of ethnic lobbies and full participation by ethnically identifiable players such as Armenians, blacks, Greeks, Indians, Jews, and Cuban Americans, who no longer are regarded chiefly as political exiles awaiting return. Moreover, until most recently many countries felt threatened by citizens with allegiances to multiple countries, and withdrawal of citizenship was commonly adopted around the globe as a weapon against political exiles and even nonpolitical expatriates as a way of undermining the foundation of their national identity. Today, more and more countries extend dual nationalities and even voting rights to their kin abroad in the hope of fostering homeland loyalties from afar and harnessing financial and political support from their organized diasporas. The aversion to dual citizenship is undoubtedly in sharp decline.[6]

After Mohammad Khatami and other reformist politicians won elections in Teheran and as Iranian radicalism was said to be waning, Iranian American Negar Akhvi wrote that twenty years after the revolution that brought Ayatollah Ruhollah Khomeini to power the younger generation of Iranians in the United States are no longer affected by "the fatigue and the stress that enveloped the [exile] generation that fled Iran" and can now see themselves as "American enough" to organize as an ethnic American lobby, yet "Iranian enough to care about what happens in our homeland."[7] On the whole, by the year 2000 the signs of a more flexible world of multiple loyalties were evident in many countries, including those with an ethnic-based identity, such as Germany, where, for example, usual statistics fail to reflect the subgrouping and political shadings within the largest diaspora group, the Turkish community, numbering 2.5 million. Political preferences of German Turks vis-à-vis the government in Ankara indicate not only a wide diversity that inevitably emerges in a sizable diaspora but also how disparate identities, ideologies, and culture typically curtailed in the homeland political context are searching for free expression in the environment of the liberal state. Hence, numerous Turkish groups have established themselves in Germany, where an anti-Kamalist exile opposition exists side by side with those who enthusiastically support the regime in the homeland and are mobilized by it.[8]

Indeed the mixing of exile politics (i.e., opposition from abroad) with "transnational" economic and political lobbying of "normalized" diasporas (addressed in this book in chapter 4) fluctuates over time, not only in the struggle to unseat nondemocratic regimes, as in the case of Castro's Cuba, but also vis-à-vis countries whose democracies are new or fragile. This phenomenon became particularly evident among the large Latin American communities in the United States, which by nature of culture, proximity, and strong economic clout inside their kin states are deeply involved in the process of consolidating their homelands' new democracies. In the case of El Salvador, for example, former members of the U.S.-based political opposition that in the 1980s supported the indigenous guerilla struggle of the leftist Frente Farabundo Martí para la Liberación Nacional (FMLN) and ultimately helped its leaders to gain international recognition as a legitimate political party in Salvadoran affairs—in conflict with Washington's official policy—have assumed the role of democratic guardians of their former FMLN compatriots. Recently these exiles-turned-diaspora-activists warned the former FMLN guerilla commander, Schafic Handal, who during his campaign as the party's presidential candidate vociferously courted the two-million-strong Salvadoran diaspora in the United States, to break with his revolutionary past and make sure that his policies do not diverge excessively from Washington's own priorities.[9]

Yet in the last few years, we also witness the pathologies of what Jim Hoagland calls "Globalization's Evil Offspring." We see this with political entrepreneurs, like Osama bin Laden, exploiting radical Islamism to recruit alienated migrants to engage in terrorism in a way that transforms traditional exilic struggles associated with the rhetoric and symbols of nationalism into transnational utopian religious movements that ultimately seek to undermine the nation-state and modernity altogether. This new mode of transnationalism is reminiscent of Lenin's exilic internationalism of the early twentieth century—though Lenin was a modernist and a pragmatist who recognized the power of the nationalist sentiment (see chapter 8).[10] At the same time, and perhaps because of the tremendous perils associated with transnational terrorism and crime—that so readily access the resources of globalized networks they have built and activated—there is also renewed appreciation of the nation-state. Even in a truly global age of information, capital, and people flowing freely across national borders, sovereign states and boundaries remain the hallmark of the international order, a point that is now especially clear after the events of September 11 and the ensuing war on terrorism and rogue states. Of course, there are many states that hardly function as sovereign, let alone control their boundaries. Moreover, the demarcation of boundaries on the basis of ethnic or geographic criteria is often arbitrary and completely ineffective "because sovereignty is many times not an innate attribute of state, but something conferred by international society and that is based . . . at least partially on how leaders hope to govern."[11] To a large extent, this has been the historical challenge of Iraq since it was forged by the British—not out of a unitary territory or peoples but out of London's desire to have its Hashemite ally securing its interest by proxy. The establishment of modern Iraq lumped together people with little interest in sharing a state. It immediately created a diaspora of Kurdish, Shii, and Christian communities (Chaldeans)—who were massacred and driven into exile when they demanded recognition and better treatment under the newly independent state. Yet, even though many nation-states are by all accounts failed political entities, the nation-state still remains the desired form for representing the aspirations of people who consider themselves or are declared to be by aspiring rulers a distinct community that ought to govern itself within its "homeland." This reality enables all states (and many aspiring nations) to employ the rhetoric of "national loyalty" as the ultimate tool for mobilizing the sacrifice of their people in defense of the homeland.

What distinguishes political exiles from other diaspora members is not only the exiles' continuous struggle to facilitate the conditions for their return but also their determination not to establish life abroad as a comfortable option, even temporarily. In the words of Judith Shklar,

exiles cannot do what most people do, accept their political obligations and loyalties as simple habits. Displaced and uprooted, they must make decisions about what sort of lives they will lead. As political agents they must at the very least think about these decisions and sort out their various and incompatible political duties and ties.[12]

The intensity with which home regimes externalize their opponents and the extent of their efforts in stigmatizing political exiles as the nation's enemies impact greatly on the vehemence and institutionalization of exile politics (see chapter 3). Yet the pain of being away and the fear of offspring's losing their ancestral identity may lead some political exiles to return even under conditions of surrender. One scholar of post-Tiananmen Chinese exiles observed that those who stayed abroad were forced "to create a mythology about their activities and successes to maintain their credibility. For many of them, any collapse of their identity as political exiles would cast doubt not only upon the value of their present situation but also upon the meaning of the sacrifices made in June 1989 by their fellow dissidents."[13] Even in the case of Iraq, some who fled the country fearing repression or death at Saddam's hand were eventually lured back by false promises of amnesty, forgiveness, and the imminent inauguration of pluralistic politics. Others, because of fatigue or continuous fear of retribution abroad or against relatives at home, abandoned their antiregime agitation over time and melted into an essentially diasporic life.

Certainly the domain of exile political activity provides the focus of identity, purpose, and hope to counter the fear of being forgotten or stigmatized by the home regime, as well as the guilt of being away from the day-to-day suffering of the people for whom the political exiles always claimed to fight. The destination of exiles, far or close to the homeland, and the nature of their host society—its culture and politics—are critical factors in mitigating or exacerbating the separation anxiety and the cost associated with the home regime's charges of national betrayal.

In the Iraqi case, political exiles in the United States and England played a crucial role in discrediting Saddam in the international arena. Over the years, these exile groups demonstrated their usefulness to the American cause by corroborating or possibly exaggerating allegations of Iraq's possession of weapons of mass destruction and Iraq's connection to international terrorism and by providing testimonials to Saddam's flagrant human rights abuses and atrocities. By organizing opposition bodies abroad, they also signaled to the world that Iraq would have a functional alternative once Saddam was deposed. Indeed, how the outgoing regime collapsed and what kind of remnants of incumbent power are left available greatly affect the exiles' role upon returning.

The experience of Iraq shows that in the twenty-first century, despite the advances of globalization and democracy, totalitarian regimes are still capable of insulating themselves from the outside world. Such regimes establish a total monopoly on their societies, controlling information and using brutality to undermine any unauthorized connection to the outside world. In that respect, they elevate the notion of sovereignty to its totality by making it impenetrable. When the Ba'thist regime finally gained power in 1968 (after an unsuccessful coup in 1963), it moved quickly to establish totalitarian rule through show trials, public executions, secret assassination (targeting real and alleged opponents), and the establishment of a pervasive network of secret police and informants. The internal forces that initially challenged the Ba'th drive to hegemony (most of all the Iraqi Communist Party) soon succumbed, and their leaders were executed or fled the country. When in 1979 Saddam consolidated his dictatorial rule, he created a reality in which virtually the only durable opposition was from abroad, by Iraqis who managed to escape the regime or found themselves outside the country. Even abroad, though, exiles did not enjoy complete safety, as Saddam's agents were able to assassinate opposition figures around the globe and intimidate those who went abroad by harassing, arresting, or executing family members who remained behind in Iraq (chapter 8). Sargon Dadesho, an Iraqi exile leader in California's Central Valley who escaped Saddam's hit man in 1990, recently collected $2.4 million from Iraqi frozen assets to compensate for his emotional distress. He now promises to use the money to rebuild Iraq.

The difficulty of identifying indigenous Iraqi leaders who have not been tainted by the Ba'th regime gave these expatriates added value shortly after the regime's collapse, but the downfall of Saddam also imposed serious liabilities upon them. The double-edged dilemma of national loyalty for those who lived abroad during Saddam's reign is a function of realities and perceptions; many of the political exiles may have difficulty earning the "credential" of victimhood required by those who stayed behind. Even worse, they could be perceived to be agents of foreigners who have inflicted great pain not only on the regime but on the people. At the same time, it is clear that indigenous contenders to power are themselves suspect of collaboration and complicity with the ancien régime and thus may lack a valid claim to power.

For years, fidelity to the dictator was a matter of life and death for the Iraqi people as fear and expediency drove many of Saddam's loyalists. Yet, the false equation of national loyalty with loyalty to the tyrant quickly collapsed with the American advance (chapter 2). Obviously the discrediting of political exiles by the home regime as "nationally disloyal" has its limits; when the regime itself completely loses its stature in the international community, as Saddam Hussein's did, safe haven and exile political activity may become immense assets if the forces with which the political exiles are allied are depicted as liberators. The question of who deserves the future, therefore, relates to a large extent to the question of who owns the past. Many of the exiles may lack the valor of endurance under suffering, while those who endured acquiesced with the regime and, in order to survive, made unacceptable compromises.

The return of Iraqi exile groups on the heels of the coalition invasion in 2003 highlights the potentials and pitfalls inherent in nationalism and the politics of exile. The competition by Iraqi exile opposition groups for positions of power inside the homeland is rife with the legacy of tainted loyalties that the Ba'th regime constantly attributed to its opponents, especially those abroad, who were charged with treason and desertion. For those returning to Baghdad after long years in London, Teheran, Beirut, and Detroit, the challenge of time and destiny is highly complicated. While they enjoyed safe havens in foreign lands and even developed new affinities, time has been frozen for them in regard to the homeland. Their advantage of being away, where they prospered and assembled a challenge to the home regime, could not forestall the fact that they and their offspring were growing distant from the realities inside their *patrie.* The passing of time made many of them both foreign to their native land and fearful of becoming too comfortable in their new country of domicile.

The Frontier of Loyalty shows how the question of international recognition and sponsorship is of immense importance to the political exiles' ability to distinguish between their loyalty to their people and their opposition to the native home regime that controls the homeland. The test of loyalty is magnified manyfold in times of war and peril to the homeland, especially when the home regime is at war with the exile's host state (chapter 7). Lewis Edinger, a scholar of anti-Nazi exiles during World War II, describes this conundrum when he writes that the political exile is "torn between an almost instinctive desire to see his people spared the agony of death, destruction, and defeat and the wish to see the annihilation of the regime which drove him into exile and which to him represented the incarnation of evil."[14] During the 2003 war in Iraq, the INC pleaded that allowing the exiles to join the fight would both be more effective for the U.S. campaign and help in the postwar rebuilding.

The coalition needs the Iraqis—Iraqis who can sneak into the cities and help organize other Iraqis, who know how to communicate with their entrapped compatriots, who can tell them why Hussein really is finished, and who are able to root out his cronies when they try to melt away into the civilian population. One cannot liberate a people—much less facilitate the emergence of a democracy—without empowering the people being liberated. It is much easier for an Iraqi soldier to join other Iraqis in rebellion than it is to surrender his arms in humiliation to a foreigner. . . . The more that Iraqis help, the less the coalition soldiers will have to engage in house-to-house fighting in cities.[15]

When the question of who constitutes the people is itself at stake, and when state boundaries are challenged by sectarian or secessionist claims, divisions among exiles may become even more explosive. Saddam Hussein governed under the veneer of pan-Arabism and spared no repressive means to erase minority, religious, and secessionist aspirations. In fact, his ideology altered even the original pan-Arab Ba'thist concept and instead developed a vision of nationalism that elevated the Iraqi people as the supreme body of the Arab world "who would never dissolve and disappear." Amatzia Baram writes that Saddam's ideology described an Iraqi nation that "had been born many thousands of years ago: it had established the earliest and greatest civilization on earth . . . culminating in the Ba'th regime. [Thus] it would be more important to pursue Iraqi interests than to sacrifice Iraq on the altar of Arab causes."[16]

With each of Saddam's incursions into Iran and Kuwait, and with the final confrontation with the United States in 2003, the exile opposition saw opportunities to exert influence at home but had great difficulty articulating a convincing alternative to Saddam's vision of national unity. The Shiis labored under the suspicion of being "shu'ubi" (self-hating Arabs) or Iranian agents. The Kurds were widely assailed as secessionist and, as a non-Arab ethnic group, hardly evoked sympathy from other Iraqis.[17] Saddam's cult of personality and his recruitment of direct loyalties within all ethno-sectarian groups inside Iraq were quite successful in splitting and undermining indigenous Iraqi affinity for exile leaders. In the post-Saddam era, the question is whether the secessionist spirit maintained by some of the exile groups will feed divisions at home or whether the exiles' desire to establish a united front will eventually help promote domestic unity. During the Spanish transition from Franco's authoritarianism to democratic rule in the mid-1970s, pacts between antagonists were required to reduce nationalist tensions. It was at this juncture that the country benefited from the collaboration between the exiled president of the Generalist de Catalunya and the transitional prime minister Adolfo Suárez. The two agreed to provide the Catalans with an autonomous stature in return for Catalan's loyalty to Spain. Despite his thirty-eight years in exile, the aging Catalan leader returned as a victor to Barcelona and was perceived by the majority of Catalans "as the legitimate embodiment of Catalanism."[18] After the disastrous suppression of the March 1991 uprising, the Iraqi INC similarly adopted a vision for a federated democratic Iraq that would provide significant autonomy to the Kurds and Shiis. Whether this pact will be adhered to by other contestants in post-Saddam Iraq will determine Iraq's fate in the years to come.

The destination of political exile is always a great factor in determining not only the character of the exiles' struggle from abroad but also their political and cultural outlook as returnees. In recent years, we have witnessed many examples of both successful and frustrated returns by exiles and diaspora members, some of whom were absent from their homelands for decades. In the 1990s, Eastern European countries have evoked kinship ties when inviting their expatriates in the West to take leading posts in helping to democratize homelands emerging from the shadow of communism. Whether the returnees ascend to positions of power inside their homelands with the blessing of their people often depends on the circumstances leading to their departure and the symbolic and real status they maintained while abroad. Past democratic mandates of deposed leaders always help, although by no means are they a guarantee for renewed access to power and legitimacy. Sometimes, democratic prestige may endure for generations, even if only symbolically. On December 21, 1990, Poland's elected president Lech Wałesa sent a plane to London to carry home members of the Polish government-in-exile, who since 1939 had maintained the seemingly pointless body that preserved the ghost of the free Poland betrayed to Stalin at Yalta. These émigrés brought back with them the state insignia that their distant predecessors had salvaged in 1939.[19]

One of the challenges for the future of Iraq is the conflicting messages that the exiles transport from their host societies, ranging from liberal democracy, to constitutional monarchy, to a workers' state, to Islamic republicanism. Indeed, a critical component in this equation is the behavior of returning Shii exiles from Iran. These exiles are in principle less susceptible to charges of national disloyalty because they draw largely upon religious (and not national) affinity. Yet, even they may be targets of competing contenders who stayed behind and paid a heavy price under repression. These political contestants portrayed the exiles as deserters as was recently shown by the rhetoric and actions of Muqtada al-Sadr, the new young radical cleric who claimed to be the most legitimate voice of Iraq's Shiite majority. Al-Sadr and his loyalists moved to replace the traditional factions of Iraqi Shiites and allegedly killed pro-U.S. cleric Abd al-Majid al-Khoi shortly after his return from exile in London. Although al-Sadr denies any involvement in the killing, he still argued that "religious people who went into exile should not have left. The country needed them."[20] On the other hand, the posture of some returnees from Iran, where they have formed affinities and alliances with Teheran's theocrats and came out in favor of an Islamic republic for Iraq, may be unpalatable to secularists and non-Shiis and ultimately undermine the creation of a unified, democratic society.

Political exiles who have found refuge in liberal democracies, where they have gained access to, knowledge of, and appreciation of free societies, may become a great asset in the rebuilding of their homelands. Broad-based diasporic support is also vital to the rebuilding process, especially when diaspora members are ready to invest economic and intellectual resources in the renewal of their homelands. At a time when financial flows of diasporas and their entrepreneurial spirits serve as engines for many economies around the world, new enthusiasm among awakened expatriate communities may turn diasporas into vanguards in the rebuilding of the homeland.

The Iraqi case shows the great impact that host countries have in shaping the exile opposition (chapter 6). Host countries can hamstring exiles and keep them subservient to their own national interests. As one scholar wrote about the pre-1991 Iraqi exiles, "The removal of Saddam Hussein's regime was not a foreign policy objective for [Syria and Iran]. What they really sought was a weak but territorially integrated Iraq, stripped of its capacity to pose a regional threat or foment crisis. It was within this context that regional countries offered their support to the Iraqi opposition. Consequently, the opposition camp fell hostage to the national agenda of these countries."[21] Additionally, affiliation with countries hostile to the home regime can stigmatize political exiles as nationally disloyal and put their families inside the homeland in grave danger. Ayatollah Muhammed Baqir al-Hakim, a high-ranking Najaf cleric who established the Supreme Council for Islamic Revolution in Iran (SCIRI), had eighty family members arrested and several executed by Saddam as retribution for his refusal to stop his anti-Ba'th activities. His command of the Badr Brigade, a militia recruited from the 100,000 Iraqi Shii refugees expelled because of their "Persian heritage" and Iraqi deserters and prisoners of war who were offered freedom by the Iranians if they would denounce Saddam and fight alongside the Iranians, however, may have haunted al-Hakim's future leadership in Iraq as he was ordered by the U.S. forces to break up the militia soon after the fall of Saddam. Yet when al-Hakim was assassinated with scores of others in a car bombing outside the Imam Ali shrine in Najaf, in late August 2003, his stature was elevated, and the role of his brigade as the defenders of the Shiite was certified once again as they deployed their armed men in a challenge to the U.S. forces that sought to disband them.[22]

Al-Hakim's group is somewhat reminiscent of Andrei Andreyevitch Vlasov's exile army during World War II (chapter 7). Vlasov, a former general in the Red Army and the heroic defender of Moscow, was taken prisoner by the Germans and was ultimately recruited by them with many other Soviet prisoners of war to join the Nazi war effort against Stalin. Vlasov collaborated with the Nazis as leader of an independent Russian army and portrayed himself as a Russian loyalist. "It became clear to me," he said, "that Bolshevism has involved our people in a war on behalf of interests that are not our people's. . . . Is it not the first, and sacred, duty of every honor-loving Russian to take up arms against Stalin and his gang?"[23] The foot soldiers that joined the Badr Brigade made similar choices. Yet, while Vlasov was ultimately executed for "treason and espionage" against his homeland, members of the Badr Brigade have yet to face questions of national loyalty. Indeed, no matter what the cause, when would-be loyalists side with another nation-state in a war against their own country, suspicions of disloyalty linger. Thus those exiles seen as having supported the American invasion are likely to face similar suspicions.

Even when the political exile serves as an instrument in his host country's efforts to bring about the downfall of the regime at home he is not ensured of receiving his sponsor's future support, let alone the appreciation of his kin inside the homeland. Indeed, the American use of exiles led those who remained inside Iraq—including Shiite leader Grand Ayatollah Ali al-Husseini al Sistani—to believe they would be sidelined by the returnees, a measure that also increased their suspicion toward Washington. A year after the war in Iraq there were growing voices in the United States that questioned the usefulness of the exiles and the accuracy of the information they gave to the Americans before coalition forces invaded Iraq. Growing charges of mismanagement of U.S. funds as well as faulty intelligence continued to dog Chalabi and his colleagues and became a focus of critics of the Bush administration.

The questions of what constitutes authentic representation and the nature of the exile's loyalties are constantly hovering and are likely to become more serious as the length of the time abroad stretches over generations. For example, the case of Elian Gonzalez in 2000 was a fascinating reminder of how some Cuban diaspora leaders have tried to safeguard the exile mentality against the atrophy that would be natural for a community of immigrants after two generations in the United States. It was at that juncture that many

Cuban Americans found themselves and their identity split between political exiles, who have tried to set the boundaries of what it means to be Cuban in the United States by nurturing the old exile rhetoric and the hope of return, and those who have reconciled themselves to their new life in America. The difficulty was further exacerbated when some of the Cuban exile activists were perceived as acting outside American laws on child custody or in opposition to congressional policies to relax economic sanctions against Cuba. Abiding by the wishes of the host country can come at the cost of loyalty to the exile's cause.

One of the most critical factors that makes Iraqi exiles important at this stage is that they are seen by some in the American administration as upholders of the American cause. As they seek to create a democratic Iraq, Americans must contend with the power vacuum resulting from the lack of incumbent claimants to power, and the question as to what extent the former exiles can forge strong ties with well-positioned insiders is looming. A similar challenge is also evident in the case of Afghanistan, although Hamid Karzai's return from exile was accompanied by strong opposition to the Taliban from within (e.g., the Northern Alliance). In Afghanistan, the problem was the difficulty of governing an ungovernable, almost completely underdeveloped state. In Iraq the challenge is not so much the failed state syndrome but rather the creation of reliable and effective control while dealing with newly reemerging ethnosectarian cleavages. In both cases, we have seen appeals to the respective diaspora communities (particularly in the United States) to assume leading roles in the politics and economics of their native land and in the exportation of democratic values and entrepreneurial spirit to the homeland.

There are striking similarities and yet very serious differences between Masaryk and the careers of returning Iraqi political leaders that may hint at the prospects for a future democratic Iraq. Like Masaryk, Iraqi exiles (especially Chalabi) were able to harness American interest in containing and eventually deposing Saddam by creating a durable exile coalition and building the support of large sectors of the Iraqi diaspora. Indeed, Chalabi in particular was the first to provide a voice to the sizable community of expatriates in the West who hated Saddam but were too timid either to speak against the tyrant or to organize abroad as a diasporic lobby. Like Masaryk, Chalabi found a sympathetic ear in the corridors of power in Washington and ultimately in the White House, as he sold his vision of an Iraq in concert with the American principles. Chalabi presented himself and his movement as secular, democratic, and Western oriented. He stressed his own Shii roots, Western education, and liberal ideology as proof that Iraq's Shii were secularly oriented, not fundamentalists like the Shii of Iran. He argued that unlike Afghanistan, a patchwork of warring tribes, Iraq has historically enjoyed a high standard of living, gender equality, and a tradition of multiethnic parliamentary democracy dating from the monarchial era.

As political exiles, Masaryk and the Iraqi exiles could not afford to present their views on the shape of their multiethnic states too specifically. Masaryk was so successful and influential among the Western states that the Slavophilic wing of the independence movement conceded control of the nationalist movement to him. This triumph effectively yoked the Slovaks' demands for self-determination to those of the Czechs but also guaranteed that those demands could never be completely fulfilled.[24] Masaryk paid tribute to both Czech and Slovak contributions to the cause of independence, but he was mute on questions such as the greater integration of the poorer Slovak community or the large German minority in the Sudetenland into the political and educated elite and often lapsed into mild forms of Czech chauvinism. For Iraqis today, the vision of a federal state (laid out by the exiles in Vienna in 1992) remains the touchstone in the ongoing constitutional negotiations. Still, the plan lacks crucial details, such as whether representation will be based on geographic or confessional bounds and how smaller minority groups, such as the Assyrians, Turcomen, and others, will be represented at the provincial and national levels.

In one crucial way, though, the Czechoslovakian and Iraqi tasks are exactly opposites. Masaryk "invented" a state from the diplomatic anarchy of the disintegrating Austro-Hungarian Empire. The task for all Iraqi exiles is not to invent the Iraqi state but to alter the definitions of Iraqi peoplehood and identity from their previous meaning of loyalty to Saddam. Revising the frontiers of national loyalty is always a difficult task, especially for political exiles. Whereas the state can use its control over the educational system and citizenship laws to invite those considered "foreign" into the national body or expel them from it, exiles lack the coercive power of the state and are already considered by many to be outside the national body. Functioning outside the nation-state, though, can provide exiles the freedom to be intellectually innovative that may be impossible inside the homeland. Arabs and Muslims living abroad have historically produced significant political movements that ultimately led to the creation of new political identities in their homelands. Major exponents of pan-Arabism began their careers as student leaders in French universities, where they were deeply influenced by notions of *völkisch* nationalism. Exiles like Michel Aflaq, the intellectual godfather of Iraqi Ba'thism, returned to their homelands bent on replacing the boundaries of the numerous Middle Eastern states, which they viewed as an imperially imposed artifice, with a single unified state incorporating all Arabic speakers.[25] Pan-Islamism, the notion that religion, not ethnicity, language, or country of origin, should unite Muslims around the world, has also played a prominent role in the intellectual life of exiles and diaspora members. In the past thirty years, at least, pan-Islamism has been the strongest competitor to the Muslim state, leading many states to seek the arrest, exile, or execution of Islamic activists. This state-mosque conflict has caused the Muslim diaspora to be populated by dissident Islamists, such as Osama bin Laden, Sheikh Omar Rahman, and Ayatollah Khomeini, who oppose the current Arab and Islamic state structure. In recent years we have seen Muslim and Arab diasporas in the United States, Britain, France, and Germany prove ripe recruiting grounds and safe harbors for movements that violently attack their homelands for being too liberal. At the same time, though, there are voices in the diaspora calling for a higher premium on freedom in the Arab and Muslim world and expressing the wish to return and rebuild their homelands along democratic lines. One scholar, reviewing the career of Ayatollah Abd al-Majid al-Khoi, the son of the former grand ayatollah of Iraq, who lived ten years in London but was murdered upon his return to Najaf in April 2003, concluded that "the experience of exile in the United Kingdom [and elsewhere] . . . seem[s] to make a rising number of Iraqi Shi'is realize that a democratic solution in Baghdad may help them practice their legitimate rights in a future Iraq."[26] If the example of Czechoslovakia is any indication, the exportation of the Western creed abroad will be a critical factor in the exiles' success or failure in building a free society at home.[27]

Washington, DC
August 30, 2004

NOTES

Part of this new preface was published in "The Frontiers of Loyalty" (with Ariel I. Ahram), *Orbis* 47, no.4 (Fall 2003).

1. Aviel Roshwald, *Ethnic Nationalism and the Fall of Empires: Central Europe, Russia, and the Middle East* (New York: Routledge, 2001), 129.
2. Just before the outburst of American nationalist sentiment in the aftermath of September 11, Walter Berns lamented (perhaps prematurely) the decline of patriotism in America—where in his view cultural relativism and individual selfishness undercut the new generation's sense of love of country. See *Making Patriots* (Chicago: University of Chicago Press, 2001). The quote from Adam Smith is on p. 60.
3. See Yossi Shain, *Governments-in-Exile in Contemporary World Politics* (New York: Routledge, 1991), 9.
4. Edward W. Said, "The Mind of Winter: Reflections on Life in Exile," *Harper's*, September 1984, 50.
5. See Myron Weiner, *The Global Migration Crisis: Challenge to States and to Human Rights* (New York: HarperCollins, 1995).
6. See, for example, the special issue of *Foreign Service Journal* (October 2000) entitled "A Question of Loyalty: In a Multicultural World, What Does Loyalty Mean?"
7. Negar Akhvi, "Exile," *The New Republic*, 12 June 2000.
8. See Nedim Ogelman, Jeannette Money, and Philip Martin, "Immigrant Cohesion and Political Access in Influencing Foreign Policy," *SAIS Review* 22 (Summer–Fall 2002): 145–65.
9. Marcela Sanchez, "Salvadoran Exiles' Warning for the Homeland," *Washington Post*, 20 September 2003, A31.
10. *Washington Post*, 14 May 2003, A29. For a similar observation, see Fiona Adamson, "Displacement, Diaspora Mobilization, and Transnational Cycles of Political Violence," in John Tirman, ed., *The Maze of Fear: Security and Migration after 9/11* (New York: New Press, 2004), 50–51.
11. Jeffrey Herbst, *States and Power in Africa: Comparative Lessons in Authority and Control* (Princeton: Princeton University Press, 2000), 269.
12. Judith N. Shklar, "The Bonds of Exile," in Stanley Hoffmann, ed., *Political Thought and Political Thinkers* (Chicago: University of Chicago Press, 1998), 57–58.
13. Shu-Yun Ma, "The Exit, Voice, and Struggle to Return of Chinese Political Exiles," *Pacific Affairs* (Fall 1993): 384.

14. Quoted in chapter 7 of the current volume.
15. Kanan Makiya, "Iraqis Must Share in Their Liberation," *New York Times*, 30 March 2003.
16. Amatzia Baram, "Broken Promises," *Wilson Quarterly* (Spring 2003): 51.
17. Ofra Bengio, *Saddam's Word: Political Discourse in Iraq* (New York: Oxford University Press, 1998), 103–6.
18. See Yossi Shain, ed., *Governments-in-Exile in Contemporary World Politics* (New York: Routledge), 9.
19. *The Economist*, 21 December 2001, 63–64.
20. Quoted in Juan Cole, "The United States and the Shi'ite Religious Factions in Iraq," *Middle East Journal* 57, no. 4 (2003): 557.
21. Robert G. Rabil, "The Iraqi Opposition's Evolution: From Conflict to Unity?" *Middle East Review of International Affairs* 6, no. 4 (December 2002): 13.
22. See Anthony Shadid, "Shiite Militia Deploy Forces," *Washington Post*, 6 September 2003, 1.
23. See chapter 7 of the current volume.
24. Roshwald, *Ethnic Nationalism*, 131–32.
25. Bassam Tibi, *Arab Nationalism: Between Islam and the Nation State* (New York: St. Martin's Press, 1997), 42–48, 204.
26. Jean-Uwe Rahe, "Iraqi Shi'is in Exile in London," in Faleh Abdul Jabar, ed., *Ayatollahs, Sufis, and Ideologues* (London: Saqi, 2002), 218.
27. See Yossi Shain, *Marketing the American Creed Abroad: Diasporas in the U.S. and Their Homelands* (New York: Cambridge University Press, 1999).

Introduction

When I place myself in the hands of another, and permit him to determine the principles by which I shall guide my behavior, I repudiate the freedom and reason which give me dignity.
Robert Paul Wolff, In Defense of Anarchism, 1970

The Political Exile and the Evolution of National Loyalty

This book provides a systematic overview of exile political activity in established twentieth-century nation-states, concentrating for purposes of theory on the activity of exiles who strive to overpower a native government without challenging the existence of the nation-state or its boundaries. A study of the dimensions of exile political activity enriches our understanding of political struggle between governments and oppositions, and of competing claims to be the legitimate object of political loyalty in the nation-state.

Exile opposition groups play a significant and usually unrecognized role in shaping the character of "national loyalty." Indeed, the large variety of political exiles who try to delegitimize and overthrow a native home regime include dramatic cases such as the Russian exiles in the Stalinist era, the Italian anti-Fascists, the anti-Nazi Germans, the Spanish Republicans, and the exiles from dictatorships in the Caribbean. Among significant recent examples are the Portuguese exile opposition to Antonio Salazar's dictatorship, Iranian exiles before and after the Islamic revolution, anti-Castro Cubans in the United States, Chileans in the post-Allende period, the external opposition to the former Filipino president Ferdinand Marcos, and Koreans working abroad against the government of Chun Doo Hwan. These and other cases of exile political activity, though appearing disparate and unrelated at first glance, upon close examination manifest great congruence and consistency across the span of the past century.

Exile political activity has a long historical lineage, dating back to the division of the Davidic kingdom in the tenth century B.C. and to ancient Greece of the fifth century B.C., where factional strife forced

1

political rivals out of their homelands. Governments born of such strife have claimed political loyalty; their claims in turn have been contested, reshaped, and advanced by the activity of exile opposition. Exiles have challenged not only the authority of regimes to define the object of political loyalty, but also their right to establish criteria for inclusion in and exclusion from the polity.

Political exiles have played an important role in molding the idea of political loyalty. When, in tenth century B.C., Jeroboam challenged Solomon's kingdom by claiming to represent the disenfranchised of the northern tribes, and Solomon threatened to execute him, Jeroboam sought refuge in Egypt and aligned himself there with Shishak, the king. After Solomon's death (ca 925 B.C.) he returned to lead the resistance to Rehoboam, Solomon's designated successor, who was attempting to coerce the loyalty of the northern tribes. Jeroboam's success in diverting the loyalty of the people of Israel from the Davidic dynasty led to the establishment of the independent northern kingdom of Israel.[1]

In the fifth century B.C., contestants for power in the Greek city-states sought political loyalty in the name of a partisan agenda, not in the name of the city or polis, though Socrates in the *Crito* spoke of the polis almost as of a parent or fatherland. The conflicts between democrats and oligarchs were factional struggles for power. The ruling faction—oligarchy or democracy—commonly ostracized political rivals whose rising power threatened their rule. Aristotle recorded that the sentence of banishment from the state was executed "in a spirit of mere faction."[2] The ruling faction in the democratic polity of Athens legalized the practice of ostracism: those regarded as potential tyrants and other powerful individuals seen as a threat to the will of the majority were expelled (following a majority vote in a quorum of 6,000 in the assembly) and sent into "honorable" exile for a period of ten years.[3]

A similar pattern of factional loyalties characterized political struggles in medieval Europe. In Italy at the turn of the fourteenth century, the city republics' ruling authorities were in constant strife with an opposition in exile; indeed, authorities and exiles often reversed roles. These struggles reflected a historical shift from government *in libertà* (an independent republic) to government *a signoria* (strong, unified rule by a despot).[4] Most notable among these rivalries was the triumph of the Black Guelph exiles over the White Guelph regime in Florence in 1301, generating the resistance in exile of Alighieri Dante's Whites to the Blacks' propapal government and its imposition of power as "God-ordained."[5]

In sixteenth-century England, during the last years of Henry VIII and again during the reign of Catholic Queen Mary (1553–58), committed Protestants refused to conform their religion to that of the Crown (which defined itself as the church's head) and sought refuge in Switzerland and the Rhineland. These expatriates, known as the Marian exiles, campaigned to undermine the queen's quest for loyalty and in the process transformed Calvinism into a revolutionary doctrine.[6] The radical clergymen among them, based in Calvin's Geneva, considered their opposition activities to be God's own mission. They smuggled into England books and political tracts that called on their countrymen to break their earthly loyalty to the "idolatrous" Crown. The political radicalism of these ministers-in-exile laid the foundation for the revolutionary upheavals of the 1640s. Michael Walzer has pointed out: "In a sense, modern politics begins in England with the return of the Genevan exiles."[7]

With consolidation of the territorial state in the seventeenth century, the sovereign ruler succeeded the faction as the supreme object of political loyalty. Loyalty no longer meant allegiance to the ruling faction, as in the Greek polis, or personal submission to a lord, as in the feudal system of rule. And, unlike under the Renaissance and absolutist regimes of the sixteenth century, the "posts carrying specific political responsibilities and faculties" were "no longer assigned directly on grounds of wealth, rank or religious standing."[8] The French Revolution and the secularization of power dealt the final blow to the personification of a regime embodied in the idea, *L'état c'est moi*. This revolutionary change in the concept of loyalty produced a large aristocratic exile community, many of whom united abroad in a fight to restore the Bourbons. After the Declaration of Pillnitz, issued in August 1791 by the Emperor and the King of Prussia, promised intervention on behalf of the French nobility, supporters of the monarchy crossed the Rhine to join the Koblenz exile community and prepared for armed intervention on behalf of the monarchy. These aristocratic exiles, unlike the revolutionaries, saw French patriotism as linked to the person of the king. They had refused to accept the oath of loyalty to the "People" imposed on them by the National Assembly. "Honour, more than life, far more than the hope of regaining their lands and their property, the fantastical point of honour, was the supreme inspiration for which so many Frenchmen forsook their homes and their families to seek new destinies."[9] But this army of exiles quickly discovered the fragility of foreign alliances. The decisive victory of the revolutionary French army over Austria in September 1792 forced them to seek asylum in England, where they soon encountered the animosity of descendants of the French Huguenots, pushed out of France by Louis XIV just a century before. The exiled aristocrats, grandchildren of a kingdom that had revoked the Edict of Nantes and thereby linked loyalty to the monarchy to Roman Catholicism, found little compassion among the descendants of their earlier victims.[10] The exiled Bourbons returned to power in 1815, but by the 1820s the aristocratic notion of loyalty had lost the day. Revolutionary turmoil and the ferment in the world of ideas had launched the nation as the ultimate object of competition for loyalty.

Political exiles have thus had a significant impact upon the definition of political loyalty in the city-state, the empire, and the papal monarchy. Their importance in defining the shift of political loyalty toward the nation became indisputable. In the early nineteenth century, as the notion of a unified sovereign state striving to enhance its own self-perceived interests by expansion became closely connected with the idea of a culturally and demographically defined nation, political exiles throughout Europe, Latin America, and East Asia led the resistance to imperial rule, advocating national self-government in a recognized homeland. The failure of the revolutions of 1830 in Germany, Italy, and Poland forced many revolutionaries into exile. In Paris, Brussels, Geneva, and London they set up bases of agitation against the monarchical powers of Russia, Prussia, and Austria. Giuseppe Mazzini's Young Italy, founded in 1831, provided the organizational model.[11] German exiles established Young Germany, and exile Poles Young Poland, both defined as authentic representatives of their "enslaved" nations. The European exile experience reached Latin America through Giuseppe Garibaldi's adventure to defend the new nation of Uruguay, and influenced José Martí, the romantic prophet of Cuba's national independence, who from the late 1860s until the 1890s led the exiled Cuban revolutionary movement in the United States against Spanish colonial rule. He established in New York City La Liga de Instrucción, a special training school to teach Cuban workers the principles of independence.[12] Killed early in the Cuban war for independence, on May 19, 1895, the month after he reached the island, he became the martyr of Cuban nationalism. So too the exiled leader of Filipino nationalism, José Rizal, banished by the Spanish colonial government for leading the Propaganda Movement, a group of dissident intelligentsia, became a martyr to his cause. His political novel *Noli me tangere* (1887), condemning the government in Madrid for distorting Catholic doctrine to justify colonial oppression, became a landmark in the mythology of the Filipino independence movement. Nine years after its publication, when Rizal returned to take part in the revolution, he was arrested, and was executed on December 30, 1896, for complicity with the opposition.[13]

Mazzini's exile federation, Young Europe, founded in Bern in 1834, marked the beginning of transnational collaboration among exiled revolutionaries. Such collaboration accelerated after the European revolutionary failures of 1848–50, but with the growing pace of industrialization, international cooperation among exiles soon shifted its focus from nationalistic struggles to international proletariat and class loyalties.[14] It was within the circles of political exiles—intellectually exposed to (although physically removed from) the variety of national experiences of the working masses—that the idea of loyalty to the nation found its principal challenge. The new exile thesis maintained that solidarity of the working class transcends national frontiers and national allegiances. By the 1860s Mazzini was already "identified with the discredited notions of nationalism and bourgeois republicanism, which were being superseded by strategies and tactics oriented around the theories of class conflict and a proletarian social revolution."[15] The new prophet of the exiles in Europe, chosen in 1864 to lead the international Workingmen's Association, was the German exile Karl Marx.

The attempt to make the object of political loyalty not national but international in the last quarter of the nineteenth century found its strongest expression in the struggle of exiled Russian socialists against the czarist regime. Ironically, the triumphant return of Lenin's exiled Bolsheviks in 1917 led to the "nationalization of socialism." The collapse of the Second International in August 1914, and the overwhelming victory of national loyalties over proletarian solidarity in World War I, forced the Bolsheviks to come to terms with the magnetic attraction of nationalism itself. The 1917 coup d'état in the name of the world proletariat generated an exodus of about two million Russian refugees, but Bolshevism, in its drive to consolidate power, was unable to dispense with the nationalist legacies of the old regime. As Benedict Anderson points out: "Despite Trotsky's unease, the capital of the USSR was moved back to the old Czarist capital of Moscow" from Petrograd, and in the past 70 years "CPSU leaders have made policy in the Kremlin, ancient citadel of the Czarist power—out of all possible sites in the socialist state's vast territories."[16]

The nineteenth-century evolution of nationalist exile movements striving for political sovereignty on behalf of a nation reached its climax with the post-World War II period of decolonization of Asia and Africa. The last wave of anticolonial "wars of liberation" in Africa was dominated by revolutionary exile movements demonstrating the ongoing power of nationalism as a vehicle for political mobilization.[17] Although the struggle for power within the new African states has been seen by certain leading students of ethnicity as a continuation of the struggle for independence,[18] the triumph of the nation-state seems incontrovertible.

One must go on to ask: what is the role of exiles in the shifting character of political loyalty in the already established nation-state? Within the nation-state, the idea that political loyalty should be directed toward the nation is intimately linked to the relationship between the national community and the state's power. The translation of political loyalty into an expression of national loyalty serves primarily as a legitimizing mechanism to justify the particular claims of the native power seekers who compete to represent the general interest of national community as a whole and to protect and preserve its existence and integrity. In the world of the nation-state, where each native government claims to promote the national interest, the struggle for state power is no longer (at least at the ideological level) between partisan claims to loyalty—oligarchs vs. democrats, Catholics vs. republicans, aristocrats vs. the people, the bourgeoisie vs. the working class, or a nation struggling for self-determination vs. colonial rule. Within the established nation-state, where the national community controls its own political unit, and where the national and the political are congruent,[19] political loyalty is sought in the name of the national community as a whole. In this effort, exiles have played an important role.

The phenomenon of exile political activity demands systematic study and the imposition of a theoretical order, yet political science has not developed any comprehensive crossnational analysis to identify the behavioral and theoretical implications of such activity. Historians, social scientists, and legal scholars, while producing works invaluable to this project, have dealt with numerous single-country case studies, often indirectly, and have offered little comparative discussion of the forms and characteristics of exile activity.[20] Studies of political behavior, international politics, and political theory have almost totally disregarded the significance of exile political activity. Scholarly works on the relations between governments and political opposition, for example, seldom mention it.[21] Similarly, theorists of the nation-state customarily omit political exiles from their discussions, considering those who operate outside the state's territorial boundaries (the unit of their analysis) to be irrelevant to their studies. No doubt one of the reasons for this omission is the fact that political science tends to distinguish between national and international politics whereas exile political activity cuts across both domains.

This book responds to this neglect. It proposes, first, to provide a comprehensive overview of the political activity of exiles and to offer heuristic propositions for future studies of particular cases; and second, by focusing on exile political activity, to illuminate theoretical issues at the center of discussion in political science. By extending the scope of empirical investigation beyond the territorial border of the nation-state, this work demonstrates how the study of relations between political exiles and their national compatriots (at home and abroad), as well as of relations between exiles and the home regime, may enhance our understanding of basic political concepts such as loyalty, legitimacy, and citizenship. By examining political exiles' inter- and intraorganizational behavior, it seeks to add another dimension to the study of the strengths and limitations of ideological affinities. Finally, by viewing political exiles' relations with international figures, it explores the role of images in international relations and seeks to shed light on the ambiguity of the concept of "recognition" in international law.

Since my goal is to develop and explore concepts of political science through exile political activity, the examples I use illustrate and inform analytical statements; they are not demonstrations of already identified hypotheses. The wide range of literature and commentary on exile political activity since the nineteenth century, which serves as the paint for my canvas, provides a basis for comparison. I have found it instructive to delve into the details of certain exile activities; in these cases well-documented examples, representing a wide spectrum of contexts for purposes of comparison, are examined at length.

Who Is an Exile?

The problem begins with definition. Who is an exile? While reviewing the existing literature on exiles, it occurred to me that their political activity has not received the theoretical attention it deserves in part because of fundamental problems of definition. I was therefore led to reexamine the existing theoretical studies, to see how social and legal scholars define an exile. I found scholars offering intellectual perspectives that reflected their own disciplines. Social and legal scholars define an exile in many different ways. From a political science perspective, is the political exile the same as the refugee? For purposes of analysis of social science, is the voluntary immigrant the same as the involuntary immigrant? Law and social science define them differently, each definition based on the concerns of the definer. The special interests of political science have not been reflected in available definitions, but there have been several illuminating works of theory on immigrants in the social science literature of the last generation. The pioneering work of H. P. Fairchild,[22] for example, gave birth—albeit thirty years after the appearance of his 1927 study—to attempts to deal with immigrants and types of migration analytically, the most influential of which are the studies of Petersen, Eichenbaum, and Kunz.[23] But literature of sociology has reduced the political exile to a case of mere social deviance; the literature of social psychology has seen the political exile only as a variant of the refugee; and the literature of the legal profession, without a clear definition of political exiles, has concentrated on technical and practical problem solving.

Scholarly neglect of exile political activity is induced in part, I believe, by confusion that is terminological, conceptual, and methodological. As a consequence, a number of interesting theoretical issues have remained unexplored. Previous study has focused on (1) the psychological and social experience of exiles before departing from their homeland; (2) the causes, motivations, and means of departure; and (3) the adjustment and assimilation of exiles in the country of asylum. These three traditional approaches assume political status quo. They fail to recognize a distinct subset of exiles: those who engage in political activity designed to end their exile, those who seek victory over their opponents so as to reverse and/or advance history.

Because social scientists, for example, focus on identifying causes of and motivations for departure as an initial step in identifying groups of exiles, they distinguish, first, between voluntary and nonvoluntary emigrants. But how can one distinguish between personal motives and external causes? William Petersen tries to overcome this complexity by positing a difference between "pushed" emigrants and "pulled" emigrants.[24] Pushed emigrants are nonvoluntary; suffering a critical change in their lives, they have no recourse but to relocate in another country. Hansen and Oliver-Smith note that the causes of critical change may range "from natural disasters to socio-political upheaval."[25] Pulled emigrants, on the other hand, are voluntary emigrants who have positive original motivation to settle abroad. As Egon Kunz elaborates: "The country of choice provides them with a purpose and a wish to migrate."[26] The motivation is usually seen as economic. Scholars have also noted levels of urgency for emigrant flight, Petersen drawing a distinction between "impelled" and "forced" refugees,[27] Kunz, between "anticipatory" and "acute" emigrants.[28] Impelled-anticipatory emigrants are limited in their power to decide whether to leave their homeland or not. They flee their country fearing that a deterioration in the political or social situation may preclude their leaving freely later. Barry Stein points out that an "anticipatory refugee senses the danger early, before a crisis makes orderly departure impossible."[29]

Impelled or anticipatory political refugees are seen as on the boundary between voluntary and compulsory emigrants. Kunz suggests that their status might be determined by examining their personal history. One might ask how much their ideologies clashed with those of their society or of their government. A good example of such refugees would be the teachers who left Cuba after the Castro revolution. Approximately 50 percent of the entire teaching population of Cuba fled to the United States. Faced with Cuba's new regime, these teachers "found themselves confronted with a necessity of either radically changing their attitudes, values and approaches to their profession, or of no longer being part of the school system and the large society of which it was a part."[30] Forced-acute emigrants, on the other hand, face an immediate choice between emigration and a threat to their existence (or at least, constraints on their departure). In Stein's terminology, such emigration results from an "overwhelming push."[31] War, internal revolution, civil war, persecution, expulsion, and sudden and severe oppression instituted by a new regime or by new policies of an old regime, may create such an overwhelming push. Such emigrants are those usually called "refugees," "political refugees," or "exiles."

Sociological literature also notes different levels of assimilation and adjustment in exiles' country of asylum. Lewis Coser, for example, distinguishes between refugees who intend to settle permanently in their new country, and exiles who regard their exile as temporary and live abroad for the day they may return.[32] Because this definition touches on the matter of intention, it seeks both subjective and objective signs of the degree of assimilation. Coser looks for efforts to establish new relations in their new environment, the refugees' "network."[33] Nor is assimilation entirely a matter of free choice. Personal "opportunities," the receptiveness of the society, and policies of the host country are essential elements in refugees' adjustment and thus in their status. Hans Speier finds a considerable difference between technically trained specialists like engineers and chemists, who are independent of any particular locality and hence can be accepted in their new environment relatively quickly, and diplomats or military officers, whose role is wholly dependent on their country and who therefore will be regarded as aliens, often find themselves "nationally useless," and end up "writing their memoirs or as taxi-drivers."[34]

So also the host government's policies toward immigration determine the status of refugees. Kunz argues that "monistic societies are less likely to be hospitable to people who cling to their differing cultures, than pluralistic societies of broader experiences."[35] Positive policies toward refugees can shape refugees' attitudes in favor of assimilation and change their negative self-perception about their exile. An antirefugee policy, on the other hand, perpetuates the refugee's status as an outsider or exile. After World War II many Poles who were anti-Russian and refused to return to their country found asylum in England. Although they had serious difficulties with the English language and culture, and were thus prevented from achieving rapid assimilation, they were warmly accepted by the British authorities. The government established special institutions to assist their adjustment and even appointed two ministers for this task.[36] In contrast, Spanish refugees who fled after the civil war and sought refuge in Stalinist Russia were considered outsiders. Many suffered arbitrary persecution and were denounced as "counterrevolutionaries" and "traitors to the Socialist Fatherland" whenever they requested to leave the Soviet Union.[37]

Other social scientists have distinguished between refugees and exiles on the basis of emotional, attitudinal, and other psychological criteria. They have concentrated on the refugees' level of attachment to the homeland and their realization that they may be required to live abroad longer than expected. Lewis J. Edinger argues that "what distinguishes the exile from an ordinary refugee . . . is, above all, a state of mind. . . . [T]he exile does not seek a new life and a new home in a foreign land. He considers his residence abroad strictly temporary and will not and cannot assimilate to a new society."[38] A "political" exile for Edinger is one whose motivations for departure are political and/or social; "exile" simply refers to the psychological status of the refugee in the host country. For Kunz, an "exile" is a refugee behind whom "doors are closed." The transition from "temporary refugee" to "exile" occurs when the refugee arrives "at a spiritual, special, temporal and emotional equidistant no man's land of midway-to-nowhere and the longer he remains there, the longer he becomes subject to its demoralising effects."[39]

Edward W. Said, a Palestinian activist, scholar, and literary critic, distinguishes among exiles, refugees, expatriates, and émigrés. Refugees, he says, are the creation of the twentieth-century state. "The word 'refugee' has become a political one, suggesting large herds of innocent bewildered people requiring urgent international assistance." Expatriates, on the other hand, live voluntarily in alien countries, usually for reasons of their own. Emigrés "enjoy an ambiguous status. Technically, an émigré is anyone who emigrates to a new country. Choice in the matter is certainly a possibility." Emigrés have not been banished and can always return, but they may still live with a sense of exile. Exiles, in Said's classification, are forced to leave their home, land, and roots, and are cut off from their past. They are in a "discontinuous state of being, [carrying] . . . a touch of solitude and spirituality."[40] To Peter Rose both refugees and exiles are "reluctant leavers forced to flee, driven by the prospect of unacceptable fate, should they choose to stay behind."[41] They must live with the realization that they may never be able to return.

Scholars have measured feelings and commitment of exiles to their homeland by distinguishing among levels of eagerness to assimilate or not assimilate, the principal criterion being the level of identification and attachment the exile holds toward the country of origin. Kunz suggests a direct link between the causes that lead exiles to depart and their ideological and mental commitment to their nation. He identifies four subgroups of refugees: the first comprising "event alienated refugees" who are rejected by the nation as a whole, or at least by an important segment of its population, and three other subgroups made up of "self alienated" refugees whom Kunz identifies as people who did not consider themselves as part of the nation even before they fled.[42] Coser, in *Refugee Scholars in America*, cites two examples that seem to me to illustrate Kunz's classification. Vladimir Nabokov wanted to be considered as an American from the moment he reached his asylum. He "did not wish to live and work in a subcultural enclave in America. He wanted to immerse himself in the mainstream of American intellectual and artistic life, [and] in this he succeeded superbly in a very short time."[43] On the other hand Hannah Arendt, who fled Nazi Germany and settled in New York, regarded herself as a "pariah." She refused stubbornly, at the beginning of her stay at least, to take any permanent job in the American academic world, preferring to maintain her independence as an autonomous outsider.[44]

Kunz's second subgroup comprises "integration realist" refugees, people who usually hold deep feelings for their fatherland and nation, but for whom there is no choice but to adjust. Realizing that the loss of their homeland may be permanent, they seek to create a substitute form of existence (an effort that usually takes five years or more). Such refugees can remain exiles mentally. Stein notes that even after five years "many will be embittered and alienated. Many will be just surviving, acculturated enough to function but far from assimilated or integrated."[45] Kunz's third "level of eagerness" are the "passive hurt" refugees, persons who have lost their sense of life's vitality. Identified by members of their new society as anomalous and eccentric outsiders, many idealize their past and give up on their future. Some of the Russian refugees from work camps, Hungarian refugees in Canada, Polish and Yugoslav refugees in Norway, Cuban and Indochinese refugees in the United States, and others have been found to exhibit similar characteristics resembling psychiatric symptoms like paranoia, "reactive depressive states," and "somatic pains." Many tend to be aggressive; some show a high inclination to suicide.[46]

Kunz's final subgroup of refugees are those who commit themselves to overthrow the home government. "Majority identified refugees" identify "themselves enthusiastically with the nation, though not with its government,"[47] and refuse to recognize that their exile is permanent. They conceive their stay abroad as a historical mission and feel responsibility and guilt for those left behind. He includes also a second group of "self alienated revolutionary activists," "founders of utopias" who try to bring about a revolution to change their home government or, "if possible, the whole world."[48] Marxists who reject the idea of a nation-state and identify with the international proletariat may be such refugees, their revolutionary activism a part of their struggle to destroy all nation-states.

The United Nations High Commission for Refugees (UNHCR) sees a political refugee as any person "who is outside the country of his nationality, or if he has no nationality, the country of his former habitual residence because he has or had well-founded fear of his persecution by reason of his race, religion, nationality or political opinion and is unable or, because of such fear, is unwilling to avail himself of the protection of the government of the country of his nationality, or, if he has no nationality, to return to the country of his former habitual residence."[49] A refugee is defined according to need for protection. UNHCR attempts to create clear criteria for identifying those who suffer from certain kinds of violations of human rights (as defined by the Universal Declaration of Human Rights) and who are therefore entitled to legal protection and assistance in finding a permanent home. UNHCR distinguishes between two subgroups, statutory refugees and displaced refugees. Statutory refugees are those who flee their country because of "well-founded fear of persecution on certain grounds."[50] Displaced refugees are people "who can be determined, or presumed to be without, or unable to avail themselves of, the protection of the government of their state of origin."[51] Status of the refugee is determined by the reasons for departure or for not returning, as for example if a change in the political situation at home has made return dangerous or even impossible.

The key to UNHCR's success is its ability to guarantee that no refugee will be forced to return to the country of origin, as long as there is danger of persecution. But according to international law, no country is obliged to grant asylum; the only obligation is that it not return refugees as long as there is a threat of persecution. This freedom not to grant asylum, on one hand, and the prohibition against forcing refugees to return, on the other, may place the refugees themselves in a "political non-status."[52] Refugees may be granted only temporary shelter ("country of first asylum") by a host who regards their stay as illegal. Others may refuse asylum altogether or violate asylum (*refoulement*), compelling refugees to return to their former country. Jaegar points out that *refoulement* has occurred even among liberal democracies.[53] In all cases, "the determination of eligibility for refugee status remains entirely in the hands of the country in which asylum is being sought."[54]

Ambivalence about granting asylum is reflected in terminologies of distaste. Countries that seek to avoid refugees usually refrain from using the term at all, classifying refugees instead, as Goodwin-Gill says, as "displaced persons," "illegal immigrants," "quasi-refugees," "aliens," "departees," "boat people," or "stowaways."[55] Those who accept refugees, on the other hand, call them "freedom fighters."

The Political Exile as a Political Activist

The criteria that shape the definition of exiles as sociological deviants, psychological variants, or a special category in international law, make no reference to what exiles actually do abroad politically in an attempt to return to their home country. To a political scientist this may be the primary question, but the classification of exiles in accordance with their day-to-day activities and state of mind has caused social scientists great difficulties. The distinction between the exile as deviant and as variant has been unclear and imprecise. What is the exile's state of mind? It is hard to say without examining the exile's emotional ties, commitment, and level of attachment to the country of origin. Such an analysis includes so many additional variables and requires so many answers to subquestions that any attempt to perform it is difficult. For example, to distinguish among levels of inclination to assimilate or not assimilate, one must draw a prior distinction between what Herbert C. Kelman calls the "sentimental attachment" and "instrumental attachment" that one feels for one's homeland and/or the new country of residence. Accordingly, sentimental attachment reflects cultural integration and national identity, and instrumental attachment refers to social and economic integration.[56]

So too, the "symbolic language" used by social scientists in regard to exiles leads to imprecision. Randolph Starn has pointed to the biblical metaphors and literary images used by many social scientists to describe exiles.[57] Paul Tabori has recognized the lack of clarity and the inadequacy of such definitions, arguing that the variety of variables resembles an "impenetrable jungle, a kind of super-maze."[58] He believes that "no perfect or complete definition is possible—or perhaps, even desirable."[59] He has created six characteristics to describe his "ideal type" of exile. The definition of the exile varies with the disposition in the host country. Circumstances constantly change the exile's attachment toward the homeland and new society, and determine the mobility of the exile's self-definition from an exile to an emigrant and vice versa.[60] Kunz, who classifies exiles into subgroups according to background and path of resettlement, does not establish a special category for politically active exiles. Indeed, he regards political activism as a minor aspect of exile dynamics.

The legalist, unlike the social scientist, has not sought any classification beyond the initial intention, that is, to distinguish between refugees and nonrefugees—a guideline for assisting those who deserve assistance.

The question remains, how can the exile phenomenon be approached in a way useful to political science? What, for example, are the motives, forms, and consequences of political activity, and the theoretical implications and questions that derive from such activity? It is often difficult to identify the motives behind, and the consequences of, political activity, but the political activity itself is accessible, thus simpler to identify.

If we agree that the exile's political activity should be the principal concern of the political scientist, we must then define who is in fact a political exile. No exiles should be regarded as political unless they participate in exile politics. The reasons for the exiles' status—that is, why they left their country—then become secondary, or at least they must be held in suspension, while attention shifts to exile activity abroad. It may turn out, of course, that a propensity to become a political exile refers back to the motive for departure, but this is another story. Many who have studied cases of exile activism have adopted such a definition of the exile as political participant commonsensically and implicitly. Yet in these studies the term "political exile" has been used randomly and interchangeably with other terms, and without grasping its real meaning. Martin A. Miller has recently offered a classification of exiles that divides them into *refugees*, who will resettle; *expatriates*, abroad by choice; *exiles*, who cannot go home but will not resettle; and *émigrés*, a subgrouping of exiles whom he describes as "political exiles." But the question is not pursued.[61] Thus previous studies have been followed by little analytical investigation; they have overlooked the questions such activities raise for political theory.

I define expatriates as political exiles if they engage in political activity directed against the policies of a home regime, against the home regime itself, or against the political system as a whole, so as to create circumstances favorable to their return. Such a shift from previous frameworks of discussion should enable political scientists to raise new questions about the political status of exile activity and its place in the study of politics. Political exiles, so defined, range from the fully committed, self-conscious, consistent political activist to one rarely motivated and only marginally active. My primary concern is with the fully committed, but the interaction between these and the border cases is of utmost importance. As a political scientist I am particularly concerned with collective behavior, therefore this study pays less attention to enterprises of individual political exiles who remain aloof from organized exile politics than it does to activities of exile groups, especially "revolutionary" exile organizations as distinguished from "reform" exile groups.[62] Both kinds of organizations seek to change their home countries' political and social order, but their objectives and tactics differ significantly in scope.

Reform exile organizations, which make only partial claims, protesting specific policies and forms of state administration, accept the basic tenets of the social and political order. Such groups are characteristic of democratically governed nation-states, which, because they can incorporate dissent, may not require revolution to effect change. An example of a reform exile organization was the Union of American Exiles (UAE), founded in Toronto, Canada, in April 1968, by young Americans facing the draft who argued "that it was not necessary to go to jail to demonstrate opposition to the [Vietnam] war." They considered it more effective to flee their country and maintain an active antiwar campaign from abroad.[63]

Revolutionary exile organizations, on the other hand, strive to overthrow and replace the home regime and usually to reconstruct the entire social order. I distinguish three major groups of exile revolutionary organizations, according to their ultimate objectives and how they justify their demands: (1) organizations that struggle from abroad to overthrow a native home regime; (2) organizations that fight from outside a claimed national territory to gain independent political status inside an international order of sovereign states ("prestate self-determination" or "decolonization" political exiles); and (3) organizations that fight from outside their country's borders against an alien conqueror to regain political independence or territory lost in a war. Examples of the first are the exile organizations of the Italian anti-Fascists, the anti-Nazi Germans, the Spanish Republicans, and the anti-Soviet Russian monarchists. Examples of the second are Mazzini's Young Italy in the era of the Risorgimento, exile liberation movements operating against colonialism in Africa, Basque nationalists demanding complete independence for the Basque state in Spain, and the Palestine Liberation Organization (PLO). Examples of the third are the antifascist governments-in-exile during World War II.

Exiles who seek to replace their country's native regime claim to have a historical, legal, or moral right to represent their national compatriots; they argue for the delegitimation of the home regime as nonrepresentative, while recognizing the legitimacy of the state itself and its territorial boundaries. This type of resistance is usually exerted when the home regime is nondemocratic. Oppositions committed to the destruction of a democratic entity, on the other hand, need not resort to exile struggle, since the system usually allows for other strategies of opposition, including revolutionary expressions.[64] In ancient Greece Athenian democracy employed exile as a protective measure against citizens considered to be too powerful and therefore potential tyrants. In our days the exile of deposed Filipino President Ferdinand Marcos by the government of Corazón Aquino is a unique example of a democracy that prevents its opponents from challenging the system from within. The refusal to allow Marcos to return from exile in Hawaii has been justified by President Aquino's newly elected government as a protective measure to promote political stability during the initial period of redemocratization.[65]

"Prestate self-determination" or "decolonization" political exiles base their claim for self-determination on the argument that nations can express themselves fully only on their own national soil and under the rule of their own national government. Claims by political exiles who seek to overpower their country's foreign conqueror become complex, when the occupying forces diminish the independence of the occupied nation-state and incorporate its people within the conqueror's own national community. Political exiles' struggle is then directed both toward regaining national independence on national territory and affirming their right to national self-determination.

An exile organization can belong to more than one kind of group, simultaneously or at different periods of its existence. The Free French of de Gaulle, the Polish government-in-exile, and the exile liberation organizations of the Baltic states and the Ukraine all had multiple goals. The Free French, for example, fought to delegitimize Vichy France, the country's home regime, and at the same time to free metropolitan France from Nazi occupation. The Polish government-in-exile has struggled against two foreign dictatorships, the Nazi and the Soviet, and over the last forty years has engaged simultaneously in an often futile and sometimes obscure struggle against Polish rulers in Warsaw. Organizations representing the Baltic states and the Dalai Lama's Tibetan government-in-exile based in India (which since the early 1960s has endeavored to recover Tibet's independence from China) are both noted examples of exile organizations struggling for the independence of their native countries and the right to self-determination.

This book deals principally with clearcut cases of exile organizations that struggle to overthrow and replace their home countries' native regimes. Such cases are more likely to illuminate relations between governments and oppositions, and questions of "legitimacy" and "loyalty," in the context of the nation-state. However, I do refer occasionally to "prestate self-determination" or "decolonization" exile groups, and to those who fight against their country's foreign occupier.

To study exile political activity as part of the broader context of governments and oppositions, I introduce a theoretical framework that describes the competition among contestants for power in the state as a struggle for loyalty and recognition, for national and international support of their claims to power. Aspiring to power from abroad, political exiles are in a peculiar position. They are removed from the domestic political arena from which they attract potential loyalists, and they are especially vulnerable to charges of "national disloyalty."

CHAPTER ONE

Who Represents the Nation's Will?

Former leaders of the Social Democrats [in exile] . . . call for foreign armed intervention against Germany. They had finally allowed the mask to slip and the German workers can now recognise what scum, and that word is far too generous, has determined their fate in the past decade. These émigrés have so forgotten the Fatherland that they have shamefully revealed themselves as preferring that Germany should be put to flame and fire under a French and Polish invasion rather than being deprived of their sinecure.

—Hermann Göring

Representing national Russia, we do unique service to our country. Owing no allegiance to anybody, we are ready to advance with all those who are against Communism and Socialism. We seek nothing for ourselves, and do not desire the restitution by force of the old preferential rights of the governing classes. As servants of our country, we are ready to join all Russians who have fought and are fighting now against the Bolshevists, and all those who to this day have been forced to remain in Russia under the yoke of the power they hate and are obliged to obey.

—Gen. Baron Peter N. Wrangel, leader of the
Russian White armies in exile

The essence of politics in the nation-state is the conflict between groups who try to capture or maintain political power—that is, the authority to command. I describe manifestation of support for any claim to power within the national community as "loyalty," the struggle over political power as the process of "loyalty building," and international support for a contestant for power as "recognition." All power seekers try to attract "loyalists" to their cause (empowerment) or at least to reduce the loyalty to other claimants. Loyalty is an asset, independent and scarce, parceled out among different contestants for power. No ruling government or nonruling group enjoys absolute loyalty—no contestant can have the whole pie. Each seeks to engender and preserve loyalty among potential supporters, employing a multiplicity of means. Rulership itself is but one, although the most important, among a variety of available tools, but the mere fact of holding power in the nation-state is only a preliminary indication of loyalty. Thus loyalty cannot be properly understood unless one takes into account factors that transcend the boundaries of political domination.

In order to identify supporters or nonsupporters among the potentially loyal, one has to develop a criterion for interpreting behavior as loyal, antiloyal or nonloyal.[1] One first has to follow the claimants' interpretation of the behavior of those whose support they seek, and then one must evaluate it. Opposing aspirants often interpret loyal behavior differently. For example, some may hold that those who do not oppose them tacitly support them. Others may regard popular indifference as a potential threat to their claim. Obviously, when the claimant is really clear as to what loyalty means, it is more difficult to misinterpret.[2]

To induce loyalty among potential supporters or to reduce the support for rivals, each group employs a multiplicity of means, varying in accordance with the competing political positions. The ruling group, of course, has a tremendous advantage over all others because it possesses what Weber has called the monopoly of the legitimate use of violence within its territorial jurisdiction. Its control over the means of violence within the nation-state—in itself an indication of loyalty given—enables the government to *command* loyalty. A shift in the loyalty of the army and the internal security forces away from the existing authorities leads to a breakdown of the monopoly of coercion. As Katherine Chorley notes, "whatever government or party has the full allegiance of a country's armed forces is to all intents and purposes politically impregnable."[3] The ruling claimant becomes the sole authority within the nation-state in determining when that state is in crisis or when it feels threatened from within or without. Thus its institutions establish the limit between national loyalty and treason. The regime is also the source of communal symbols transmitted to the public. By controlling the educational system and at least part of the media, and "by the encouragement of national holidays and festivals, [and] . . . by fostering patriotic organizations and activities,"[4] the state develops loyalty in its citizens.

On the other hand nonruling contestants, who often experience difficulty in inducing loyalty to their cause, try to advance their claims by undermining loyalty to the rulers. The strategy is to provoke popular unrest by propaganda warfare and other methods of peaceful protest, or by forms of violence and subversion such as terror, political assassination, and guerrilla warfare. A major weapon at their disposal is manipulation of countersymbols of authority and identification.[5] A flag, a hymn, or a ceremony may be powerful instruments in challenging a regime's authority.

Loyalty and Disloyalty in the Nation-State

It is very difficult to maintain power by sheer coercion. Other means must be used to cultivate loyalty among the citizens. In the age of the nation-state where, as Ernest Gellner says, the notion prevails that the "political and national unit should be congruent,"[6] nationalism becomes a major tool for recruiting loyalty. Almost all groups understand that a nation can maintain its existence and truly become manifest only within the defined territorial boundaries of the nation-state. Those who support radical internationalism, on the other hand, advocate abolition of the nation-state, often as part of a class movement for "emancipation of all workers." Irredentists urge incorporation within the national boundaries of territory of which their nation has been "deprived," or sections of a population with close ethnic affinities to those of their nation. Secessionists uphold the right to challenge the national integrity of the state itself and to establish a separate nation-state on all or part of the nation-state's existing territory.

For the nationalist, the nation-state represents the collective interest. It implements and cultivates the national values and protects the cultural boundaries of the nation from penetration by other national cultures. The ruler of that nation-state is considered to be in charge of its manifest destiny. Thus the major task of a government, as the nationalist sees it, is to represent the "national interest."[7]

To gain loyal support, every group in power tries to convince the citizens of the nation-state that it most authentically represents the national interest. Its principal strategy is to identify loyalty to itself with loyalty to the nation-state. Because it contends that, by definition, eminent domain protects, cultivates, and incarnates the national interest, it assumes that all citizens will feel bound by its decisions and will equate national loyalty with such conformity.[8] A regime tends to regard attempts to challenge its "national mission" as acts of "national disloyalty." It will derogate political opponents as being linked to alien interests and therefore nationally disloyal. It seeks to impose a psychological as well as a material penalty on citizens who reject the regime's authority. Albert Hirschman notes: "Such a price can range from loss of life-long association to loss of life, with such intermediate penalties as excommunication, defamation, and deprivation of livelihood."[9] Yet to opposing aspirants competing for the support of the state's citizenry, the existing regime is a false prophet of the nation's spirit; far from representing the national interest, the regime itself is the principal reason for national decadence.[10]

Regimes offer citizens certain benefits of nationalism: citizenship, the pride of belonging to a national community, national awards and decorations, perhaps even a share in determining the national future. Aspirants for a share in the "loyalty pie" must deal, therefore, with the basic fact that the effective "exercise of power creates its own loyalties and common interest."[11] Those who seek to repudiate a regime's equation of nationalism with itself (i.e., the assertion that the regime and the nation-state are one), must offer citizens another, more attractive option than compliance with the existing regime. They must offer citizens new foci of identification and alternative organizations like national parties, national committees, provisional governments, countergovernments, governments-in-exile, and revolutionary armies. Such groups all have in common the realization that organization is the key to political power.[12] Aspirants less organized than this may refer to the national liege in more abstract and at times ambiguous terms, seeking to redirect loyalty of the citizens from an existing regime to the country, the nation, or the fatherland—notions that transcend the present regime. The opposing groups present themselves as national patriots who zealously love and are devoted to their homeland, and brand the existing regime as disloyal to that homeland.

Nonetheless most citizens, knowing little about revolutions and coups d'état, recoil from total opposition to their government, and consider the benefits of accepting its interpretation of national loyalty to be greater than the cost of opposition. Michael Ledeen points out: "It is difficult indeed for any citizen to come to the conclusion that his own country has become a menace to human progress and human society, and even when one suspects that his government is behaving terribly, the commitments to national tradition, family, and friends are very potent ones."[13]

In the age of nationalism, culminating in the triumph of the nation-state, loyalty to the state has become the predominant imperative. Even the greatest universalists of our times have acknowledged that the notion of national loyalty has more appeal and is more tenacious than its less nationalistic competitors.[14] Even Lenin said, "Scratch a Communist and you will find a Great Russian Chauvinist."[15] The Ayatollah Khomeini, the modern prophet of universal Islam, was careful throughout his exile not to alienate Iranian nationalists. In his campaign against the shah, as Shaul Bakhash says, Khomeini preached "state and religion, Iran and Islam, in the same breath."[16]

The process of legitimation,[17] by which competing groups attempt to equate loyalty to their cause with national loyalty, requires special analysis. One must distinguish, for example, between loyalty as a behavioral manifestation of support, and national loyalty as a value-laden concept that power seekers use to rally support and undermine opposing claims. Only such a distinction will enable us to understand the real dynamic of governments and oppositions within the state. An interpretation of loyalty as a behavioral manifestation would exclude by its very nature any moral evaluation of the object of loyalty. One's support of claimant X, Y, or Z has little to do with value judgments of loyalty or disloyalty. Such value judgments are imposed instead by the claimants who seek support or by the supporters themselves. The mere support of a contestant's claim to power is of less importance than questions of how national loyalty should be manifested or who should be regarded as a national loyalist. John Schaar observes: "Actions which seem to be disloyal by one standard may be justified as entirely loyal by another. In all these ways, individuals are able to 'save the appearances,' to regard themselves as loyal and to defend themselves against charges of disloyalty."[18] These value judgments about national loyalty and national disloyalty are used by the contestants for power to impose costs or award benefits for support (for being "loyal" to them). National loyalty is often defined by defining its negation, national disloyalty. The ruling government will interpret any support for other aspirants to power as an act of national disloyalty. The distinction between loyalty as a manifestation of behavior and national loyalty as a moral commitment is thus blurred. No member of the national community inside or even outside state territories can award support to those not in power, without considering the consequences of being stigmatized by the government as nationally disloyal. Nonruling claimants themselves tend to refrain from labeling those who do not support them as "national disloyalists," lest they alienate potential supporters. They may call on the members of the nation-state to follow their cause, warning them against active or passive cooperation with the regime and its atrocities, which might contaminate the "national soul." Aspirants to power reserve their opprobrium for the ruling regime and any rival aspirants to power. They have less power to manipulate the national symbols in their behalf or to induce loyalty or impose costs on those who oppose them.

Political Exiles: National Loyalists or Traitors?

The political debate within the boundaries of the nation-state expands and gains in intensity when it involves opponents of the home regime who are abroad. Political exiles have escaped legal control of the ruling claimant. They cannot be the objects of legal sanctions, although the regime can act against them indirectly. They are subject to the laws and the policies of their host country. Their ability to impose or reward loyalty is drastically limited. In most cases, indeed, "there is nothing to induce members to remain [active] . . . other than their voluntary commitment"[19] to the cause of return.

The need of political exiles to establish their image as national loyalists is crucial not only for mobilizing purposes, but also as a defensive device to protect their national identity. For many political exiles the retention of national identity means living as strangers in their host country. Divorced from contact with their national milieu and culture, they are forced to adapt to a foreign environment and at the same time to negate it. While engaging in a constant struggle to organize and effect a return, the exiles seek to maintain a normal family life. Conflicting commitments, to their national cause on the one hand and to their family on the other, jeopardize their ability to serve either adequately. They often lose contact with the political realities in their home country, and fall victim to sharp generational as well as cultural conflicts with their children. Of Latin American political exiles in Europe in the late 1970s, Andrew Graham-Yooll, an Argentine exile in London, writes:

Many Latin American political exiles in Europe ceased to be militant, blaming distance, language, lack of time or the host country for a decline in interest. . . . As the months passed . . . the language of home became marked with accents or dialects or, in places of foreign tongues, the native speech became faultier and patchy. The jokes, songs, music, that were so dear, so filled with remembrances, became lost on the children. The distinguishing asset that is another nationality was at first disguised, then mentioned to boast of a greater worldliness; finally used only to escape generalisations.[20]

To overcome a contradictory life, as Lewis Edinger writes, the political exile must try "to identify his cause with the national interest, to give himself the psychological support to survive the constant political and socioeconomic pressures pushing him to abdicate his exile status."[21]

In addition to operational difficulties in engendering loyalty to their cause (inside and outside the nation-state boundaries), and their initial inferiority in projecting their image as national loyalists, these exiles must also cope with the value attached to the state's boundaries and the home regime's authority in protecting them. Those in power transform the nation-state's boundaries into a critical element of national self-definition for which people are willing to sacrifice their lives. As the sole authority in protecting the integrity of their territory and their nation's often precarious status internationally, the rulers of the home regime for their own political purposes promote the attachments of the people to the land. The boundaries become the landmark between "us" the insiders and "them" the outsiders, a dichotomy that makes the political exiles extremely vulnerable to the charge of national disloyalty. In an attempt to reduce internal pressure and also to justify future discrediting their opponents as nationally disloyal, many power holders, as Hirschman notes, "have long encouraged their political enemies and potential critics to remove themselves from the scene through voluntary exile."[22]

In this century the idea that national loyalty can be sustained from abroad has been broadly questioned. It is assumed that the more an individual is nationally committed, the less likely will that individual consider emigration. In his noted work *Exit, Voice, and Loyalty,* Hirschman tries to solve the puzzle of why people who are expected to leave a corrupt organization or state do not in fact do so. He describes two alternative responses by members or clients of corporate organizations or states to their system's declining performance: they can express their dissatisfaction by leaving ("Exit"), or they may try to put their organization "back on track" by protesting their dissatisfaction in various degrees to force the management to stem the decline ("Voice").[23] Loyalty in Hirschman's model is the intermediate variable between Exit and Voice: "Loyalty holds exit at bay and activates voice."[24] Exit, according to Hirschman, reflects disloyalty.[25] Hirschman's concept of loyalty and disloyalty has been severely criticized by A. H. Birch and Brian Barry, who argue that by using Exit and non-Exit as the boundary between loyalty and disloyalty, Hirschman has overlooked the possibility of Voice from without: it does not occur to him that at times "exit was not an alternative for voice but a necessary condition for the exercise of voice."[26]

Many nationalists see departure from one's country as "a shameful and even treasonous act."[27] In the nineteenth and twentieth centuries, if not earlier, military service and participation in a country's wars have been considered direct manifestations of patriotism and national loyalty.[28] Americans who chose exile in Canada or Sweden over fighting in Vietnam were regarded by many as "unpatriotic and cowardly."[29] So too, attempts to overthrow a home regime from abroad in the name of the national interest are often viewed skeptically, especially when would-be loyalists side with another nation-state in a war against their own country. (See chapter 7.)

Largely dependent on the assistance of their host country and the support of other international patrons, political exiles are primary candidates for the title of "national disloyalists"; their activities are considered by the home regime as conspiracies against the national interest. In its attempts to discredit internal opposition, the home regime tends, as Juan Linz found in Spain, to "discriminate between internal opponents according to whether they did or did not have contact with [exiled] leaders abroad . . . making them appear to be tools of exiles without contact with reality of life in the country . . . perhaps even subject to foreign manipulation and therefore anational."[30]

To protect themselves against such charges of national disloyalty and the danger of national exclusion, political exiles reject the idea that the home regime manifests the national interest; for them, the regime is a temporary usurper. Responding to Castro's labeling of them as counterrevolutionaries, Cuban exile groups in the United States declared, for example, in April 1961: "We are not, nor could we be, counterrevolutionaries. We are revolutionists who fought against the previous regime, which had impoverished the whole country for the benefit of a minority lusting for gold and power. It is with the same convictions that we now oppose the present regime, which has betrayed our country and plunged it into chaos."[31]

Exiles consider their position not as a final abandonment of the nation-state but on the contrary as a temporary expedient or a makeshift strategy to express their positive commitment to further their nation-state's welfare in a time of crisis.[32] Political exiles regard their struggle as a patriotic mission to save their national community from the home regime's distorted and corrupt representation of the national interest. They distinguish between their "home nation," the national community with which they identify and to which they want to return, and the "home regime," the nation-state's political system that they seek to transform for the sake of the national interest.

Political exiles must struggle to evoke loyalty to their cause inside the home nation and among their national compatriots abroad. Establishing and maintaining an image as national loyalists upholding the national interest is a key factor in that struggle. So too, they must attempt to mobilize international support for their struggle by gaining recognition as authentic representatives of their nation-state.

CHAPTER TWO

Exile Organizations

Competing Claims to Represent the National Interest from Abroad

> *Organization is the road to political power. . . . In the modernizing world he controls the future who organizes its politics.*
> —Samuel P. Huntington, *Political Organization in Changing Societies,* 1968

Exile groups, like all political groups, vary greatly in the structure of the organizations they establish to carry on their collective struggle. Some are informal, amorphous, and fragmented, without a hierarchy between leaders and followers and with constant reshaping of ideologies; others have well-defined and highly bureaucratized structures. Differences in the structure of exile organizations are related to a number of factors, as for example the organizations' justifications for their claim to represent their national constituency, their political origin, and the length of time the organizations have spent abroad.

Governmental and Nongovernmental Claims

Organizations that claim to represent the national constituency are either governmental, including governments-in-exile and exiled monarchical courts, or nongovernmental, consisting chiefly of political parties and their variations of factions or coalitions. An intermediate, semigovernmental form, combining both governmental and nongovernmental claims, includes national committees, national councils, and other similar groups. Such broad classifications do not necessarily reflect differences in the origin of these organizations or in their "targets of mobilization,"[1] but rather differences in the types and degree of support they hope to attain and the justifications they provide in their quest for such support.

Governmental and semigovernmental exile organizations claim to be the sole, or at least the most viable, alternative to the home regime. They appeal for international recognition and vie for the loyalty of their national compatriots at home and abroad, maintaining that they are either (1) lawful, elected rulers of their nation-state, (2) traditional and thus "legitimate" representatives of their national community, or (3) the "authentic" spokesmen of the national interest.

Max Weber's sociology of legitimacy can be applied to an analysis of the institutional framework of these diverse claims. There may be internal divisions between the innermost core of the elite and the organizations' prime loyalists, the staff. An exile organization that claims to be the lawful sovereign of its nation-state, because its members were duly elected and appointed representatives of the last legally constituted and internationally recognized government, usually includes functional superiors and a staff of bureaucrats. The Polish and the Spanish governments-in-exile maintained strong institutional structures characteristic of democratic governments, with cabinets of prime ministers and varying numbers of other key ministers. To emphasize their democratic characteristics, they established and maintained various parliamentary bodies whose members were usually veterans of the pre-exile legislative system.[2] Exile organizations that base their claim to loyalty on their traditional representation typically include exiled monarchs (or their heirs) and their loyal retainers. The Bourbon and the Romanov courts-in-exile provide convenient illustrations for the pomp and circumstance typical of aristocratic rulers.[3] Exile semigovernmental organizations that claim to represent the authentic national interest, but without any legal or traditional claims to power, often are led by a charismatic self-appointed leader with a staff of disciples and followers, as for example the Iranian exile movement in Europe and the United States under Khomeini before the Islamic revolution.

A nongovernmental exile organization, on the other hand, may consider itself only one among several alternatives to succeed the home regime. It may be led by executives or exile leaders (sometimes they are one and the same), assisted by loyal functionaries abroad or inside the home nation. These organizations usually claim to represent a segment of the national electorate in a democratic system and for this reason regard the question of succession as premature. Occasionally they combine forces with other exile groups to establish a more effective organization against the regime at home. Such alliances leave open the matter of what kind of government will supersede the current regime.[4] Several exile coalitions have appeared in the form of "national committees," "national councils," or "national fronts," indicative of a transition in the organizations' claims from nongovernmental to governmental. The idea of forming national committees as counterelite organizations can be traced back to the Comite, an international exile organization founded by Mazzini and other exiled European revolutionaries in 1850, its major objective to promote "republicanism and international revolutionary activity." It advised each country to establish a "National Committee of its own to be the veritable and regular expression of the wants, the wishes, and the general tendencies of that country. . . . The delegates of the National Committees will constitute the Central Committee of the democracy in Europe."[5]

In adopting such labels, political exiles seek to project an image of group unity, crucial for attracting national or international support, and to undermine competing claims of other nonruling aspirants at home or in exile. Such was the case of the Cuban Revolutionary Council, an exile coalition formed in the United States in March 1961. According to its president, the former premier José Miro Cardona (as paraphrased by Peter Wyden), the council was "to be transformed into a provisional government once it had gained a military foothold in Cuba."[6] The council consisted of major exile groups from the center and left of the Cuban exile colony in Florida. It sought to counter the claims of right-wing exile organizations to authentic leadership, and to persuade the American administration to help plan and launch an exile expedition to Cuba. The Americans had long wished to use Cuban exiles in a military operation against Castro, but had been troubled by their lack of political unity; in the Revolutionary Council they found a solution. The council soon became the core of the exile invasion force involved in the Bay of Pigs fiasco.[7]

The opposite transformation in exile organizational claims, from a governmental to a nongovernmental claim, almost never occurs. This can be illustrated by the Polish government-in-exile in London, whose old members as a matter of principle still oppose any suggestion to transform their status into that of a national committee. Although the Polish government-in-exile lost its last diplomatic recognition in 1963 and became no more than a fictional entity,[8] the group still claims to be a government-in-exile. What seems an anomalous stance to an outside observer is perceived by the old members of the group as a vital tactic in maintaining their prewar status. They refuse to abandon their fictional existence and their claim to be the legal representatives of the Poles, lest they endanger their future relevance should the home regime collapse. As with the Norwegian and the Benelux governments-in-exile in the aftermath of the German occupation, so members of the Polish government-in-exile maintain their legal claims and the power of their political forum in anticipation of a possible transition to a democratic regime. In a 1986 interview Count Edward Raczynski, the aging president of the Polish government-in-exile, expressed confidence that at the moment of national liberation his exile organization, as paraphrased by Eva Hoffman, "would ride in on white horses to take the reins of power; it would merely pass on the symbols of its legitimacy, which it inherited from the pre-war government."[9]

It is apparent that the claims of both governmental and nongovernmental exile organizations are an integral part of these organizations' tactics and their rhetoric to mobilize support, and do not necessarily reflect other fundamental differences among them.

The Role of Origin

There is often a close connection between the form of exile organizations and their historical origins. Origin often determines both material resources and recruiting policies, especially during the initial period abroad. Significant differences may exist between exile organizations that grow from groups established prior to exile, and organizations formed abroad with no pre-exile following of any kind. The material resources an exile organization has at its disposal may themselves reflect origin. Thus pre-exile organizations, especially deposed governments, are more likely to have reserves of state capital abroad. The Spanish Republicans managed to smuggle part of the Spanish treasure from Spain to Mexico on the pleasure yacht *Vita*.[10] The governments-in-exile in London and the United States during World War II also provide clear examples. Dutch and Norwegians living abroad paid taxes to their exiled national governments, whether or not they also paid taxes to the countries where they resided.[11] Members of exile organizations with little pre-exile background, on the contrary, are largely dependent, especially during their formative period, on individuals' personal possessions, or on extensive fund-raising campaigns abroad. Justice and Liberty, the Italian anti-Fascist exile organization, was such a group. Its founder and leader, Carlo Rosselli, also served as its financial patron.[12]

Leaders of organizations that predate the period of exile devote much of their effort to perpetuating the mere survival of their ongoing organizations; they work to preserve their political identity, secure key contributors and resources, and protect their roles as leaders. Problems of distance and dispersal, and limitations in their ability to reward their followers, stand in the way of renewing and rejuvenating loyal cadres abroad. The first task of their leaders is to regroup their scattered ranks and establish communication networks with followers at home. This was the primary undertaking of many Latin American parties in exile after the imposition of authoritarian regimes in their countries.[13] They sought first to preserve their organizational apparatus and its symbols abroad.

The problem of maintaining the authority that existed in the home country is especially acute for organizations whose loyalists are now in exile. Many of these refugees will be lonely, homesick, and needy. Longing to be led, they look to exile organizations as an oasis of national companionship. One student of Russian refugees in the post-revolutionary period observed that such collective support counters the sense of inferiority a refugee may experience in a foreign environment.[14] To perpetuate such comradeships and keep old loyalties and symbols alive among the refugees, many exile organizations may assume the role of welfare and social agencies. They organize mutual aid groups, public lectures and conferences, and means of maintaining social, cultural, and home language ties. Leaders try to promote participation in political acts through the manipulation of material rewards and by distributing a variety of collective symbols of solidarity. For example, they may provide jobs and health care, or finance children's education, or award other material benefits that reduce economic distress. All such efforts help preserve the national identity of nationals abroad and enhance the position and power of the exile organization itself. The activities of Spanish Republican refugee organizations in Mexico is a good example of this dynamic (see chapter 4).[15] Leaders of exile organizations often try to reinforce the sense of "historic responsibility" toward those who were left behind in their homeland. They seek to instill a sense of duty or a feeling of guilt that will impel their compatriots abroad "to work for the cause and compensate for their freedom, by speaking up for those silenced at home."[16] The military clubs of the White army veterans in France in the 1920s exemplified such an effort; their high command tried, though futilely, to keep the army's nucleus intact. (See chapter 4.)

The Validation of Claims to Power

Many pre-exile organizations hold an unusual (sometimes distorted) vision of history and time. On the one hand, they maintain that the passage of time abroad is insignificant as a criterion for evaluating the validity of their claims to power. On the other hand, they operate with a sense of urgency, wishing to force the future into the present while at the same time trying to preserve the past.

These paradoxical desires find powerful expression among organizations that strive to preserve pre-exile status and form, particularly those governments-in-exile and exiled parties that have fled after the imposition of authoritarian rule at home. They try to maintain the democratic-legal character molded in the pre-exile period. Exile aspirants who do not make claims to power based on elections, on the other hand, have less need to validate their claims as national representatives—at least at the theoretical level. For exiled monarchical courts, which are examples of traditional authority, legitimacy is bound up in the person of the monarch or his successor(s). The exiled king, through his dynasty, "is the living flag of his nation."[17] Those who claim to be the supreme national representatives but without providing legal or traditional justifications appeal for support in the name of moral or political principles of universal validity. Ideologies and personal creeds serve exile groups as ongoing manifestations of their legitimacy; de Gaulle, for example, claimed to represent the honor of France. These kinds of validation alone are obviously insufficient in justifying legal claims of pre-exile groups. Leaders of such groups may, for example, face serious difficulties in maintaining democratic procedures and authority, as did Chilean socialist leaders in exile whose parties had been severely handicapped since the fall of Allende.[18]

In contrast with periodically elected bodies in a democratic parliamentary system, exile organizations are faced with the problem of how to renew their legal status without elections, plebiscites, or other popular mandates. With their claims to power unvalidated, strong loyalties both at home and abroad are of instrumental importance. By demonstrating the strength of such loyalties, the organizations seek to strengthen their peculiar self-legitimizing position. They may urge the international community to recognize them in various ways: declarative, diplomatic, and operational.

Pre-exile organizations that try to perpetuate their democratic legal character while abroad will insist on maintaining their internal order in accordance with old constitutions and provisions regarding succession in leadership. But over time, adherence to democratic formalities of legal continuity and bureaucratized procedures, common to governments- and parliaments-in-exile, may become an obstacle or a threat to organizational unity. The operation of rules of succession may become undesirable or unacceptable to certain elements within the exile organization. In the 1940s the Spanish Republicans in Mexico faced constant turmoil over the question of legal succession after the resignation of the Spanish president, Manuel Azaña. (See chapter 4.) The longevity of exile succession can also be jeopardized by lack of generational continuity after the death of the organization's original cadre. In the early 1980s the old leaders of the Polish government-in-exile, fearing that their organization was fading, tentatively approached high-ranking Solidarity activists in exile to test their willingness to inherit their posts.[19] The case of the Paraguayan Febrerista Revolutionary Party (PFR), on the other hand, is an extreme example of how an exile party has dealt with the complex issue of validating and perpetuating its legal status while abroad. The Febreristas succeeded in maintaining contact with their followers both inside Paraguay and in exile in Chile and Argentina. They established a sophisticated organization that operated in accordance with the party's constitution. This constitution sought to ensure that the leaders abroad remained accountable to policies laid down by the party's members. The supreme authority of the exile Febreristas, a National Convention that named the party's National Executive Committee, was elected every three or four years by both regional and local committees that were themselves elected periodically in a legal-democratic process in Paraguay and abroad.[20]

The success of the Dalai Lama in heading a Tibetan government-in-exile based in India is even more fascinating. Its raison d'être is to work for the reestablishment of Tibetan sovereignty through democratic procedures. The Tibetan cabinet-in-exile, the Kashag, consists of seven ministers subordinate to a body of representatives elected by the large and cohesive Tibetan refugee community in India. Like the former General Assembly (Tshokdhu Gyezom) in Tibet, it is elected for a period of three years to represent the three major geographical regions of Tibet and its five religious orders. The Dalai Lama and the Tibetan diaspora have nurtured an alternative democratic polity in India, and "provided a beam of light and hope . . . for the six million Tibetans remaining in the Chinese-dominated Tibet. [They have] not abandoned their faith or [their] loyalty to the Dalai Lama, who has come to personify more than ever the Tibetan religo-political order and national identity."[21]

The Hope of Return and International Recognition

The observation "Time in politics like in life is a resource and therefore scarce"[22] is especially relevant to pre-exile organizations. The likelihood that such an organization will preserve its cadres intact decreases proportionately as the group stays outside its home nation; in an exile environment there is a constant danger of erosion of the hope of return. Removed from the immediate conditions that motivate their political struggle, and living in an indifferent environment, pre-exile groups frequently find their collective energies dissipating into sterile and meaningless activity. Moreover, with the growing acknowledgment that the home regime will not lose its grip, the revolutionary spirit of the organization's loyalists is gradually consumed by participation in their host country's life. There will be a decline of interest among the younger generation, many of them born abroad. Old followers will die. Indeed, the fear of dying before reaching the promised land affects all political exiles. "I feel as if I had come here to be buried,"[23] Lenin murmured to his wife Krupskaya upon beginning his second period of exile in January 1908 in Geneva.

When there is no immediate prospect of return, leaders of pre-exile organizations are more likely to be challenged by followers abroad and by opposition leaders at home who deny the exile leadership's right or ability to maintain its leading status. Many exile leaders are forced, in consequence, to devote much of their energy to healing internal divisions. This was the predicament of the exiled leadership of the German Social Democratic Party (SPD). Throughout its time abroad the party chairman, Hans Vogel, and other members of the SPD executive insisted they were the only authorized speakers for the legal party, a right they had legally earned in the 1933 elections. Nonetheless, the legality of the SPD leadership prior to its departure from Nazi Germany was constantly contested by many new socialist groups, some of which rose abroad, while others predated the exile. These groups refused to recognize the authority of the old leaders. Only toward the end of World War II, after tortuous negotiations and division, was a union formed of all socialist groups, including the old executive.[24]

Time has an effect not only on political exiles but also on the resistance at home. The internal opposition may encounter great operational difficulties while the opposition abroad, under the shelter of a supportive host state, enjoys relative immunity from the home regime's repression. Political exiles may "not only [be] unharmed by the pressure and trauma of exile but [may] actually [prosper] because of it."[25] A student of the African National Congress has observed: "Underneath the shelter afforded by sympathetic government, the organization has developed resources well beyond the capacity of internally based South African political movements."[26]

Leaders of exile organizations ideologically related to other parties in the international community will try to exploit their pre-exile international connections so as to maintain their status abroad. Recognition by ideological allies in the international community is often sought by exile party leaders as a means to discredit rival party factions and cliques of other would-be leaders. Carlos Altamirano, an exile leader of the Chilean Socialist Party, which was severely shattered by Pinochet's 1973 coup, appealed for support from European socialist parties at the first congress of the Spanish Socialist Party in the post-Franco era. This was part of Altamirano's campaign to delegitimize the exiled socialist faction in Caracas, Venezuela, headed by Aniceto Rodríguez and Clodomiro Almeyda.[27] The exiled German socialists in London during World War II, however, "were cold-shouldered by the [British] Labour Party, mainly due to the hostility of the then International Secretary of the Labour Party, William Gillies, to everything German." Gillies was also behind the exclusion of the German and Austrian socialist exiles from the international socialist gathering that took place in London during the war. He "favoured a small group of German writers and journalists, preaching the gospel of Vansittartism," that is, the view that the majority of Germans were responsible for the war and must therefore bear the consequences.[28]

The organizational elite of pre-exile organizations whose leading members held state positions before departure will try to maintain the elite's sovereign status in the eyes of the international community. Spanish Republicans in Mexico and the governments-in-exile during and after World War II were examples of this. So was the Council of Russian Ambassadors, founded in Paris at the end of 1917. This group, consisting of ambassadors to important European states from the deposed Provisional Government, succeeded for several years in maintaining recognition by French authorities of its status as Russia's official proxy.[29]

In highly ideological pre-exile organizations, leaders will often try to protect their position by restricting membership to loyalists who have demonstrated ideological commitment—a selective recruiting policy justified by the need to maintain ideological purity. Or they may restrict membership, fearing spies and agents provocateurs in the service of the home regime.[30] Max Nomad, an exiled revolutionary and disillusioned devotee of Waclaw Machajski, a quasi-anarchist-Marxist philosopher, described the relations within exile groups in Europe in the 1930s: "In some people the ever present danger of betrayal calls forth a mild form of insanity, or mania, of seeing stool-pigeons everywhere—even in one's closest friends."[31]

Founders of exile organizations who have no solid pre-exile ideological or political background, on the other hand, are less likely during their groups' initial months to concentrate their efforts on matters of organizational forms, leadership, and loyalty. They often leave such matters to circumstance. Only after these forces find roots inside the home country and abroad will they try to build organizational networks, create leadership groups, and formulate programs for the future. Instead, they frequently use their energies for mass appeals to arouse their compatriots and stir international opinion against the home regime. Such exile organizations often consist of a handful of followers of a single charismatic individual, or intellectuals forced to flee because of antiregime activity. These groups hope to establish a popular revolutionary movement to mobilize their compatriots and challenge the home regime's mass appeal. Justice and Liberty, an Italian anti-Fascist exile group, is a good example of such a mass-oriented movement. Founded in Paris in 1929 by Carlo Rosselli with a few of his closest friends, many of them intellectuals, Justice and Liberty called itself a movement and not a party, reflecting Rosselli's tactics to appeal to as wide a national constituency as possible.[32]

Exile organizations that are closely tied to a charismatic leader and do not maintain a structured headquarters with full-time staff are extremely fragile in times of political uncertainty and crises. This was true of Justice and Liberty during the Ethiopian war and especially after Rosselli's assassination in 1937, when the organization almost collapsed. (See chapter 5.) In terms of ideological outlook, exile groups with little organizational history often find it difficult to maintain ideological consistency. Their leaders may see the organization's cause as better served by articulating vague or broadly stated goals, and tend to reshape their ideologies in an attempt to gain more support. An illustration of this is the policies of Rómulo Betancourt, founder and leader of Venezuela's Acción Democrática (AD), in his first exile period (1928–36). Betancourt was then involved in the activities of the Communist Party of Costa Rica, but steadily moved toward a nationalistic doctrine advocating cooperation with the United States in the fight against Caribbean dictators.[33] Ideological ambiguity and inconsistency, however, may threaten an organization's credibility and internal cohesion. Rosselli's ideological opportunism, for example, was severely criticized by many of his closest loyalists, who subsequently deserted Justice and Liberty. (See chapter 5.)

Finally, exile organizations that lack a strong and consistent ideology cannot sustain themselves for long, unless able to produce rapid and dramatic developments in the conditions of their constituencies at home and abroad. Ideologically uncommitted loyalists who join the organization in a burst of enthusiasm will remain active only if they receive quick compensation. When the excitement wanes and the organization fails to deliver, followers may either become disillusioned or withdraw their support altogether. This was the case of the Cuban exile organizations in the United States in the early 1960s. Lourdes Casal, a student of such organizations, has noted how at the beginning they managed to engage a large segment of the refugee community in their activity to overthrow Castro. After the Bay of Pigs fiasco, however, "[a]s these organizations failed to reach their goal— and the international situation plus the internal consolidation of the Cuban regime made it progressively more unlikely that they would— the Cuban communities became disenchanted with such [exile] activities and withdrew their support."[34]

CHAPTER THREE

The Politics of Schism

Exile is a hothouse where conflicts grow wild and hairsplitting dog-matists luxuriate.
—Louis Fischer, *The Life of Lenin*, 1964

The political world of exile is anything but united. It frequently resembles a lion's den. Indeed, the intensity of the inter- and intraexile conflicts often diverts energy from the attainment of the ultimate group goal, a return to the homeland.

Fierce disputes arise among exile organizations about who exactly is the authentic representative of the national interest. Competing organizations offer opinions on their historical, legal, or moral justification for representing the national will at home, and each on the basis of its particular perspective competes for recognition and loyalty from prospective contributors. Most conflicts among and/or within groups stem from issues of leadership, ideology, and tactics.[1] Constant animosity has existed since the early 1980s between the two exile groups opposing the Islamic regime in Iran: the Mujahedeen and the monarchists. Until June 1986 in Paris, and since then in Iraq, the exiled Mujahedeen under the leadership of Masood Rajavi have claimed to represent the authentic popular will of the entire Iranian nation. Rajavi considers himself the leader of the domestic opposition to Khomeini and regards his organization's struggle from abroad as a "historical mission to save Iran." The exiled monarchists, headed by former Iranian prime ministers Ali Amini and Shahpour Bakhtiar, see in the shah's son, who has proclaimed himself Shah Reza II, the only legal alternative to the Islamic regime. According to the monarchists' legal-traditional claim, "a return to the monarchy is the only solution for Iran . . . for it is the institution that everyone knows."[2]

Rivalries between and within exile organizations continue pre-exile political disputes, intensified by the exile environment. Pre-exile organizations bring with them mutual prejudices, animosities, and resentments stemming from their failure to emerge as political victors at home. Unity within a group abroad is affected significantly by the cohesion that existed within the group before exile. Organizations without a cohesive leadership and a developed sense of internal unity at home are more likely to split in exile abroad.

Autonomy and Identity

Compelled to contend with a new environment, exile organizations by their very nature operate under a great deal of uncertainty. The task of maintaining pre-exile symbols of unity or of generating new ones is particularly difficult and complex. The binding power of the exile leaders themselves is extremely limited; conformity to their rule must depend principally on the genuine consent of their loyalists. The operational vacuum occasioned by the exiles' dependency on their host state's policies, or on those of other international patrons, may undermine the exile organization's cohesiveness and weaken the status of its leadership. Many exile leaders therefore find it difficult to assure the survival of their organization and at the same time adopt policies that might help realize their national aspirations. Their limited ability to assure control over developments either in their home nation or among their followers and prospective followers abroad, often engages all their energy in guaranteeing the survival of their organization. In consequence, leaders often avoid compromises on theoretical and tactical issues that they believe might threaten their organization's survival abroad or its position on returning home. Ideologies tend to harden into dogmatic creeds.

Like political organizations in general, those in exile often become ends in themselves. As James Q. Wilson points out, "Whatever else organizations seek, they seek to survive."[3] The desire to promote political goals may seem diametrically opposed to efforts to maintain an organization's character; in some cases, constant strife to preserve that character actually compromises the political goals. Operating under a constant shortage of autonomy and resources, political organizations, Wilson notes, "are among the most competitive, and they will, . . . freely attack other groups, including, and perhaps especially, those whose goals they do not oppose but whose resources they envy."[4] Exile organizations are such competitive groups.

One of the most noted cases in which exile debate took on the character of competitive disputation involved the Russian Social Democratic Labor Organization in exile before the October Revolution. From the first days of publication of *Iskra*, the first exile newspaper, Lenin had become the protagonist behind the historic Bolshevik-

Menshevik rupture. The leader of the Bolshevik faction, who became known for his "splitting mania,"[5] that is, his obsession with fragmenting as a technique for maintaining his own power, did not avoid bickering and squabbling with his fellow exiles but in fact, as Louis Fischer writes, "welcomed it."[6] In his drive toward ultimate control of socialist opposition to the czar, Lenin rejected any attempt by the Mensheviks to establish a united front to overthrow the monarchy. This man who devoted himself religiously to the idea of a professional revolutionary elite had exaggerated out of all proportion the ideological differences with his exile rivals, as part of his tactics to maintain absolute control over his party.

In a situation of prolonged exile, which is often characterized by political sterility, ideological gratification serves as an essential mechanism to perpetuate loyalties. Exile leaders must appeal to some set of moral and political principles that their prospective and active followers acknowledge as having universal validity. But if devotion to principles is not followed by substantive accomplishments, loyalties can be preserved only for a limited period of time. Defeatism and dissension may grow, even extremism and political blindness.

Exile leaders may find themselves abandoned, especially with the turnover of generations, because of increasing disenchantment with the organization's performance. Fellow loyalists in exile—especially among the younger generation, who search for solutions without maintaining continuity with the past—may try to discredit them abroad, protesting that the traditional leadership is either too restrained or too heavy-handed and rigid. Or exile leaders may find themselves challenged abroad and at home by younger and more militant members. After years of vacuous ideological conflicts, by 1909 the majority of Lenin's devotees had deserted the Bolshevik faction, and the party in exile almost totally crumbled. In retrospect Zinoviev wrote, "at this unhappy period the party as a whole ceased to exist."[7] Potential and active followers who have remained at home and newly emerging internal opponents of the regime, with no connection or commitment to the 'exiles or their loyalists at home, may dispute the exiles' claim to represent the domestic opposition. They may seek to discredit these exile organizations on the grounds of their ignorance of new realities at home.

Exiles who have lost faith in the political leaders of the older generation may try to organize themselves along different lines, perhaps advocating a new and more violent strategy against the home regime or, at the other extreme, seeking reconciliation with it. More often this new exile force will strive to establish contacts with potential reformers within the home regime. After the British withdrew their recognition of the Polish government-in-exile in 1945 and transferred it to the Soviet-sponsored regime, followers abroad increasingly questioned the exiled government's legality and its effectiveness in the fight against communism. The internal controversy split Polish exiles in London into two camps: both the "legalistic" and the more militant "pragmatic" exiles claimed to represent the real Polish interest.[8] Among the young Russian exiles, however, some groups repudiated the anti-Bolshevik politics of their fathers after the Nazi invasion of Russia, and at that time of patriotic defense adopted the extreme policy of acknowledging the Soviet regime as an "authentic national phenomenon."[9]

In the early period of their activities abroad, groups from different political backgrounds may feel the disadvantage of appearing as a divided community in the eyes of their potential supporters, and thus seek to form alliances. Such exile coalitions often preempt the labels "government-in-exile," "national committee," or other titles intended to symbolize overall national representation. But like any other political organizations that operate under conditions of uncertainty, the exile coalitions face extreme difficulties in preserving unity. Exile groups with divergent views that seek to operate together in a single organization frequently are beset by even deeper division, particularly in the absence of an immediate prospect of return to the native land. Mitigating against exile unity are memories of recent bickerings; disagreements as to the character of the social and political system to be established on return; opposing views on foreign policy or domestic exile issues; fear of losing influence within a large exile conglomerate; lack of financial resources; fear of agents provocateurs; and most of all, the role of the internal opposition to the home regime, and the possible consolidation of the latter. For these reasons, in the late 1940s and early 1950s Czech, Hungarian, Bulgarian, Rumanian, Yugoslav, and Polish exile organizations all failed in their effort to maintain a united exile front against the communist regimes at home.[10]

Exile Coalitions

Bringing political exiles together are a number of incentives: financial need, availability of military resources, policy promises, and the emotional satisfaction of solidarity. Exile unity can increase the credibility and prestige of the overall exile struggle in the eyes of prospective national and international supporters. Some exile coalitions are formed during the organizations' formative stage abroad. Others are an act of despair, a response to a prolonged inter- or intraexile conflict that has exhausted competing exile forces. More frequently, an exile alliance is established as a consequence of dramatic internal changes in their country or as a result of international events. Competing exiles then join together to appeal to prospective contributors whose support, so the exiles calculate, may increase if their forces are united. This was the case among the Spanish Republicans in Mexico after World War II, who tried to iron out their old internal rivalries in a vain effort to convince the Western powers to help them topple Franco.[11]

By and large, political organizations in parliamentary frameworks operate under conditions that guarantee victory to a winning coalition and that make the benefits from a coalition victory highly certain. Under exile conditions, however, "the probabilities of and the payoffs from coalition victory are uncertain."[12] Moreover, exile coalition partners often disagree over how to allocate the resources of power, material or symbolic, and differ in their evaluations of each coalition member's contribution to the collective effort. The administration of financial resources, in particular, is a common cause of exiles' disputes. Since exile leaders often receive personal support from anonymous outside elements, questions often arise about their management of organizational resources, and distrust about the misuse of funds for personal or factional gains may induce schism. Apprehensiveness about financial trustworthiness is often abetted by the home regime's effort to discredit the exile leaders as crooks who exploit their compatriots in order to "live in 'princely fashion' in 'golden exile.'"[13] Hence potential and active partners in exile coalitions frequently exhibit suspicion and jealousy toward one another and are extremely protective of their precoalition identities. Participants in exile coalitions often tend to exaggerate their ideational and tactical identities by overemphasizing their differences with other exile groups that actually share much in common with them.

The case of the exile Concentrazione Antifascista may serve as an example. Established in Paris in 1927 as an exile umbrella organization, the Concentration included representatives from a wide spectrum of Italian anti-Fascist exile groups. In 1931 the Concentration merged with Justice and Liberty, then a fairly new exile organization that had earned a reputation as the most effective organized opposition to Mussolini inside Italy. Upon merging with the Concentration, Justice and Liberty's leader Carlo Rosselli assured his coalition partners that he was willing to dissolve his own group's independent status. He authorized the Concentration to outline and direct "the over-all anti-Fascist strategy outside of Italy," while his faction became the supreme authority for anti-Fascist activity at home. But the new coalition soon encountered a grave conflict over the distribution of power. Other coalition partners, particularly the exiled Republican Party, whose "Mazzinian program . . . had been copied by Rosselli's group, became envious of the leading role given to Justice and Liberty." Justice and Liberty, for its part, "did not live up completely to the agreement that it had struck with the Concentration, whereby the latter was to have full authority over the supervision of anti-Fascist activities abroad." By March 1932 the Mazzinian Republicans had withdrawn from the Concentration.[14]

Exile responses to the choices between unity and going it alone range over a wide spectrum. At one extreme are attempts to establish an inclusive exile front consisting of the largest coalition possible; at the other extreme, policies of total separatism. Efforts to establish and preserve a "grand coalition" are strongest where a central exile body coexists with smaller peripheral groups. The largest organization's leadership attempts to absorb peripheral and rival leadership in a wider coalition that can present itself as the sole, authentic national voice. Yet preserving exile unity around a central leadership may threaten ultimate goals. The smaller coalition participants, who fear being stripped of autonomy, may seek to limit the coalition's authority to speak on their behalf. Or a coalition's leaders who fear the outbreak of factionalism may find their attempts to satisfy all coalition members extremely costly. Under the constraint of organizational unity it becomes almost impossible for exile leadership to respond swiftly to changing circumstances by altering or reformulating policy; in turn, this inability to act intensifies the factionalism always present within exile organizations.

Ideological Purity

The failure to establish or to maintain political unity is often rationalized by exile leaders on ideological grounds. For ideological purity is often considered a key tactic in sustaining a leadership's power. Attachment to a "fundamental ideology"[15]—an integral phenomenon in the politics of nonruling aspirants, especially nonruling pressure groups in parliamentary democracies and in certain marginal opposition groups in multiparty parliamentary democracies—is often at its most extreme among exile organizations. As a consequence of its revolutionary character and the involvement of intellectuals, exile politics has a strong ideological component. Moreover under exile conditions, especially in times of an operational void and lack of control over developments at home, ideologies meet social, psychological, and tactical needs of the exile rank and file. Ideology helps to protect organizational identity, defining who you are (or, more important, who you are not) and who you can appeal to. Ideology also serves to define loyalists' responsibility, enabling exiled followers to see their struggle as a sacred mission to bring about national salvation. Ideologies can then provide exile leaders with a body of doctrine by which to justify and protect their position against the threats arising out of any operational stalemate or internal dissent. As Paul Lewis has observed, exile leaders "try to use ideology to smother criticism and read the dissidents out of the party."[16]

Unlike opposition organizations abroad, an internal underground movement frequently has neither the time nor the incentive to engage in ideological debates that can lead to factionalism. While it needs to establish institutional procedures to cope with problems of loyalty and unity, the rigor imposed by daily struggle against the regime tends to oblige the clandestine opposition to set aside abstract discussions so as to devote its energies to survival. Political exiles, on the other hand, often being free from severe challenges to their very existence, can take the risk of factionalism. Their politics often shifts from genuine action to sterile planned action. The discord that often weakened joint action among anti-Fascist groups in exile was not reflected in the anti-Fascist struggle inside Italy, where internal opposition to Mussolini collaborated closely and effectively. As an anti-Fascist observed: "Having lived twenty years under Fascism, [the internal opposition] is united by a community of experience which inevitably created a mentality no exiled group can share."[17]

Also, the exiles' limited ability to affect their political and social environment back home causes enormous frustration, which in turn may lead to heavy-handed and rigid policy. Denied the ability to engage in meaningful political activity, exiles sublimate their frustrations in arid debates about procedures, charters, and constitutions. Hence many political exiles tend to express their ideological uniqueness, as opposed to rival groups, in divisive ways. They are more prone to engage in ideological debates that produce factionalism, splinters, and in extreme cases even killings, as happened in the 1960s among organizations in exile, from Angola's MPLA (Popular Movement for the Liberation of Angola), Mozambique's FRELIMO (Liberation Front of Mozambique), Zimbabwe's African People's Union and African National Union, and, most recently, South Africa's Pan-Africanist Congress and ANC.[18]

The "escape" to theoretical purity is often the only way an exile organization can maintain itself in the face of strong opposition from outside groups and internal dissent. As Paul Lewis has observed, many of the theoretical disputes within and among exile organizations are "simply glitter to distract attention from the real battle over some narrower concern—such as dispute over tactics or personal feud."[19]

The Insider-Outsider Dilemma

A major practical consideration dividing exile organizations along theoretical lines is the respective roles of the political exiles and the domestic opposition in the struggle against the home regime. Use of exile-motivated violence in overthrowing the home regime, as opposed to domestic forces for delegitimation and final rejection of the regime, is a central issue in the disputes among political exiles. Two clearly defined exile camps emerge. One consists of political exiles who claim that the home regime can be overthrown only by the continuous activity of people who remain inside the country. Those who hold this view usually argue that exiles' roles should be restricted to aiding and abetting internal revolutionary activities of the opposition forces, and to establishing and promulgating foreign-policy programs. They reject the idea of overthrowing the home regime from outside, sometimes maintaining that such violence merely worsens the lot of those whom the exiles seek to liberate. The other camp usually gives little consideration to opposition to the regime at home. It advocates a return to the homeland "weapon in hand"; it calls for outright violence, originating abroad, and seeks to destroy the hated regime violently.

The different approaches to the insider-outsider dilemma often hint at opposing claims for national representation. They indicate the nature of the situation under which the exile organizations are operating, their foothold among domestic opposition to the regime, and the operational resources at their disposal. The idea of overthrowing the regime from without appeals mainly to exile organizations removed from the people at home and to those who have little faith in the internal opposition's ability to overthrow the regime. Exile organizations that stress the role of popular resistance inside the country, on the other hand, have either retained a foothold at home or concluded that there are no external alternatives in the struggle against the regime. This second category includes organizations hoping that those who overthrow the home regime will give them an important role in the new government. Exile organizations that play or claim to play an active role among the underground opposition try to belittle the political importance of rival exile organizations concentrating on externally induced change. This was, for example, true of the Spanish exile communists who took pride in their close relations with the opposition to Franco in Spain. The exiled communists "accused members of other partisan groups in exile of excessive talk about bringing down the Franco government and a minimum of concrete action."[20] Similarly, the Banderivtsi, the Ukrainian "nationalist-revolutionaries" exile faction, withdrew from the Ukrainian National Council in May 1950. After the end of World War II the faction had demanded a greater role in the Ukrainian government-in-exile, as the only exile group with active links to domestic revolutionary forces. They sought at the same time to minimize the political effect of the council in international politics.[21] The insider-outsider dilemma was also a chief dividing line between leftist and rightist Cuban organizations in the United States in the early 1960s,[22] and it was the principal theoretical issue fueling the futile debates among Russian exiles in Europe after the October Revolution. (See chapter 4.)

Foreign Intervention

The insider-outsider debate among and within exile organizations often acquires ideological tints that perpetuate cleavages when the debate involves third-party intervention. Competing exile organizations heavily dependent upon different international benefactors may find themselves agitating against one another on issues that have nothing to do with their own struggle. This was the case among African exile organizations polarized into two rival leagues according to their affiliations with Peking or Moscow. As John Marcum points out, the deterioration in Sino-Soviet relations in the late 1960s "introduced ideological discord, reinforced factionalism and thereby undermined both collective purpose and organizational stability within some of these [exile] movements."[23]

Of more critical importance is the question whether all means are justified in the struggle against the home regime, a question that often irrevocably splits political exiles. Many organizations avoid cooperation with foreign elements declared by the home regime to be "national enemies," for fear of abdicating their claim to be national loyalists. Others view cooperation with the hostile body as preferable to continued rule by the home regime. The tactical and ideological disagreements between and within the exile organizations on the subject of foreign intervention reach an extreme, when the exiles' native country is engaged in an external war with another country or with national liberation movements fighting to secede from colonial rule.

Thus the outbreak of war in Angola in 1961 between African nationalist insurgents and the colonial government in Lisbon intensified discord among Portuguese exile groups opposed to Antonio Salazar. They were divided into two camps—for and against independent Africa. Gen. Humberto Delgado, who fled to Brazil after challenging Salazar's government in the fraudulent elections of 1958, and his close friend Capt. Henrique Galvão, who spent years in a Portuguese prison for alleged conspiracies before finding refuge in Venezuela, collaborated abroad in the National Independent Movement (Movimento Nacional Independente, or MNI), the leading organization of the Portuguese democratic opposition. In January 1961 Galvão and his exile loyalists captured the world's imagination when they hijacked the 25,000-ton Portuguese liner *Santa Maria*. This act, which was intended to arouse domestic opposition to Salazar and expose his regime to world criticism, ended with no real victory. Galvão was forced to turn the ship over to the Brazilian authorities. Delgado, as head of the opposition who had initially lent his authority to the operation and even joined the ship near Brazilian shores, later acknowledged the *Santa Maria* affair was a fiasco. He accused his old friend of pursuing publicity and of conducting "an action very damaging to the preparations of the revolt of Portugal. He displayed an exhibitionism almost without measure."[24]

The revolt in Angola that broke out shortly after the *Santa Maria* affair[25] further aggravated the split between the two exile leaders, and Delgado, acting from his new headquarters in Rabat, Morocco, dismissed Galvão as secretary-general of the National Independence Movement.[26] Delgado, who later united his exile forces with the exiled Portuguese Communist Party (PCP), expressed readiness to recognize Angola's right to self-determination; he had established contacts with the leaders of the Popular Liberation Movement of Angola (Movimento Popular de Libertação de Angola, or MPLA). Galvão, however, rejected the idea of self-determination. His anticommunist exile faction in São Paulo, Brazil, the Frente Antitotalitária dos Portugueses Livres Exilados (FAPLE), and Galvão supporters in the United States adopted a procolonial nationalist position, maintaining that "whatever culture . . . exist[ed] in Portuguese Africa [was] of Portuguese form and expression."[27]

In time of war (see chapter 7), political exiles are forced to reexamine the distinction they make between their national compatriots and their opponent government. This dilemma results in a spectrum of opinions ranging from those who collaborate with the foreign forces, to those who fight in defense of their home nation despite its being ruled by their opponents.

The limited ability of exile organizations to determine their own political future often makes theoretical questions central to their lives. Adherence to subtleties of theory—especially when it serves as a refuge from political realities—often seems to work against the exiles' objectives. Prospective national and international supporters may withhold or withdraw their support upon noting the exiles' lack of leadership and political experience. Moreover, the home regimes may try to exploit and encourage the exiles' internal divisions for propaganda uses. They will portray any exile schism as proof of extremism and the narrow political interests that these exiles represent. A failure to present a unified exile leadership indicates, according to the home regime, an inability to lead the nation. For this reason, many home regimes do all in their power to induce schism and splits among exile groups. (See chapter 8.)

The threat of splits hangs over the heads of exile leaders. Many understand perfectly that their mere existence and their chance of realizing their goals depends heavily upon the strength and unity of their organizations and on massive support for their leadership among the exile community. Thus Gen. Humberto Delgado, who after splitting from the pro-Galvão camp was chosen the first president of a new exile coalition, the Frente Patriótica de Libertação Nacional (FPLN), expressed his fear that rivalries between his exile loyalists and his partners, the communists, would compromise the FPLN cause in the eyes of their new Algerian host government. He recalled the schism between Portuguese exiles in Spain in 1934, which had provoked the previously supportive Spanish government to cut off all assistance, and now in December 1964 warned his fellow exiles about the Algerian authorities' growing impatience with exile quarrels. Delgado saw the writing on the wall. Several weeks later he was ejected by the Algerian government from his FPLN office. A few months later he was found dead, most likely the victim of Antonio Salazar's secret police, the Policia Internacional de Defesa de Estado (PIDE).[28]

The desire to maintain exile unity holds most forcefully in situations where a stronger exile group coexists with smaller peripheral organizations and aspires to absorb them, and presents the differences within and among the various factions but within a broader unity as a sign of the exiles' undiminished energy for their cause. Describing the rivalries among anti-Bolshevik exile groups during the 1920s, Gen. Baron Peter N. Wrangel, the high commander of the Russian Armed Services Union (ROVS), declared in 1927: "To-day the Russian emigrants are divided into several political clans which go on talking with passionate zeal. These discussions surprise foreigners; they do not realize that the very existence of these differences shows that the difficult life of the exile has not killed his spirit; that we are seeking eagerly the larger hope; and that our sentiments turn with ardour to our country."[29]

Finally, exile leaders who seek to lead the greatest exile coalition possible—as an indication of their overall national representation— may find their fear of exile factionalism a serious obstacle to attaining their primary political goals. Their desire to maintain a grand coalition under their leadership can harm their ability to formulate policies rapidly and to respond to changing situations. Thus the central leadership might find itself in a trap, since political stagnation in itself is conducive to splits. Subordinate groups, and especially extremist forces, will then harp on the organization's failure to advance the exile cause and hence will challenge the leadership.

CHAPTER FOUR

Political Exiles and the Diaspora

[I]n order that there may be a tribunal of one's own people one must first of all have one's own people.
          —Alexander Herzen, *My Past and Thoughts*, 1855

Faced with difficulties in mobilizing supporters in the home nation and obstacles in gaining international recognition, political exiles often turn to their fellow nationals abroad—their national diaspora—as their organization's most valuable source of legitimacy. Public acknowledgment from this diaspora, especially its prominent members, can be used by the exiles as a prime indicator of an organization's national representation. Moral and material backing from compatriots abroad may strengthen the determination of loyalists who already possess some degree of commitment. Equally important, in mobilizing the national diaspora to act on their behalf, exile organizations hope to attract greater international attention; they seek to convince international patrons that they exercise or have the potential to exercise political power. Reflecting on the tactics that East European anti-Soviet exile groups ought to employ in order to mobilize the support of Western nations, a political exile in the postwar period wrote:

On what may [our] claim be based, apart from [our] patriotic feelings, to appear as mouthpieces for [our] nations? Such a claim can be based only on the confidence of the majority of the nation: this is an essential condition both for regular governments and national centers in exile. As in the latter case any direct verification is out of the question, it is necessary to keep to indirect evidence on which an opinion could be formed as to the degree of representativeness of a given center. . . . Such proof is the fact that the majority of the emigrés recognise the national center.[1]

To analyze the relations between exile organizations and members of their national community abroad, one must broadly characterize the major segments of the national diaspora whose resources the exile groups seek to mobilize, and the chances of achieving such mobilization with help of the "recruiting incentives" used by exile groups to foster loyalty abroad. One must bear in mind that relations between exile groups and their compatriots abroad vary dramatically from one case to another, and are affected by variables such as the organization's own character, the host state's policies toward the exiles' activities, and the home regime's counteractivities to discourage dissent among the national community abroad. (See chapter 8.)

In studying relations in the 1920s and 1930s between exile anti-Fascist organizations and Italian nationals abroad, one must take into consideration the Fascist government's efforts to earn the support of Italian expatriates, and the government's response to exile attempts to sow dissent among them. In early 1927 Mussolini established the Direzione Generale degli Italiani all'Estero (General Bureau of Italians Abroad) as a special agency to organize and "protect" Italian communities abroad. The term "emigrant" was replaced by "citizen" as part of the Fascist policy "to redeem the emigration from the political ineptitude and social irresponsibility of the liberal state," and to achieve "the spiritual recovery of all Italian communities spread throughout the world by strengthening those material and moral contacts between Italy and her citizens abroad."[2] In 1934 Piero Parini, the general secretary of the Fascist offshoots abroad, declared: "Anti-Fascism with the assistance of the *fuorusciti* set out to conquer the emigrants in order to bring Fascist Italy face to face with the moral drama of millions of Italians outside the frontiers declaredly opposed to the regime which had charge of the fate of their country, but the campaign had failed."[3]

Also, to combat the German exiles' anti-Nazi campaign among German nationals in Argentina, Joseph Goebbels's Propaganda Ministry spared no effort in seeking the sympathy of the large German community in Buenos Aires. Prominent members of the old German emigration in Argentina were invited to visit Hitler's Third Reich as honorary guests and were encouraged to publish glowing accounts of the new Germany in the Argentine press.[4]

National Diaspora

In political terms, a national diaspora can be understood as a people with a common national origin who regard themselves, or are regarded by others, as members or potential members of the national community of their home nation, a status held regardless of their geographical location and their citizenship status outside their national soil. Members of a political national diaspora are called upon periodically by various contestants for power, within or without the borders of the nation-state, including the home nation's existing regime, to award their loyalty to a particular cause as an expression of their national loyalty.

The importance ascribed by various political factions to the national diaspora can be exemplified by the efforts made, since the early 1970s, by the rival governments of Taipei and Peking for the support of the twenty million Chinese scattered around the world in resolving the historical dispute as to who are the authentic representatives of the Chinese people, the immediate issue being Taiwan's reunification with the mainland. Peking sought to exert pressure on Nationalist Taiwan to end the Chinese civil war formally. By opening its borders to "our fellow countrymen abroad," especially in the United States and Canada, to see the communists' economic and social achievements, Peking has tried to undermine Taiwan's own status in the West. The Nationalists, who refuse to negotiate with Peking on the question of reunification, have been constantly alert to the potential danger of a shift in the minds of Chinese abroad. "There is an urgent question for us," a Nationalist official said. "If we lost the support of Chinese-Americans, for example, we will find ourselves in a very difficult position. They help us to explain why the Communists' proposals are not acceptable and to make clear that it is not just we 'stubborn Nationalists' who do not want China to remain Communist forever and ever."[5]

In her work *Exiled Governments*, Alicja Iwańska identifies three major groups within a national diaspora according to their active or potential role in the undertakings of exile groups. The "core members" are the active members of the exile organization. I term these people "political exiles." The second stratum, in Iwańska's classification, comprises the "rear guard members," including proven loyalists who "have been members in the past but have drifted away." The third layer of the national diaspora consists of all national members whom "core members assume may be aroused and mobilized in case of need."[6] This group is composed mainly of overseas students and emigrants and their descendants who, for economic reasons, reside or are naturalized outside their home nation. Its members may give the political exiles material and moral resources, and may influence the international community through the authority of their country of residence—especially if they are naturalized citizens—by awarding recognition to the exiles at the expense of the home regime. Thus, for example, Filipino political exiles succeeded in rallying the large

Filipino diaspora in the United States, which mobilized American politicians and public opinion against the Marcos regime.

Alex Esclamado, an outspoken critic of the Marcos regime and the publisher of the *Philippine News* of San Francisco, the largest Filipino community newspaper in the United States, attacked Marcos in the pages of his paper. Afterwards, one of the exile leaders in opposition, Steve Psinakis, charged that Marcos was involved in efforts to bring pressure on the newspaper through its advertisers. The incident led to requests by California Senator Alan Cranston for an investigation by the Attorney General's office. The FBI, assigned to the matter, found no basis for prosecution.[7]

The Filipino exiles' success in mobilizing their diaspora has become a model for South Korean exile activists in the United States in their struggle against the Chun government.[8] Since the early 1970s, with the increased repression of the opposition inside South Korea, mobilizing the Korean community in the United States has gradually become the primary goal of Korean exile groups in their struggle for democracy. The influence of the political exiles among the U.S. Korean community increased significantly after the principal opposition leader to the Korean government, Kim Dae Jung, was exiled to the United States on Christmas Eve in 1982. From Washington, D.C., Kim and his followers established a network within the U.S. Korean community to influence American politicians and media organizations to exert pressure for reform on the South Korean government. The South Korean authorities, alarmed by these activities, acted to combat the exiles' attempts to mobilize the U.S. Koreans with a variety of coercive and propaganda measures "to get rid of those who seriously undermine the government and intimidate and buy the rest."[9]

Overseas students, in particular, are important assets as potential recruits for opposition activities against a home regime. From the earliest organized exile opposition to the czarist government in Western Europe in the 1850s until the middle of World War I, Russian students throughout Europe constantly rejuvenated the émigrés' revolutionary forces. In the early 1860s the Russian student colony in Heidelberg was the first to challenge the liberal individualism that dominated Alexander Herzen's exile generation by introducing international radicalism.[10] From the 1870s on, waves of Russian students flooding the continent, and especially Switzerland, revitalized the exile socialist groups until the final victory.[11] Many who encounter great difficulty in acquiring higher education at home, and who are reluctant to express political and intellectual views freely, take advantage of educational opportunities afforded by foreign countries in a free environment. For a variety of social and psychological reasons, these students tend to organize abroad along national political lines. They are especially prone to demonstrate against the home regime,[12] as did Iranian students in Europe and the United States in the struggle against the shah's dictatorship. Thousands of young Iranians who left their country's poor educational system to complete their studies abroad became "a fertile base, sometimes the only one, for the Iranian opposition against the Shah."[13] Their militancy became critical during Khomeini's exile in Iraq from 1964 to 1978. Through his loyal emissaries abroad, Khomeini established contacts with Iranian student organizations in Europe and the United States, urging them "to shun secular ideologies and to devote themselves to the promotion of an Islamic government in Iran."[14] Not all Iranian students supported Khomeini's theocratic ideas, yet they "saw in him a possible leader in their common cause against the Shah."[15] Khomeini was in a favorable position to enjoy the Iranian students' "contacts among the American and European press, among parliamentarians in various European countries, and with international human rights organizations; and they were able to call attention to human rights violations and other negative aspects of the Shah's regime."[16]

The demographic aspects of the national diaspora are the chief factor in determining the composition of the pool from which exile organizations will draw support, but it is often extremely difficult to produce accurate information on the size of the diaspora, its composition and distribution. A decisive influence on the nature of a diaspora pool is the home regime's policy of migration. Home regimes that encourage or force nationals to go abroad expand the pool of potential exile supporters but calculate that, by externalizing dissent, they will reduce the ability of their opponents to undermine the regime. The externalizing of dissent proved successful for Castro's revolutionary government.[17] On the other hand, regimes that selectively encourage members of the national diaspora to return home, and that succeed in this policy, deplete the political potential of the pool. Since the late 1970s the Chilean government has formally permitted Chilean refugees to return home, with the exception of several thousand political exiles "suspected of being a potential threat to state security." Inviting exiles to return may have contributed to the growing opposition to Gen. Augusto Pinochet inside Chile, but at the same time it weakened the opposition abroad.[18]

Another strategy through which home regimes may affect the exile pool is the restriction or denial of exit to those who may become troublemakers abroad. Thus apprehensions about the activities of political exiles led the government of Nicaragua "to discourage the foreign travel of anti-Sandinista figures, South Africa to forbid the exit of prominent black leaders, and Iran to quarantine the Baha'i 'virus' within its own borders."[19]

By and large, the greater its scope and the more complex its demographic makeup, the less likely it is that a diaspora pool will consist of a homogeneous population holding similar political opinions. Hence, in estimating the probability of mobilization within their national diaspora, political exiles must first distinguish between those who overtly support the home regime and those who hold, or are assumed to hold, an opposing political stance. In designing their recruiting policies among fellow Greeks abroad, Greek political exiles operating from Europe and the United States to overthrow the military dictatorship of George Papadopoulos (1967–73) had to take account of the fact that many Greek nationals abroad, especially in the United States, were fervent anticommunists and thus potential supporters of the colonels in Athens. Those who fled Greece because of conviction or political necessity probably numbered several thousand out of larger numbers who left for economic reasons; among them only a few hundred were willing and able to devote their time and effort to undermining the Junta.[20]

The more immediate pool from which exile groups assume they will draw followers is that segment of the national diaspora forced to flee their nation-state for political reasons, especially those who, before their departure, were engaged in antiregime activity, or were regarded by the home regime as troublemakers. This group is usually known as political refugees. The collective national and political sense of these refugees, and the antiregime feelings that they retain, are assumed to be stronger than among members of the national diaspora who left freely with the intention of settling permanently abroad. Therefore refugees—"rear guards," in Iwanśka's terminology—are always, in the eyes of political exiles, prime targets for mobilization. In gauging the probability that refugees can be successfully recruited as political activists, exile groups may discover, however, that opposition to the home regime is their only common denominator. Other diaspora characteristics such as amount of time abroad, places of dispersion (especially in relation to the exile organization's headquarters), different waves of departure, size of the community, and sociological and political composition, are critical factors in determining the availability of refugees as prospective supporters, and the recruiting measures required to mobilize them.

There were fundamental differences, for example, between Spanish refugees from the civil war who were accommodated in Mexico in more or less cohesive communities, and anti-Nazi Germans who were forced to seek asylum throughout the world. The Republican refugees received a hearty welcome from the Mexican government, and through formal and informal associations were able to maintain their old ties for a long period of time. German anti-Nazi refugees, by contrast, were a fragmented community without a receptive host. The German refugees were divided according to previous political affiliations, but primarily between "Aryan" (those who fled "in order to plan for the day they could return"), and "non-Aryan" (those who had been excluded from the nation by their home regime and were therefore compelled to build a new life abroad).[21] One must also distinguish between the anti-Castro militancy of the earlier Cuban refugees and the attitude of post-1964 émigrés. Although both opposed the regime in Havana, the latter were increasingly depoliticized and came to America principally for economic gain.[22] Similarly, there is a sharp difference in numbers and composition between Russian refugees who fled their country in the mid-nineteenth century when the czar was in power, and refugees from the 1917 revolution. The older diaspora was insignificant in size: "it included representatives only of certain definite classes, and was made up of individuals who lived outside their native land as a protest against the forms of state administration then existing."[23] The postrevolutionary diaspora, far larger, scattered Russians around the world for over two decades. These refugees included every social class, a great variety of professions, and a wide spectrum of political affiliations that could be traced back to the pre-exile period.

The Incentives for Mobilization

The incentives manipulated by exile groups to mobilize members of their diaspora are largely determined by the specific acts the exiles want their prospective followers to perform. Exile groups may ask members of their diaspora for declarations of support for the exiles' activities, for public denunciation of the home regime's human rights record, for financial contributions, for participation in demonstrations, and in some cases for direct involvement in acts of violence against the home regime. The effectiveness of the mobilizing incentives is largely a function of the recruits' spiritual and material needs, and the extent of sacrifice asked of them.

In his work on organizational behavior, Amitai Etzioni distinguishes three major ways of producing compliance among potential members: coercive force, economic control over material resources and rewards, and normative control through the manipulation of symbols. According to Etzioni, "while most organizations use all three kinds of power, each organization tends to rely heavily on one, and the type of power relied on depends on the nature of the organization."[24] In his work on political organizations, James Wilson makes further classifications of incentives. He distinguishes between "tangible" rewards, material benefits such as jobs, taxes, and market opportunity, and "intangible" rewards such as "solidarity," used by different organizations "to induce various contributors to perform certain acts."[25]

In many cases exile groups are very limited in their ability to reward their supporters materially. Hence they often end in complete dependence on the voluntary commitment of their compatriots abroad and on the manipulation of intangible rewards in generating loyalty. For the most part, exile organizations have neither the effective power nor the acknowledged right to employ coercive means to induce compliance among their fellow nationals abroad. However, there are two notable exceptions. In rare circumstances, governments-in-exile maintain legal jurisdiction over their nationals abroad. For example, governments-in-exile under the protection of the British Crown during World War II were granted limited authority by their British host to enforce their decrees among their citizens abroad. However, even in these cases "the legislative enactments of the territorial sovereign [the host state] always prevail over those of the personal sovereign [the exile organization]."[26] At the other extreme are examples of exile groups that use terrorist methods to engender loyalty to their cause or to penalize those who do not share their outlook. The use of violence against diaspora members may prove extremely costly and counterproductive. This is best exemplified by the activities of Cuban exile terrorist groups in the United States. Since the early 1960s Omega 7, the Miami-based Cuban exile group, has failed to recruit supporters for its anti-Castro struggle among the U.S. Cuban community. Omega 7, which rejected any appeasing tendencies among the Cubans abroad toward the regime in Havana, adopted terrorism to "convince" Cubans abroad to abandon their conciliatory policies. Its agents were apparently responsible for the murder of two members of the Committee of 75, a group of Cubans in the U.S. that endorsed reopening relations with Cuba. This act, which was condemned by many in the Cuban community, did not stop what was called the *diálogo* with Castro on the subject of the reunification of families.[27]

Most exile organizations rightly insist that material benefits are only a minor incentive for those refugees who take part in exile politics; active refugees are motivated primarily by their national commitment. Material benefits of participation, exile groups and leaders maintain, merely help reduce the hardship of refugee life abroad, and thus enable them to maintain their political energy for the cause at home. Still, there are recent cases in which refugees have been compelled to take part in exile activities mainly for economic reasons and not necessarily as an expression of national or ideological commitments. As Aristide Zolberg and others note, Eritreans in the Sudan and Afghan refugees in Pakistan "usually lack the means for even subsistence production, [and] . . . are heavily dependent on international or local assistance to stay alive. [These refugees] may find [that] the most socially meaningful and economically rewarding"[28] course is to join their compatriots engaged in military operations across the border. Under duress these people "move from the category of mere displaced persons into that of the politically active and conscious."[29]

For the most part, exile organizations try to use their economic resources as a mobilizing instrument in two major ways: (1) as a long-term investment in human resources, and (2) as compensation for participation in their activities. The exile groups' long-term investment policy is employed generally among refugee communities. Such a policy was adopted by the two rival factions among the Spanish Republicans in Mexico, Servicio de Emigración para Repúblicanos Españoles (SERE), headed by the former Republican premier Negrín, and the Junta de Auxilio a los Refugiados Españoles (JARE), headed by Negrín's major exile opponent in the Socialist Party, Prieto. Serving as exile and refugee relief organizations at the same time, "each, controlling a portion of the funds remaining to the Spanish Republic, vied with each other to win the gratitude and the trust of those who accepted the aid and services they offered."[30] To be sure, the exile policy of "cast your bread upon the waters" may yield unintended results. It may promote assimilation, especially when refugees are enjoying warm hospitality in their host country while the prospect of returning to their home nation appears unlikely. However, as a student of South African refugees in England has observed, certain refugees fail or decline to establish a new life abroad, thereby concentrating their energies on revolutionary activity rather than on personal advancement.[31]

The ability of exile groups to provide material reward for loyalty becomes critical in attempts to overthrow the home regime through military operations from across the borders. In such circumstances the exile organizations must provide a means of livelihood to their ranks and their families. Describing the difficulties in organizing the scattered forces of the White army in exile and its gradual transformation into an army of volunteers (after the French government recognized the Soviet Union and withdrew its support of the Russian exiles), General Wrangel wrote:

At the beginning the High Command had to be responsible for the needs of all the officers and under-officers whose all time [sic] was taken by general organizing. As the various units got to work, and the men got accustomed to the new order of things, the cost of keeping the chief lessened; officers and under-officers set to work in their turn, and the number of persons whose needs the High Command saw to was reduced. . . . The support of the families of the soldiery, the women, the wounded and the sick who had been incapacitated for work during their services in the ranks, required a large expenditure. But this help was regarded by the Army as a debt of honour.[32]

The exiled Russian monarchists continued to give material benefits to their followers abroad until the early 1950s. In the late 1940s they released a special fund, transported abroad by General Wrangel after the 1917 revolution, to provide financial support to the remnants of the Vlasov Army, which sided with the Nazis in World War II and help them maintain their anti-Soviet radicalism.[33]

Material incentives can be a scarce asset in the exiles' recruiting arsenal. When exile organizations lose their capacity to provide material rewards, the danger arises that support will decrease or even completely evaporate, especially among militants less ideologically involved. Furthermore, the capacity of exile organizations to contribute to the well-being of their followers abroad is largely dependent on the financial support they receive from international sources. Since these creditors frequently seek to use the exiles for their own policy objectives, home regimes tend to label political exiles as "mercenaries." This is particularly common when exiles join sponsoring governments in a military invasion to topple the home regime. However, as Robert D. Tomasek, a student of Caribbean exile invasions, has observed: "It is inaccurate . . . for governments being attacked to brand all exiles as mercenaries, which they have frequently done for propaganda purposes. The exiles, no matter how dependent they are on their sponsoring government, have a fervent desire to free their homeland. Their zeal is explained by much more than mere monetary rewards or a search for adventure."[34]

Although material rewards are often critical for mobilizing national followers abroad, ideological commitment and nationalistic attachments to the home nation are the primary reasons why refugees join the exile ranks. To develop the sense of national partnership in a common undertaking within the diaspora community, exile organizations try to manipulate national symbols and exploit other intangible rewards.

Political exiles' ability to generate loyalty through the manipulation of symbols begins with their organizational appearance. By its very existence, the group invokes emotional identification among its national compatriots, but in mobilizing refugees it is vital to have a central authority transplanted from the home nation around which life abroad can be organized. Refugees are often grouped abroad according to their pre-exile affiliations with political parties. If they are bound together by a unifying ideology, they are less likely to separate. Exile groups also acknowledge the symbolic importance of presenting their organizations in "state-governmental" forms. By preempting labels such as "government-in-exile," "national committee," and "national council," and by continuing the use of familiar sentimental symbols, flags, slogans, songs, cheers, poems, hymns, expressive gestures, and uniforms, exile organizations and their leaders encourage their prospective contributors to think of their organization as having national stature and authority.

A common device for evoking loyalty among refugees is a ceremonial calendar. Ceremonies, writes Morton Grodzins, "are symbols which function 'to draw all people together to emphasize their similarities and common heritage, to minimize their differences, and to contribute to their thinking, feeling, and acting alike.' The rituals of Memorial Day, for example, are a symbols system that integrates the entire community by emphasizing the sacredness of those who died for the nation."[35]

Hence the exile leaders of the Acción Democrática held periodic public meetings on the Venezuelan independence day and proclaimed October 21 "The Day of the Heroes" to commemorate fallen exile leaders who gave their lives "on behalf of the people's struggle against tyranny."[36] The anti-Khomeini Mujahedeen announced in 1984 that June 20 would be "The Day of Martyrs and Political Prisoners." On this day the organization's leader, Rajavi, reported to Iranians abroad about the apparent increase in international support for the exiles' struggle, and about the growing erosion of the legitimacy of the Islamic regime in Teheran.[37] Among the exiled Paraguayan Febreristas, special memorial days were established "as reminders of the party's dramatic past . . . to invoke a feeling of solidarity."[38]

In dealing with discouraged refugees, exile groups must produce a quick political change or at least the image of one. Symbols help exile organizations and their leaders present the appearance of action and some evidence of accomplishment in the face of slow progress (or none) toward the envisaged return. Refugees search desperately for reinforcement of their belief that their exile is only temporary, and they worry continuously about those they left behind. Thus exile organizations will never admit that they are not going back home someday; their own existence is contingent upon their ability to induce or maintain faith in the victorious return in the hearts of their active or assumed followers.

Some exile organizations, limited in their ability to provide concrete evidence of progress, may resort to producing exaggerated, even fictional, information about accomplishments. Such imaginary achievements may be presented in the form of minor gestures by the international community on behalf of the exile organization and its leaders, or in stories about the apparent collaboration of the organization with the underground forces at home. For example, in the early 1920s *Dni* (Days), the organ of Alexander Kerensky's exile Social Revolutionary Party in Europe, constantly provided "secret" accounts about its clandestine missions inside Russia. These self-proclaimed achievements were never verified. By concealing the identity of *Dni's* sources, Kerensky's exile group for a short period succeeded in creating a halo of mystery and admiration around its activities. *Dni* earned a reputation as a reliable source and its reporters were seen as courageous patriots who shared the risks with the internal opponents of communism.[39]

There is always a danger of gradual erosion of the hope to return. The time the refugees have spent outside their native country and the time they expect to stay abroad erodes the energy of potential supporters. In their attempts to reduce such erosion, exile organizations manipulate symbols so as to tie the refugees to their past and perpetuate in them a sense of guilt and of national responsibility toward those who are silenced at home, but there are pitfalls in relying so exclusively on the past. Exile organizations that fail to update their symbolic arsenal, building solely on personalities of the past, incur the risk of petrifying their own role as national representatives. Such organizational rigidity may intensify the difficulties in rejuvenating their cadres, especially if exile is prolonged.

By and large, pre-exile symbols that speak to the needs and political consciousness of the older generation of refugees gradually lose their meaning and relevance for a younger generation out of touch with their content. Moreover, with the passing of time comes a growing risk that a new symbol system preempted and manipulated by the home regime to enforce its formula of national loyalty at home will slowly penetrate the minds and hearts of the national community abroad. A home regime's new symbols may gradually come to be the identifying marks of the national community as a whole, and may exacerbate the identification crisis among refugees, many of whom are already troubled by the question of their loyalty. Trying to maintain their identities as national loyalists, refugees may become psychologically disposed to see the positive side of the home regime whenever possible, despite their hatred of it. In their dealings with foreign nationals they will often refrain from attacking the home regime's policies and sometimes even express pride in its accomplishments. This happened, for example, among many anti-Soviet refugees who fled in fear of their lives. While abroad they spoke with admiration of Soviet accomplishments and found pride in the strength of the motherland.[40]

For the younger generation of refugees, searching for their nationality and future rather than striving to recapture a past, the old national symbols and attachments appropriated by the exile organizations may become obsolete. The attempt to perpetuate old symbols can provoke alienation among the young generation, who may consider them an obstacle in their attempt to reestablish a national bond with their compatriots at home.[41]

The Case of the Russian Diaspora

> *Pink and Reddish, green and whitish, the Russian exiles were all waiting for the Bolsheviks to fall so that they could go back to Russia and resume their feuds interrupted by the October Revolution.*
> —Grand Duke Alexander

The stories of the Russian exiles and the Spanish Republicans reflect the difficulties of large, diverse, and widely dispersed diasporas in forming united political fronts in the face of strong home regimes and the constraints posed by international developments. They also demonstrate the problems that exile organizations experience in maintaining and rejuvenating pre-exile structures abroad without the recognized criteria of institutionalized procedures and rules of succession. Indeed, the exiles' failure to unite behind a recognized and cohesive leadership allows the debate on fundamental strategic and tactical issues to take the form of personalized battles and ad hominem attacks among the exile aspirants to power.

An enormous number of exile organizations emerged within the Russian diaspora, for example, many of them descended from parties of the Duma. These groups all cherished the hope of an imminent return to the homeland after the collapse of the Bolshevik system, which they confidently anticipated, and claimed to speak for the Russian people. They were addicted to fruitless theorizing debates on how bolshevism should be abolished, whether the future form of the Russian state should be a monarchy or a republic, and the status of the leadership abroad. The ideological and tactical discrepancies between the different movements and the tensions within the movements themselves were so deep "that the establishment of a supra-national body including all groups, even for purely representative purposes, has been out of the question."[42]

By 1925 more than two million Russian refugees had spread to Europe, the United States, and Asia; the largest number had found temporary homes in Germany and later in France. This massive emigration included men and women of all parties and social classes: liberals and conservatives, former members of the socialist parties, the aristocracy, the middle classes, professional classes, and Russian workers. They all waited impatiently for the day when they would be able to return home; they refused to be described as émigrés, a title that to them implied voluntary exile. They considered their condition to be *izgnanie*, or banishment.[43]

The republican exiles included former members of the Social Revolutionary Party, the Constitutional Democrats or the Kadets (under the leadership of Prof. Paul Miliukov), the Social Democrats (including the exiled Mensheviks), the Populist Socialists, and also nonsocialists. All these groups confined their political activities to propaganda warfare and the maintenance of certain political ties with revolutionaries at home.

The chief claimant for the leadership of the Russian democrats and republicans in exile was Kerensky, who had succeeded Prince George Lvov on July 20, 1917, as the head of the Russian Provisional Government and was virtually the dictator of Russia during four of the most dramatic months of the revolution. Kerensky, the political exile, spent most of his time in Paris as the editor of *Dni*, the Russian exile daily regarded as the official organ of the anti-Bolshevik Socialist Party.[44] *Dni* and other leaflets, allegedly smuggled into Russia through underground channels, informed the Russians about "the fallacies of Bolshevism."[45]

In March 1927 Kerensky, on a trip to the United States to raise money to expand the activities of his exile organization, predicted "the eventual overthrow of the Communist regime through economic forces gathering strength 'as the result of their absurd economic system.'"[46] Advocating the overthrow of bolshevism from inside Russia, he opposed any armed intervention by the Russian diaspora, advising restriction of opposition activities to international propaganda warfare. Kerensky maintained that the exiles' role was to inform the free world about the nature of the communist regime and its economic difficulties, and most of all to teach "fundamental principles of freedom" to the Russians at home.[47]

In 1921 Paul N. Miliukov, a leader of the exiled Kadets, formed a coalition with Kerensky's organization, seeking "an inclusive governing body to represent the Russian diaspora in the struggle against Bolshevism."[48] This national committee crumbled almost immediately because Kerensky loyalists could not tolerate a coalition with Miliukov's "bourgeois" group.[49]

The majority of the Russian diaspora, including the influential Orthodox church, which obstructed friendly relations between the Bolshevik regime and European governments in the early 1920s, supported the restoration of the Romanovs.[50] For the exiled monarchists the restoration was an attainable political goal, not merely a nostalgic desire. The Bourbons and the Bonapartes had both been restored in France, and for a time, the Stuarts had recovered the throne of England. And most significantly, Lenin, the monarchists' greatest enemy, had spent fifteen years as a political exile before he became the master of Russia. The monarchists were looking for a lawful sovereign of the Romanov house who would restore the crown to its original glory. But throughout the 1920s the exiled monarchists were split into two rival factions loyal to different pretenders. The large number of monarchical groups and the plurality of opinions presented in the first Supreme Monarchist Council in Berlin, in the summer of 1921, demonstrated how fragile their endeavor was. Recognition of a would-be czar at that stage could have had a devastating effect on their overall struggle for return.[51] A rupture within monarchist ranks was evident at the second meeting of the council in Paris in November 1922. The views and political activities of the two largest colonies of Russian monarchists, in Germany and in France, each responded to the climate of opinion in their host countries. The anticommunist position of the monarchists' colony in Germany was abetted by extreme German nationalism and anti-Semitism;[52] the monarchists in France followed the political pattern established by the Council of Russian Ambassadors.[53] Each community stood behind a different pretender to the throne.

The principal controversy was over the question of legitimacy. The German faction accepted Grand Duke Cyril, eldest son of the late czar's eldest uncle, as the only legitimate heir. In 1924 Cyril proclaimed himself as "the sole legal Heir of the Russian Imperial Throne," and his son, Prince Vladimir Kirillovitch, as "Heir to the throne with the title Grand Duke Heir and Czarevitch." He regarded his right to the throne as a "duty before God [and his Fatherland], . . . a supreme authority which is above classes and parties." But to the utter consternation of the Supreme Monarchist Council, the Council of Ambassadors, and the rest of the monarchist colony in Paris, Cyril had already proclaimed himself the "Palace Keeper of the Russian Throne" in the summer of 1922.[54]

An opposing faction supported Grand Duke Nicholas, grandson of Nicholas I and first cousin of Alexander III, who earned his reputation as the chief general of the Russian forces in World War I.[55] Nicholas himself emphatically dismissed the "rumors" about his claim to the throne but did not renounce it—part of his strategy to undermine Cyril's conflicting claim. He left to the leaders of the defeated White armies the task of promoting his candidacy. "I am not a pretender," Nicholas said in an interview with the *New York Times*, "I am merely a citizen and a soldier anxious to return home in order to aid his fellow citizens and his country. When God gives our cause victory the nation must decide as to its form of government."[56]

The "Bolsheviks had systematically eliminated obvious heirs; neither the custom nor the law clearly prescribed who should inherit the throne under such extraordinary circumstances."[57] The animosity between the two cousins, Nicholas and Cyril, can be traced back to Nicholas's disapproval of Cyril's scandalous marriage to the divorced Grand Duchess Victoria Melita in 1905. Nicholas, chief of the Russian forces, banished Cyril from Russia and deprived him of his honors.[58] In retaliation, Cyril's loyalists accused Nicholas of treason for advising the last czar, Nicholas II, to abdicate during the first stages of the revolution, and for accepting Kerensky's Provisional Government.[59] Nicholas's loyalists, for their part, discredited Cyril's legitimacy by reminding the monarchist camp that he had accepted the Bolsheviks and been "the first to hoist the red flag over his palace." During the civil war Cyril, as the head of the navy marine, broke his oath to the czar by swearing allegiance to the Provisional Government. Later Cyril explained that it was necessary if he was to retain control over his command.[60]

Until 1927, when he moved to France, Grand Duke Cyril established himself in Germany at Coburg, settling on his wife's family estate (next door to ex-King Ferdinand of Bulgaria) and surrounding himself with a small group of reactionary exiles. He extended his influence among Russian military groups in the smaller Balkan states and Yugoslavia. But the majority of the exiled monarchists followed Grand Duke Nicholas. In the fall of 1923 General Wrangel, the last leader of the defeated White armies, formed the Russian Armed Service Union (ROVS) to preserve the military cadres of he White forces in exile.[61] As chairman, Wrangel submitted his forces to the authority of Grand Duke Nicholas, hoping that the old and respected former commander would be able to gather around him, as Dimitry V. Lehovich said, "all the 'nationally minded' elements among the Russian émigrés."[62]

Cyril, in proclaiming himself "czar by divine right," sought to discredit Wrangel's initiative as an act of treason. In a manifesto published by his representative in Paris, Cyril warned Nicholas's followers and all who refused to recognize Cyril as the sole Russian sovereign, that "they will never be permitted to return to Russia on pain of being shot instantly when they cross the frontier."[63] Nicholas, on the other hand, tried to avoid any direct confrontation; though he declined to discuss Cyril's claims, he repudiated Cyril's proclamation as irrelevant, arguing, without mentioning Cyril explicitly, that the Russian people would reject "anything forced on them."[64] From his small apartment in Choigny, a suburb of Paris, Nicholas conducted what his supporters regarded as secret and responsible diplomacy. His image as a quiet and professional leader helped give him credibility as a national figure and statesman. Nicholas was regarded as a man "who held himself above and aloof from the petty squabbling of a party politician."[65] He called upon his followers, who had urged him to declare himself Nicholas III, to direct their efforts only to the restoration of order and legality inside Russia: "Do not run ahead of the future destinies of Russia."[66]

Cyril condemned any attempt to advocate a nonmonarchical regime in Russia; Nicholas, however, called on the other exile organizations "to present a united front against the common enemy,"[67] though he did not exclude the possibility of a nonmonarchical government, perhaps led by himself. He predicted a constitutional monarchy in Russia after the fall of the Soviets, and was willing to serve as the head of its government if he "would be freely chosen by the people themselves."[68]

Cyril was far less popular than Nicholas, and even among his own family some challenged his claim to the throne.[69] The Dowager Empress Marie, who refused to believe that her sons (Czar Nicholas and Grand Duke Michael) had been killed by the Bolsheviks, regarded Cyril as a "usurper."[70] "If a protector of the throne was needed," she said, "it would be her husband's cousin, the universally respected and admired Grand Duke Nicholas."[71] Nicholas visited the Dowager Empress at her home in Copenhagen, receiving her blessing and recognition as the real and official leader of the monarchist movement.[72] For Cyril, however, unpopularity within the Russian diaspora could not invalidate his claim. He argued that the Cossacks and peasants inside Russia, whom he regarded as 90 percent of the population, were totally loyal to him: "When the times comes they will speak their weighty word."[73] Yet he did everything he could to enlist new exile loyalists in his own behalf. He dressed his campaign with nostalgic monarchical gestures. During his interviews with foreign journalists, he insisted on being called the "czar"; he issued public letters warning investors against subscribing to any of the loans sought by the "Soviet Junta," declaring that "they will be repudiated by the Russian nation as soon as he recovers the imperial throne."[74] He appointed his own exile government, governors for different Russian districts, and sent ambassadors and ministers to major states and cities in Europe and the United States. He also conferred titles of nobility.

Cyril's wife, the real driving force behind his presumption to the imperial throne, used her noble connections and her family's money to surround her husband with devotees. Seeking German support for the restoration of the throne, she established connections with German politicians, including Adolf Hitler's National Socialist Party, in 1922, which later damaged Cyril's credibility.[75] In a visit to the United States in 1924 the duchess presented herself as Empress Victoria, the czarina, and was escorted by a motorcycle cavalcade through the streets of New York and Philadelphia. But she failed to meet with the American president and settled for second-rank diplomats. As Gleb Botkin, an early advocate of the Romanov restoration, sarcastically remarked: "Mr. Coolidge, a man notorious for his lack of imagination, failed to discover any such institution as the Russian Empire, and accordingly did not receive Her Majesty Empress Victoria Feodorovna."[76] Cyril spared himself no effort to consolidate his position among the Russians abroad, including provocations against Nicholas's faction. In December 1924 Cyril's faction spread rumors in the German newspaper *Münchener Neueste Nachrichten* about a secret plan of Nicholas's faction to attack the Soviet Union from German soil with the White armies and French, Czech, Polish, and Balkan military forces. The *Nachrichten*, which lent its institutional support to the publication of Cyril's monarchist exile journal *Messenger of the Russian Monarchists' Union* in Bavaria, was probably used, as the *New York Times* reported, to "prejudice the Germans

against Nicholas by hints that Germany may be used as an instrument by Nicholas and his French supporters in attacking the Soviets."[77]

The rivalry between the two exile camps added to the frustration
of the Russian diaspora, which had already suffered a great psychological setback when France recognized the Soviet Union in October
1924. Cyril rejected any exile attempt to seize power in Russia
through invasion from abroad and regarded Wrangel's military legions
as a fantasy. In a call "to all loyal Russian people" he repudiated other
leaders' ideas of going to war against their compatriots with the support of foreign troops.[78] A few months later, however, he supported
the idea of foreign intervention in a prediction of a sudden upheaval
from within; he called for a "helping hand extended to the subject
nation from the outside to rouse the millions who will ally themselves
with the helper."[79]

By the early 1920s Nicholas had become almost the unanimous
choice for czar, especially among the thousands of exiled officers and
soldiers of the White armies, who recognized him "as their trusted
leader and declare[d] their readiness to obey his order."[80] Nicholas
regarded his followers' choice as more of a duty than an honor. Although there was no "next in line" for succession (Cyril may have
been closer in consanguinity), Nicholas's advocates promoted him as
the most suitable heir. They argued that the line of succession had
been broken before in the history of the Russian monarchy. "And even
if there existed an unbroken line and an immutable law, this is not
the time for formal technicalities. *Salus Populi Suprima Lex.*"[81] He
was the only opposition leader whom the Soviets feared.[82] His legitimacy among the Russians abroad extended beyond the exiled monarchists. He received the approval of many exiled republicans, among
them members of Kerensky's old party who paid homage to his "self-
restraint."[83]

The major tactical difference between Cyril's and Nicholas's factions concerned foreign intervention. For Nicholas, the future social
and political organization of Russia could be established only on Russian soil. Cyril's position was ambiguous. He was accused by Nicholas's supporters of searching for outside intervention to restore the
monarchy without taking into consideration the will of the Russian
people, and thus alienating the revolutionary forces at home. His
position, they argued, hurt the cause of liberation in Russia and
"strengthened the confidence of the Bolsheviks. It made those who
were ready to strike doubtful and finally convinced them that it was
better to wait."[84] Most of all, the followers of Nicholas charged that,

by having himself proclaimed emperor, Cyril enabled the Bolsheviks to make use of him "as a symbol of what was evil in the Czarist regime."[85]

In early April 1926 a monarchist congress was called in Paris to create a supreme exile organization to lead the Russians to liberation. Grand Duke Nicholas was unanimously elected the monarchists' leader by the 457 delegates, gathered in a kind of parliamentary assembly. He received his nomination in his home.[86] His refusal to attend the congress's meetings indicated his absolute opposition to imposing a new form of government from abroad. "Our people themselves will find the glory and grandeur of Russia,"[87] was his reply to the congress's call.

The Kadets, under the leadership of Miliukov, the Social Revolutionary Party under Kerensky, and the monarchists under Cyril boycotted the congress from the beginning.[88] Even without them the congress failed to achieve consensus on the basic issue of organizational form, and even less so on the issue of an anti-Bolshevik campaign. The right wing supported the creation of a permanent public executive group. The left-wingers, who favored a headquarters office, argued against establishment of a permanent executive lest it arouse high expectations that might not be met.[89] A day after the closing session, the *New York Times* reported with sarcasm: "Bolshevism is secure from the power of the old regime in Russia. . . . [T]he fact that the Monarchists devoted more time to disputing among themselves than in presenting a solid front against the common enemy appear [sic] to have spelled the doom of any organized or efficient attempt to overthrow the Russian soviets from this quarter."[90]

On January 5, 1929, Grand Duke Nicholas died in Antibes. *Pravda* described him as "a long dry scarecrow who didn't frighten anyone like other clowns of the Monarchist circus."[91] Gen. Paul Alexander Kutepov, one of Nicholas's assistants, was elected honorary chairman of the monarchist's largest faction. Soon after, he was kidnapped by Stalin's secret police, the G.P.U.[92] Cyril remained as the last hope of the monarchists. On October 30, 1930, Gen. Evgenii K. Miller, president of the Russian Armed Services Union (founded by General Wrangel to support Nicholas), issued a proclamation for creation of a monarchists' "united front against the bandits in the Kremlin."[93] Cyril's personal dream seemed to be realized. He became the undisputed leader of the exiled monarchists. His coronation took place with a glittering but somewhat pathetic display of pomp and ceremony.[94]

The reconciliation between the two monarchist camps came too late; by the time they were able to mount a united front, any opportunity to influence Russian politics had long since passed. The protracted internecine squabbling had eroded support for the monarchists in the Russian diaspora, elicited condemnation from the Soviet government, and provoked expressions of contempt from the international community.

The Case of the Spanish Republicans

> *Since I left Europe, the unity of the Spanish Republicans has been my constant thought and the most fervent desire of my heart. Then as now, if I were asked what I want for Spain, I would unhesitatingly answer: I want all Spaniards in politics to forget petty, personal quarrels and think of Spain.*
> —Isabel de Palencia, *Smouldering Freedom*, 1944

Whether the Allied governments used the factional tendencies among the exiled Spanish Republicans as an excuse to avoid any commitment to aggressive action against Franco, or to deny the Republican government-in-exile official recognition in the aftermath of World War II, is still unclear.[95] Yet it is beyond doubt that the years of constant animosities between the Republican leaders Juan Negrín and Indalecio Prieto left a deep scar on the opposition to Franco inside and outside Spain and helped discredit Franco's opponents abroad. C. L. Sulzberger of the *New York Times*, described the destructive effect of the Republicans' aging in exile: "[V]iolent individualist, separatist, tribal and generally centrifugal forces which are apparently traditional to the proud Spanish character, have tended to dissipate the [exiles'] energies which otherwise might have broadly combined in an over-all republican movement."[96]

The Spanish word *personalismo*, an equivalent of the English word "faction," refers principally to personal relations that have deleterious effects on a community. The long and bitter rivalries between Negrín and Prieto, which infected the entire Spanish refugee diaspora in France, Mexico, London, and the United States, was an example of the harmful effects of *personalismo*.

Negrín, the last prime minister of the republic, was an optimist who rejected any surrender to the monarchist forces when it was widely perceived that further military resistance was futile.[97] Prieto, the minister of defense in Negrín's government, embodied the spirit of fatalism and defeat. He held with many others, including the president of the republic, Manuel Azaña, that the Republicans were doomed, and he advocated publicly the acceptance of defeat and surrender. Negrín could not tolerate the pessimism Prieto infused into the ranks and so dismissed him from office.[98]

The paramount issue abroad was that of official and legal authority, the status in exile of the last Republican government, and especially the status of its prime minister, Negrín. Prieto and his exiled loyalists argued that, after the early resignation of Azaña, the presidency of the republic should have automatically been assumed by the president of the Spanish Cortes, who also served as vice president. The failure of Diego Martínez Barrio, the former president of the Spanish Cortes, to fill the gap after Azaña's resignation as provided by the Spanish constitution, created a rupture that undermined the legality of Negrín's government. Without a government and without a parliament "there could be no ministry and therefore no Prime Minister."[99] Negrín and his exiled supporters rejected this legal claim at the outset. After the early resignations, the Negrinistas argued, "the Permanent Commission was then occupied, during meetings held in France, by one of the vice-presidents, Don Luis Fernandez Clerigo."[100] Furthermore, Negrín himself maintained that the Popular Front government was "the only authority to survive the defeat, and was therefore still in effect."[101] In his first public statement after fleeing Spain, Negrín addressed Spanish refugees in London: "Nothing will break the will of the Spanish people or make void the institutions they chose for themselves. Those who had the duty of preserving those institutions have not deserted their post. We do not consider that our duties have ended. We do not consider that our mandate has expired."[102]

The confrontation between Negrín's legal claims and Prieto's attempts to discredit him as nonrepresentative, split the Republican diaspora throughout its crucial years in exile (1939–46). In the aftermath of the civil war, when the Republicans still operated from France, the two exile leaders established competing organizations to aid the refugees. They selected and transported many refugees from France to Mexico, where they were offered political asylum, and reallocated funds to the refugees left in French camps. Prieto and Negrín vied in assisting the refugees, while repudiating each other's activities as "nationally disloyal."

The hostility was so severe that, in order to obtain a visa from Negrín's organization, the Servicio de Emigración para Repúblicanos Españoles (SERE), a refugee had to laud Negrín and condemn Prieto and his loyalists as traitors.[103] Moreover, Louis Stein has stated, the competition between the SERE and Prieto's organization, the Junta de Auxilio a los Refugiados Españoles (JARE), subverted the rescue operation and its financing. Another observer, a student of Spanish exile Republicans in Mexico, said the dispute resulted in "inefficient management of funds, duplication of efforts, and increasing personal hostility between the two leaders."[104]

Prieto and Negrín differed in the way they viewed the struggle against Franco from abroad. At the outbreak of World War II, Prieto denied any exile attempt to foment internal strife in Spain. Joining other Republican groups, he urged a passive exile approach, arguing that "Franco would fall because of his own unpopularity and inability to rule."[105] Negrín did not believe that the domestic opposition to Franco was virtually destroyed and thus offered hope and vision to his fellow refugees. Advocating external struggle to provoke the Spaniards at home, he perceived the Republicans' role abroad as a crucial component in the wider fight against totalitarianism and for democracy in Europe. Negrín frequently reported on the continuous struggle at home in words like these: "In the mountains and the fields of Spain, in village and city, in school and work-shop, the Spanish people continue their resistance."[106] Negrín avoided attacking Franco's loyalists as national enemies and preferred to regard them as sheep without a shepherd. "Things will return to their course to the good fortune of Spain, even the good fortune of those who burn incense before the 'New Order.' "[107]

These differences between Negrín and Prieto were only symptoms of the more critical pre-exile disagreement about cooperation with the Spanish communists. Negrín, supported by many of the exiled Left, wanted to include as many exile groups as possible under his command. In his attempts to portray himself as a nonpartisan national leader, he spoke of his exiled rivals as "brothers." Negrín refused to exclude the communists from his exile coalition. He remembered the assistance his government had received from Stalin during the civil war, whereas the British and French governments had been quick to recognize Franco's regime.[108] Prieto's exile faction, on the other hand, dismissed any attempts to ally itself with the exiled Spanish communists. Since the beginning of the civil war, Prieto had tried to "eliminate the Communist stigma from the image of the Republic and to convince France, the United States, and Great Britain, that they should rectify past negligence by coming to the aid of the defeated Republic."[109]

The political and personal rivalry reached a new climax when Prieto, with the collaboration of other exile groups, formed the Junta Española de Liberación in Mexico in November 1943, in an attempt to build a national committee resembling de Gaulle's Comité de Libération. As the only exile organization to include the major political parties of the Spanish Cortes of 1931, it claimed to represent the authentic voice of the Spaniards. The establishment of Prieto's Junta, which resulted in deeper division between the exiles' camps, was a direct reprisal against Negrín's "communist-tainted" government.[110] By excluding the Negrinistas, the exiled communists, the General Confederation of the Spanish Workers in exile, and the Basque Nationalist Party, supporters of Negrín argued that Prieto's national committee undermined its claim to represent the whole Spanish nation.[111] It became an anticommunist and anti-Soviet organization, a critical image for obtaining the Western powers' recognition at the end of World War II.

Responding to the challenge, the exiled communists in Mexico collaborated with the Spanish communists in Madrid in establishing a national committee of their own, the Junta Suprema de Liberación Nacional, which in its manifesto exploited Negrín's name as if he were behind it. Negrín protested vehemently; as always, he sought to maintain his image as the putative supreme leader.[112]

Prieto's Junta directed its efforts to securing international recognition as a government-in-exile. It reasoned that the overthrow of Franco could be achieved only by the great powers' intervention. Prieto believed that recognition of the Junta by the members of the United Nations (then about to be established) would help the Spanish exiles exert pressure on the governments of the world to break with the fascist government of Franco and impose sanctions.[113] Negrín remained poised for action. Relishing the role of national leader, he avoided attacking the Junta's initiative, leaving this leg work to his loyalists. "I have kept silent," he said, "because I did not want to add fuel to the political bickering within the Spanish emigration."[114] The policy of exclusion was Prieto's fatal mistake. There was no hope for a semilegal exile organization that did not garner popular support from the Spanish diaspora.

In early 1945 the Spaniards abroad felt that they would soon cross the threshold to salvation; Prieto declared his confidence in Franco's fall before the end of the year.[115] The diaspora community was almost fully united by the urgent need to form an official body that would be recognized by all Spanish exile organizations as the government-in-exile. Even at this crucial moment the political maneuvering of the exile leaders was a major obstacle.

The first political move came on January 10, 1945. Acting as next in line to the deceased former president of the republic, Azaña, Martínez Barrio took advantage of Negrín's absence in London to hold the first session of the exiled Spanish Cortes in Mexico City. Negrín learned about it only a few hours before the first session. Isabel de Palencia, a distinguished member of the Spanish exile community in Mexico, a supporter of Negrín, and a former ambassador, has observed that only "seventy-two out of four hundred and seventy-four deputies that formed the [old Republican] Cortes were present. This meeting turned out to be simply a memorial session for the one hundred and twenty-seven deputies who have died since the last meeting of the Cortes was held on Spanish territory."[116] A few days later, although he knew that Negrín was on his way from England to Mexico City, Barrio decided to assemble the exiled Cortes for the second time, hoping to be elected head of the future Spanish government. Barrio's maneuvers came to naught. He could not obtain a quorum of the Cortes's members. Moreover many exile deputies, realizing that Barrio's abuse of power would discredit their democratic reputation, raised their voice against the attempt to exclude the Negrinistas. Prieto collaborated with Barrio, hoping to achieve recognition of his Junta as the Republicans' official representative. He protested the delay in the Cortes's work while waiting for Negrín to arrive, but in vain. The Cortes adjourned without passing any resolutions, leaving Prieto's loyalists fearful for their future.[117]

Paradoxically, the only exile group to benefit from the Barrio-Prieto maneuver was the Negrinistas. By rejecting Barrio's moves, the deputies of the exiled Cortes demonstrated their desire for exile unity. They had come to the sessions not to support Barrio or Prieto, but "to identify themselves with the effort to mobilize the Republican forces."[118] The failure to exclude Negrín discredited Barrio and Prieto in the eyes of many in the Spanish diaspora, as well as many of the Republicans' foreign supporters. An editorial in the *New Republic*, for example, called upon the governments in Washington and London to recognize Negrín as the leader of the Spanish exiles and their exiled government: "The failure of the Barrio's maneuver has made it evident that Señor Negrín is now the natural leader of the work of unification. If constitutionalism is to be observed, . . . the Junta de Liberación, headed by Señor Prieto, [cannot] hope to succeed where Martínez Barrio has failed."[119]

When Negrín arrived in Mexico City, he joined the members of his former cabinet in a call for unity. At a public meeting called by the Negrinistas, an official representative of the Mexican government declared its support for Negrín as the "true incarnation of Spain."[120] The presence of a minister from Guatemala inspired the feeling that "[exile] unity is on the march and nothing can stop it."[121]

Prieto had his own plans. With the Junta's future at stake and his own political vocation shaken, he realized that the only way to redeem his precarious position in the future Spain was by a dramatic impact at the United Nations conference about to take place on April 26, 1945, in San Francisco. The Junta's representatives were invited to attend the conference as observers without a vote. They presented the Republican case in a long document reminding the Allies that they were the pioneers in fighting Fascism. They called for intervention to overthrow Franco. With Hitler and Mussolini defeated, Prieto argued, Spain "should not remain as a monstrous exception in the world free of totalitarian tyranny."[122] Prieto and his Junta left San Francisco triumphant. The United Nations had adopted a Mexican resolution that put Franco outside the constellation of nations by denying membership in the organization to all states whose governments had been installed with the help of German Nazism and Italian Fascism.[123]

The new international posture simply deepened the rivalries among the Spanish exile groups. Prieto, who now enjoyed a quasi-official recognition as observer at the United Nations, refused to have any relationship with Negrín. In San Francisco, he argued, it became evident that his Junta was the only authentic representative of Republican Spain.[124] The support of the Spaniards abroad, however, went to Negrín. Any reconciliation between the two leaders seemed impossible.

On August 17, 1945, the exiled Republican Cortes, led by Martínez Barrio as a provisional president, assembled in Mexico City to elect its cabinet. This time more than a quorum was present.[125] No one wanted to remember the feuds between Prieto and Negrín; they belonged to the past. José Giral, a well-known scientist and a man who appeared to many exiles to be the "epitome of the political spirit of the original Republic,"[126] was elected to form the new Republican government-in-exile. But at this promising and crucial moment, the political rivalries of the past overwhelmed the dreams of the future. Negrín's exiled loyalists regarded Negrín's exclusion from this post as a "betrayal of Negrín, a betrayal of the Republic."[127] Prieto and his exile loyalists, for their part, abandoned hope in the old legalistic formula and sought for solutions to overthrow Franco "without necessary continuity with the past."[128]

By rejecting Giral's government-in-exile as illegitimate, the two exile camps gave the Allies reason to deny recognition and actual support to that government. As Louis Stein put it: "The leaders of the democratic nations lacked confidence in the ability of the Spanish republican government-in-exile to blunt the communist drive to power. The image that persisted of Spanish democratic politics was one of factionalism and weakness, qualities that were not conducive to building a stable government that could contain the inevitable communist thrust."[129]

The Spanish government-in-exile continued to function until 1977, two years after Franco's death, but it declined in stature, lost most of the recognition and loyalty it once enjoyed, and fast became an anachronism in a fast-changing world.

CHAPTER FIVE

Political Exiles and the Domestic Opposition

Exile leadership, in order to be effective, must retain national roots.
Alfred Stepan, 1980

For many exile groups, survival requires the formation or preservation of an organizational skeleton not only abroad but inside the home nation as well. Most exile groups maintain that the breakdown of the home regime can be accomplished only from within the home country; they see domestic opposition as the primary force for this mission, and their own activities abroad as interrelated and complementary to this struggle. They therefore cooperate with and even direct the internal opposition to the home regime, in the process securing their own political future in any later political transition. In some cases, especially those groups removed from political realities at home, exiles initiate their own strategies to overthrow the home regime, leaving little or no room for the internal opposition. Distance from inside events, inability to retain a foothold at home, lack of faith in the insiders' ability to bring about the home regime's downfall, and sustained reliance on international assistance are the principal reasons for a split between political exiles and internal oppositional forces. (See chapter 3.)

Pre-exile Organizations and Loyalty at Home

The ability of exile organizations to perpetuate loyalties at home is greatly determined by the state of the organization before and after departure from the home country. Groups that before exile already had strong ideological bonds, a cellular organizational structure, cohesive leadership, and a developed sense of internal discipline with past experience in clandestine operations, are more likely to maintain loyalties at home. Chilean communist exile leaders in the Soviet

Union and East Germany maintained their authority over the communist underground inside Chile. On the other hand, exile leaders of the Chilean Popular Unity parties, heavily factionalized before exile, failed to retain organizational roots inside Chile after the imposition of military rule in 1973.[1]

The nature of the activity of exile groups abroad is determined by pre-exile circumstances and the events that led to departure—civil war, imposition of a new regime, and so on. A significant question is, who left, and who is left behind? Usually the organization's leaders have gone into exile while the rank and file remain behind—frequently in prison or underground. For the most part, the activities of the organizational elites control exile politics, especially among pre-exile groups. This dramatically affects the complex relations between external and internal forces. Leaders abroad who strive to maintain their pre-exile positions may be challenged by those at home who aspire to leadership and resent the exiles' claim to authentic representation. To perpetuate and promote pre-exile roles, political exiles must exhibit unique charismatic and bureaucratic leadership qualities; they must attend to their home loyalists' spiritual and material needs from a distance. Proximity is neither sufficient nor necessary.

Juan Perón is a classic example of a successful exile leader; for nearly eighteen years he maintained and cultivated home loyalties from abroad. Perón, who spent most of his exile years in Madrid, used his financial resources, manipulative organizational skills, and charismatic appeal to make Argentina "virtually impossible to govern"[2] without him. Describing the effects of Perón's exile maneuvers on his home country, Robert Alexander writes:

Perón kept in constant touch with the political leaders of his movement and the trade union officials who represented the real core of the strength of Peronisimo. He orchestrated and directed their maneuvers, he dictated their attitudes towards successive regimes, he played off one leader against another, one group of his followers against another, making sure that he kept the final control of the Peronista movement in his own hands.

From abroad he maneuvered among the various tendencies that were working to keep him away, ably manipulating the loyalty of his followers and the institutions that were controlled by them. The shadow of Perón thus lay over the country throughout the period. His followers never forgot him and his opponents could never be assured that they would succeed in keeping him from returning.[3]

Occasionally the situation is reversed, with exile groups consisting of a small number of antiregime activists abroad, while organizational leaders and affiliates operate the opposition campaign at home. Exile groups loyal to such inside leadership tend to devote their energies to mobilizing outside support—the international community and the national community abroad—leaving the internal leadership with carte blanche to direct the antiregime campaign at home. The activities of the Korean Embassy-in-Exile, located in Washington, D.C. and inspired by Kim Dae Jung, the leader of the opposition New Korea Democratic Party, is an example of such outside-inside relations. Rallying the South Korean exiles in the United States, Kim Dae Jung attempted a two-front political assault on the Chun Doo Hwan regime, forming opposition inside Korea with compatriot exiles on the international front, mostly in the United States.[4]

The Internal-External Legitimacy Nexus

Political exiles' ability to maintain a foothold at home enhances their prestige among their prospective supporters abroad, both national and foreign. Political exiles without an active organization at home (and thus forced to concentrate mobilizing efforts exclusively in the international arena) are likely to encounter severe problems in mustering outside support. To convince international forces to support their struggle, exiles must continually provide concrete evidence or at least give the appearance of their capacity to maintain strong loyalties at home. Failure to do so may lead international contributors to look at the exiles as "generals without an army who are not worth taking seriously."[5]

National followers abroad are constantly searching for information that will provide a measure of the home regime's instability and prospects for breakdown, embracing any reports suggesting a clandestine resistance at home. Such home resistance is more likely to commit its support to exile groups that demonstrate a strong presence at home. Hence many exile organizations take pride in retaining a foothold within the clandestine home opposition and discredit competing exile groups for failing to maintain such connections, often dubbing them "theoretical," "impractical," or "irrelevant."

Spanish communist exiles in the early 1950s rebuilt their organization within Spain, developing "a strategical and tactical programme which was based on the principle of struggle from within."[6] They viewed other Republican exile groups with contempt for not accepting the necessity of clandestine operations against Franco.[7] A more dramatic case involved the Trust, the Stalin-sponsored pseudoexile organization (see chapter 8) set up by G.P.U. agents. The Trust sought to track down authentic monarchist exiles in Europe. This decoy organization developed a reputation among the true Russian exiles for "heroic" deeds inside Russia—a reputation accepted by the exiled monarchists, who wanted to believe in the existence of a strong anti-Soviet organization at home?

Political exiles try to maintain at least the appearance of objectives consistent with those of the domestic opposition and resist attempts to create a breach between insiders and outsiders. Thus, while trying to save the Spanish Republicans' reputation, toward the end of World War II Julio Alvarez del Vayo, ex-foreign minister of the Spanish republic and Juan Negrín's exile confidant, portrayed the Spanish Republican exiles' internal disputes as insignificant in the context of objectives shared by antifascists inside and outside Spain:

No exiled leader who is truly a leader of his people can believe that what anti-fascists inside Spain may do and think is of secondary importance. That would be patently ridiculous. On the other hand, no serious Republican fighter in Spain will pretend that he and his comrades are the only ones who can take leadership in the reconstruction, or that the exile parties and organization of the Republic, to which they belong and from which they came, are merely refugee groups carrying no particular weight. It is the exact coincidence of the political structure and aims of the Spanish Republic in Exile and the internal movement of resistance that gives strength to the Republican cause.[8]

However, many exile groups claiming ties to inside opposition groups find themselves challenged by forces at home who gradually become disenchanted with the political exiles' activities or leadership and refuse to submit to their authority. Such domestic disillusionment with political exiles is more prevalent when the outside forces prove powerless to mobilize foreign support, or when their leadership is hopelessly divided, or when their apparatus is unresponsive to the needs of the insiders. As time passes, the inside forces are likely to look less and less to the political exiles, whose physical and ideological distance makes them unreliable as an inspirational force for internal opposition. Developments inside the home nation may produce new opposition forces that find the political exiles "dated in their ideas and style."[9]

But occasionally exiles are reborn as leaders of the internal opposition. The most astonishing case is the recent and abrupt rejuvenation of the African National Congress (ANC) as the South African government's "most adamant enemy."[10] After long years in the wilderness, in Lusaka, the ANC benefited from the government's nationwide crackdown after the Soweto uprising in 1976. With most legal black organizations in South Africa increasingly subject to harassment and intimidation, and groups such as the Pan-African Congress weakened by internal organizational rivalries, the ANC inherited internal support, partly by default but also through an international and national campaign to release the ANC's jailed leadership, and through the organization's newfound respectability and growing stature among Western nations. As a prominent white South African student of African exiles has observed, the activities of the ANC since 1976 exemplify the advantages of exile politics over internal opposition groups in attracting inside loyalists: "The terrain of exile . . . can provide protection, security, powerful forms of external support, factors and conditions which facilitate the development of a form and quality of organization unattainable in the precarious circumstance of opposition politics within the homeland."[11]

Insiders' tendency to resist outsiders' control usually increases when exile groups and their leaders "symbolically represent the pre-defeat power groups."[12] The increasing erosion of the internal legitimacy of the Spanish and Polish governments-in-exile is an illustration.[13] Another is the revolt, shortly after the imposition of the Nazi regime, of anti-Nazi socialists in the German underground against the leaders of the exiled SPD.

The party leaders of the German Social Democratic Party had gone into exile in Prague in early 1933, then seemingly the best way of ensuring the continued survival of the party. A few months later, however, young activists in the underground at home challenged the exiles' claim to leadership based on their pre-exile legal standing in the party. The internal SPD blamed the party's deteriorated domestic condition on the "disastrous policy" of the old leadership and called upon the executive in Prague to relinquish power and submit itself to the will of SPD's underground inside Germany. In May 1933 a clandestine SPD group, led by "Miles" (a soldier), published a pamphlet called *New Beginning*. It declared the leadership abroad politically and spiritually ineffective, "entirely incapable of securing the existence and the revolutionary work of the party in *Germany itself* under the fascist regime, let alone of organizing the struggle for the overthrow of fascism."[14] The inside challenge to the exiled SPD greatly blemished its international reputation.[15] The feud was later reproduced abroad where the groups competed bitterly for support of socialist and trade union circles in the U.S. It "poisoned the atmosphere in the fashion most detrimental to the socialist cause."[16]

Edinger observes: "All exiles aspiring to lead an indigenous resistance movement are seriously handicapped by appearing to call upon those who remained to risk their lives in opposition while they enjoy the safety of sanctuary abroad."[17] In November 1948, a military junta deposed the democratic government of Venezuela and forced into exile almost all of the leaders of Acción Democrática (AD), the ruling party. The younger and less experienced members of the party who remained behind became the objects of increased military repressions. The insiders and outsiders soon grew apart, developing into factions with incompatible interests. The leaders abroad sought to guide and direct the home resistance, but as Michael Coppedge, a student of Venezuelan politics, has observed, "Some of the underground leaders considered the exiles cowards or fair-weather friends for staying out of the country while [they] were risking their lives daily." He continues, "Loyalty to the older leaders in exile was weakened by their long absence, and the younger leaders . . . eventually felt justified in ignoring decisions made abroad."[18] The split between the insiders and the exiled leaders persisted throughout the ten-year dictatorship of Marcos Pérez Jiménez and dominated the ruling party during the initial period of Venezuela's redemocratization. Moreover the forces at home, striving to weaken the home regime from within, are frequently reluctant to take additional risks to maintain their contacts with political exiles, especially when the insiders do not expect to benefit significantly from such connections. When political exiles, to save face and not be forgotten, advocate violent and insurrectionary methods in the struggle against the regime, the home loyalists are the first to suffer from retaliation. Sometimes they refuse to follow the exiles' advice, noting with bitter irony, as Paul Lewis quotes Paraguayan insiders as saying in the 1960s, "it is easy to be brave when you are far away from the fire."[19] In turn, internal disinclination to adopt the violent tactics urged by the outsiders may further undermine the exiles' standing at home. In 1981, for example, the Communist Party's underground leadership inside Chile ignored the call of party exile leaders in Moscow for violent overthrow of the military regime.[20] Likewise, the Manila-based opposition to Ferdinand Marcos questioned and insisted on modifying the violent tactics and terrorist methods suggested by the exiled leadership in the United States. Later it became evident that the exiles' desire to destabilize the regime through bombing attacks had backfired. As one student of Filipino politics observed, "the bombings led to no appreciable growth in the moderate opposition while increasing government repression against it."[21]

The internal underground is usually compelled to give priority to organizational cohesion and existence over theoretical discussions.

On the other hand, political exiles, facing an operational void, often concentrate on theoretical disputation. As Charles Delzell, a student of Italian anti-Fascist exiles, has observed, many political exiles "ceased to be politicians and had become merely political theorists."[22] The gap between the inside world dominated by the exigencies of practical political struggle, and the outside world of abstract political designs, may lead to front-line fighters' resentment of the exile leaders. With the growing resistance to Mussolini inside Italy, the discord between anti-Fascist elements abroad was no longer reflected in the struggle at home. One anti-Fascist said in a pamphlet, "a young Communist inside Italy would feel intellectually and emotionally closer to a liberal revolutionary in Italy than to a leader of the Italian Communist Party abroad. A young liberal would feel the same."[23]

Exile groups are often constrained by the political and ideological debts imposed on them by their international "creditors" (their host state and other international patrons) so as to support their international benefactors on issues unrelated to their home cause. They may find it difficult to persuade their domestic followers to involve themselves in such international matters. Many home loyalists are reluctant to adopt their exile leaders' stance on international questions for fear of appearing to be tools of foreign influences. In recent years exile leaders of the Chilean Communist Party living in Moscow faced great difficulties in persuading their internal loyalists to follow them in supporting the Soviet Union's invasion of Afghanistan and the 1981 Polish military's crackdown on Solidarity.[24] As a student of Chilean exiles has noted, whereas Chilean communist exiles "have begun to espouse only Soviet communism, Chilean politics and opinions have taken the back seat to the views of the Soviets."[25]

Exiles and Hegemonic Home Regimes

Leaders who molded their organizational supremacy through democratic procedures at home have the problem of how to legitimize their decisions and authority from abroad. In the absence of democratic mechanisms for sustaining their pre-exile authority and symbols, the exiles' claims for legal representation are invalidated. They must provide alternative indications of their legitimacy at home. Exile leaders whose home loyalists operate in less hegemonic systems may encounter, in their relations with the insiders, additional complexities that derive directly from the home regime's partial openness. Exile groups struggling against such regimes maintain their contacts with home through phone calls, written messages, and a steady stream of

visitors. In some unusual cases political exiles are even allowed to
enter and reside in their home country legally. Exiled Febrerista leaders
were permitted to live for short periods of time in Paraguay. As Paul
Lewis points out, this reflects the "paradox of Paraguayan politics; it
is often violent, yet political groups seldom wage total war on their
opponents."[26]

One of the most difficult tasks of exile groups and leaders is the
perpetuation of loyalties among home followers who operate clandes-
tinely under "Hegemonic" or "near-Hegemonic" systems,[27] to use
Robert Dahl's classification. Under hegemonic rule government for-
bids all political opposition or criticism. The only opposition possible
is an internal underground or exile. Soviet Russia in the 1920s and
1930s is an extreme example of a hegemonic system where the
suppression of domestic opposition embraced all shades of political
opinion, from monarchists on the extreme Right to anarchists and
nonconformist communists on the extreme Left.[28] Rafael Trujillo's
repressive dictatorship in the Dominican Republic also exemplifies a
hegemonic system. Under Trujillo, "the only opposition parties were
organized in exile."[29]

The more hegemonic the home regime, the more difficult it is to
find evidence of strong underground revolutionary currents. Every hegemony takes pains to conceal the existence of hostile underground
elements and employs every conceivable measure to suppress information about their existence. Therefore political exiles who seek to
maintain ties with underground forces under hegemonies or near-
hegemonies must acquire sophisticated technical skills of clandestine
communication.

In this century political exiles have improved their means of communication with underground loyalists at home, keeping the exile
organization and its leadership in the minds of the home followers,
while providing the internal forces with information both on the internal situation as perceived from abroad and on exile resistance
activities. Written publications smuggled in from abroad, secret or
above-ground radio stations, coded radio messages and courier systems, cassettes, airplanes and balloons carrying leaflets to the home
country and, finally, exiles who occasionally risk their lives to sneak
across the frontier to deliver their message by word of mouth—all are
part of the tactical repertoire that political exiles employ to strengthen
their organization at home. In the era of television these efforts have
reached extraordinary levels of sophistication. Thus on September 5,
1986, Iranian television viewers were startled by the appearance of
Reza Pahlavi II on their screens. The son of the late shah, leader of

the Iranian exile monarchists, had succeeded, with the assistance of inside loyalists, in interrupting the regular programs on Iranian national television in order to send his message to the Iranian people. For eleven minutes the exiled self-proclaimed shah called upon loyalists at home to fight against Khomeini and the Islamic regime, declaring himself the authentic "leader of Iran." This insurrectionary broadcast led to street demonstrations by Pahlavi supporters that the Iranian Revolutionary Guards quickly met with gunfire.[30] In some extreme cases, political exiles resort to terrorist measures against officials and institutions of the home regime abroad, hoping to make their activity visible and morale-building for the frustrated opposition at home. The anti-Castro exile terrorist group Omega 7 serves as an example. Its leader, Eduardo Arocena, was implicated in many bombings in the United States and in the 1980 murder of Félix García Rodrigues, an attaché to the Cuban mission to the United Nations.[31]

Often there is an inverse relationship between the home regime's ability to suppress its internal opponents and the opposition role assumed by the political exiles. As long as the clandestine forces at home remain viable, the activities of the opposition abroad are designed chiefly to aid and abet the internal struggle. With the growing deterioration of the insiders, however, political exiles are likely to assume a greater opposition role, often claiming to be the sole voice of the internally oppressed. After 1948 the exile leadership of Acción Democrática supported an active underground movement inside Venezuela. However, when toward the end of 1952 the underground began to collapse, the outsiders assumed more of the burden of opposition to the regime of Pérez Jiménez, thereby making their struggle more international in scope.[32]

Total repression of the internal opposition may in fact contribute to the image of political exiles among potential international supporters, particularly among those who seek the fall of the home regime but have lost faith in internal change. These international powers tend to sponsor exile activities, mostly for their own policy objectives, hoping that when the exiles overthrow and replace the home regime, they will be remembered for their assistance. Governments that supported exile invasions in the Caribbean and in Africa are the extreme manifestation of this phenomenon. A more recent familiar example is the Arab and Western governments' support of anti-Qaddafi Libyan exiles. Libyan exile groups have neither a significant base of support inside the country nor links with the Libyan military and are themselves incapable of developing a serious military challenge to the Libyan regime. Nevertheless, many of Qaddafi's international opponents have considered them to be his most serious challengers as well as the potential successors to his regime.[33]

Foreign support is likely to decline over time, when international supporters come to realize that the home regime is stable and not apt to be affected seriously by internal challenges. On the other hand, it is likely to rise with renewed popularity of the exile groups at home.

Mixed Regime or Pluralistic Hegemony

Relations between political exiles and the internal resistance vary significantly with the nature of the home regime, in particular the tolerance afforded to domestic opposition. Under a hegemony any form of organized opposition is prohibited and the home regime enforces a policy of closed borders. Many governments "severely restrict travel abroad by their nationals. Passports are difficult to obtain, while illegal border-crossing and absence abroad beyond the validity of an exit permit can attract heavy penalties."[34] The exile-insider interaction in such regimes is confined to underground work.

In more pluralistic systems or "mixed regimes," where above-ground forms of internal opposition are permitted and a certain degree of free movement is possible, the exile-insider relations are more likely to exhibit greater variations. Mixed regimes are defined by Robert Dahl as political systems that combine limited pluralism with limited tolerance toward the opposition. The rulers of such systems permit pluralism and tolerate opposition as long as it is perceived as unthreatening.[35] In political-science literature mixed regimes are usually known as authoritarian, in contrast to totalitarian rule where no dissent is permitted. Juan Linz's account of the opposition to Franco is often considered the classic example of government-opposition relations under authoritarian rule.[36] Linz distinguishes three major types of opposition possible under authoritarian rule: legal, alegal but tolerated, and illegal-clandestine. "The borderlines [between these types of opposition] vary considerably from one authoritarian regime to another," Linz points out, "and even within the same system, depending on a great number of factors."[37] The main characteristic of the above-ground, tolerated oppositions under authoritarian rule is that they enjoy semifreedom and relative immunity from repression, in exchange for keeping their oppositional activities within tolerated or prescribed boundaries—in particular, the exclusion of any violent means of opposition.

The situation of semifreedom and partial acceptance by the home regime imposes certain costs and at the same time yields certain benefits to tolerated forms of opposition under these authoritarian-mixed regimes. Just as the regime is constrained in its repression of the tolerated opposition, so is the opposition constrained in its anti-regime campaign by the limits to dissent set by the regime. On the one hand, a tolerated opposition enjoys relative immunity from the official repression that is endemic to activities of illegal underground forces. On the other hand, the tolerated opposition may face great difficulties in presenting itself as a viable alternative to the existing authorities, since a viable alternative often requires total denunciation of the system. Linz notes that the ambiguity of the opposition under authoritarian regimes "explains the frustration, disintegration and sometimes readiness to co-optation, which contribute to the persistence of such regimes sometimes as much as does their repressive capacity."[38]

For exile groups as for the internal underground, the existence of an above-ground, "acceptable" opposition creates a special dilemma. They must decide to what extent they will cooperate with the tolerated opposition without compromising their claims to representation. Because political exiles are by their revolutionary nature reluctant to participate in the political game as defined by the home regime, they defy the home regime's distinction between acceptable and non-acceptable opposition. At the same time they often acknowledge the political advantage of domestically tolerated opposition. Exile groups, like other clandestine forces, must constantly contend with problems of organizational survival. When official tolerance is granted to forces at home, they gain considerable leverage for political maneuvering. Hence when political exiles abroad deliberately avoid collaboration with the above-ground forces at home, they run the risk of losing influence in a future arrangement, in particular, in the case of a gradual and peaceful "opening" of the political system from within.

The 1958 redemocratization in Venezuela is a prime example of a situation where leaders of a party in exile understood the necessity of compromising with above-ground rival parties at home. In the face of fierce objection from Acción Democrática members who for years carried on the day-to-day struggle underground, AD leaders abroad pushed for concessions to old enemies, thereby laying the foundation for the Pact of Punto Fijo, signed on October 31, 1958, which ensured the stability of political democracy in Venezuela.[39]

Just like domestic political opposition groups, so too must exile groups come to grips with the degree of loyalty granted to other contenders for power in the state, as well as with the relative strength of social subsystems and semipolitical forces such as religious groups, labor unions, women's organizations, and student groups. The activity of these civil society segments, especially in countries where they enjoy considerable spheres of autonomy, can be the key to the weakening and final breakdown of an authoritarian regime, and to the determination of the type of system that will succeed it.[40] The political exiles' ability to evaluate the relative strength of internal forces and to shape their policies accordingly can decisively influence the exiles' future. In 1948 the Catholic church in Venezuela greeted the collapse and exile of the AD regime as a blessing from God. The AD leadership, now in exile, recognized the need to compromise its previous anticlericalism. In order to win support of the church, AD leader Rómulo Betancourt promised to reevaluate AD's church-state policies. The church in turn reversed its position in the late 1950s and supported the return of the AD group to power as the best alternative to succeed Pérez Jiménez.[41]

One must keep in mind that, whatever the position exile groups assume regarding collaboration with the domestically tolerated opposition, interaction with political exiles involves great risk for insiders. The home regime may interpret such collaboration as a deviation from the "rules of the game" and retaliate by withdrawing the partial immunity. Franco's regime, Linz writes, "tended to discriminate between internal opponents according to whether they did or did not have contact with leaders abroad. It generally used foreign contacts to question the legitimacy of its [internal] opponents."[42]

Collaboration with the Opposition or Infiltration

The conflicting desire either to maintain a revolutionary identity on the one hand, or to take advantage of the existing regime's tolerance on the other, may produce a wide spectrum of political responses. At one extreme, exiles may adopt the "honest" approach, avoiding any collaboration with forces inside the country that accept the regime's definition of permissible dissent. At the other extreme, adopting the "genuine collaboration" approach, they may conclude that their politics has outlived its usefulness, relinquish revolutionary claims, and try to find their way back home to work for peaceful change from within. Many communist exile groups exhibit a combination of these responses. They try to utilize the opportunity to work within the tolerated space provided by the regime, usually through infiltration, in order to deepen their inside agitation. But at the same time they seek to maintain their underground struggle while discrediting the internally tolerated forces for collaborating with the home regime.

A classic example of infiltration in the exile-insider relationship was the exiled Bolsheviks' reaction to the establishment of the Russian Duma. When the czarist regime founded the first Duma in April 1906, Lenin and the exiled Bolsheviks ordered their followers at home to boycott the election: "If you preach and breathe revolution and call for partisan warfare, how can you turn around and demand patient electoral work of participation in this fraudulent parliament where voting is weighted in favor of the possessing classes?"[43]

However, after the Mensheviks and the Kadets achieved relative success in the first Duma, Lenin reversed his opposition to participation in the established order: "History has shown that the convening of the Duma brings with it the possibility of useful agitation . . . that inside we can apply the tactics of an understanding with the revolutionary peasants. It would be ridiculous to close our eyes to reality. The time has become now when the Revolutionary Social Democrats must cease to be boycottists."[44]

Lenin adopted the position that involvement in the legal procedure was simply part of the plan for total revolution. His new equation was: "You join forces with party X in order to defeat a greater enemy, party Y. But you do it also to expose and unmask X."[45] However, the Bolsheviks' participation in the czarist system, under the constant instruction of the party leaders abroad,[46] estranged some members of the ultra Left, Vperyodist Bolsheviks who continued to call for a total boycott of czarist institutions. Although this challenge threatened Lenin's leadership, he stood firm in his advice to use the Duma as a forum where revolutionaries could appeal to the masses and inspire insurrection.

For the most part, the "honest" approach of avoiding collaboration with the tolerated opposition at home is more prevalent among those exile groups that make governmental claims. Groups that claim to be the sole alternative to the home regime are less likely to cooperate with the internally tolerated opposition, unless the insiders accept the outsiders' supremacy. The unwillingness of exile leaders to cooperate with internal opponents of the home regime may produce dissension among their national followers at home and abroad, who may consider their leaders' behavior rigid. Thus from time to time, exile activists and home dissenters who strive to bring down the regime at any cost may cooperate with domestic opposition forces outside the exile organization's program.

Spanish exile leaders in 1945 were divided on the question of cooperation with Don Juan's monarchists in the struggle to overthrow Franco. Some exiled Republicans, among them Prieto, entered into negotiations with the monarchists to establish an alliance against Franco, leaving the question of the future form of government unresolved. These contacts intensified the split between Republicans who were "loyal to a 'legal' government in exile and those willing to search for solutions without necessary continuity with the past."[47]

"Nongovernmental" exile organizations that conceive of themselves as one among several alternatives to succeed the home regime are more likely to seek cooperation with above-ground domestic forces. Concerned chiefly with democratization of the political system, they seek to assist internal groups that may promote their goals. This was, for example, the case with the Filipino coalition of exiles and internal forces that aimed at eliminating Marcos's rule. In 1982 twelve opposition groups, including U.S.-based oppositionists led by Raúl Manglapus and Benigno Aquino, Jr. announced formation of the United Nationalist Democratic Organization (UNIDO) "to undo the Marcos dictatorship and restore the fundamental institutions of democracy."[48]

The importance of maintaining a foothold inside the home nation increases when the home regime moves toward liberalization and eventual democratization of the political system. Over time authoritarian regimes may acknowledge, in response to growing internal or external pressures, an inability to perpetuate their closed political systems. To protect themselves against demands for greater pluralism, these regimes may seek to establish legal forms of opposition loyal to their rule, and at the same time to exclude their bitter opponents at home and abroad from promoting the new political and societal transitions. Through the manipulation of their power, such authoritarian regimes hope to reshape the political and social realm so as to retain electoral ratification and popular support when the democratic transition takes place. In a period of increasing liberalization at home, the political exiles' sustained struggle may be viewed by the young internal opposition forces as anachronistic, and in some cases even as a threat to the opening process. Guillermo O'Donnell and Philippe Schmitter observed: "Regime opponents, having been given virtually no role within the authoritarian scheme of governance and, in some cases, having returned from exile to act in societies which have undergone substantial changes, often have had to rely on precarious past identities, outmoded slogans, and unimaginative combinations."[49]

The redemocratization of Getúlio Vargas's Brazil in 1945 is a classic example of an authoritarian system that neutralized its exile opponents throughout the transition period. Vargas's self-imposed legal opposition gradually earned support and was able to win the election at the end of the authoritarian rule.

In November 1937 Vargas, Brazil's first president under the constitution of 1933–34, canceled the elections scheduled for January 1938 and introduced his authoritarian system, the Estado Nôvo. The coup d'etat of 1937 was followed by the elimination of all political parties. Special treatment was given to the Liberals under Armando de Salles Oliveira, a leading presidential candidate who had a reasonable chance of winning the election of 1938.[50] Shortly after the imposition of the Estado Nôvo, de Salles and a handful of his loyalists were forced to flee Brazil. They went first to Paris, then later established their opposition base in Buenos Aires.[51] De Salles understood that political power in Brazil was contingent upon the loyalty of the military. Hoping to benefit from a military intervention to overthrow Vargas, in December 1939 he called on the Brazilian military command to assume the role of protectors of the "national dignity": "Outside the Army there is no solution for the Brazilian crisis. Only the Army can bring about unity because it is the only national force not demoralized by the authoritarian lunacy."[52]

In late 1943, with the prospect of an end to the war in Europe, "Vargas was foresighted enough to realize that his dictatorship could not survive the war."[53] A victory of the Allies and the fall of European totalitarianism would have a major impact on his regime. Therefore he gradually fashioned a new political and social reality capable of outlasting him after the reopening of the system—two political parties that benefited materially from Vargas's rule and were led by his trusted lieutenants. He formed the Social Democratic Party (Partido Social Democrático, or PSD) under the leadership of his war minister, Gen. Eurico Dutra, and the Brazilian Labor Party (Partido Trabalhista Brasileiro, or PTB) under the leadership of his minister of labor, Marcondes Filho. The PTB, in particular, was part of Vargas's continuing efforts to gain the loyalty of the workers at the expense of their traditional representatives on the Left.

Throughout this period the Liberal Constitutionalists and their exiled leader, Salles Oliveira, were excluded. Although most opposition leaders abroad were allowed to return to Brazil early on,[54] he remained unwelcome. Vargas was orchestrating the reorganization of Brazil (he had announced that he himself would not run for president), arming his partisans with a strong electoral machine. His Liberal opponents, on the other hand, faced the elections of December 1945 confused and disorganized, and Vargas's plan was implemented smoothly. The PSD and the PTB together won 52 percent of the vote in the congressional elections. Salles Oliveira, who was mortally ill, died before the end of 1945, a month after he finally arrived on Brazilian soil.

Exile-Insider Relations over Time

As in other political encounters, the complexity of exile-insider relationships is compounded by time. Indeed, a case-by-case analysis of their relative strengths in relation to the home regime must take into account social and political developments inside the home nation throughout the duration of exile—dramatic events such as external war, civil strife, assassination or death from natural causes of a dictator, and also processes of gradual change such as slow alteration in the structural bases of the society, modifications in the nature of the home regime (whether toward polyarchy or hegemony), and finally the turnover of generations.

As an analytic point of departure, one can imagine four theoretical examples of the strength of political exiles and the internal opposition in relation to the home regime: (1) strong opposition at home and viable opposition abroad; (2) strong opposition at home and powerless opposition abroad; (3) increasing opposition abroad and deteriorating opposition at home; and (4) broken opposition at home and deteriorating opposition abroad.

The positions of the exile group and the internal opposition vis-à-vis the home regime are usually interrelated. That is, the situation of the internal opposition affects the position of the political exiles and vice versa. Moreover, if we put these static examples into motion, to be examined over time, we are likely to find fluidity. One may observe a strengthening of the home regime followed by total neutralization of the inside opposition. This may lead to an enhancement of the exiles' position as the sole alternative to that regime. At the same time, it may force them to achieve, at least in appearance, quick and substantial gains in their struggle; otherwise, the political exiles are likely to face a gradual erosion in the international attention that their cause elicits, and an organizational dissolution resulting either in assimilation abroad or in return under conditions of defeat. Also, either gradual or dramatic developments conducive to the home regime's breakdown may accelerate the political exiles' return home, as recently illustrated in the return of South Korean political exiles from the United States after political changes were announced by Chun Doo Hwan's government in response to the huge street demonstrations of June 1987.[55]

A more dramatic example is the clandestine return to Chile in March 1987 of the leader of the radical social wing of the democratic Left, Clodomiro Almeyda, from his exile in East Berlin. The growing tendency among domestic opposition parties, especially within the socialist camp, to suspend militant protest strategies in the struggle against Pinochet and to join forces to challenge the regime in the plebiscite of October 1988, convinced Almeyda to make a spectacular homecoming. He sneaked across the Andes into Chile and turned himself in to the Chilean courts. Almeyda's return and arrest enhanced his mystique within the opposition camp; from his Santiago jail cell, he became a major advocate in the campaign for a "no" vote in the plebiscite.[56]

The role of the political exiles in developments leading (or about to lead) to the downfall of the home regime, the nature of the political transition (violent or peaceful, democratic or nondemocratic), and the timing of the exiles' homecoming (before or after the collapse of the home regime)—all are critical factors in determining the exiles' political future. However, since every regime's transition takes place in a unique set of circumstances, it is almost impossible to predict the role and impact of exiles in shaping the future of the country upon their return.

Whether the political exiles will play a dominant role in, or indeed become the future rulers of, their country, or whether they will remain marginal actors, is in many cases a function of serendipity.[57] The arrival of Lenin and his exiled fellow Bolsheviks at the Finland Station is a case of a uniquely timed exiles' homecoming. It changed the course of history. Adam Ulam points out that "the Bolsheviks did not seize power. . . . They picked it up."[58] But political exiles who return after a long absence (especially to a society experiencing a gradual transition toward democracy) may encounter great obstacles to reintegrating themselves in the new array of political forces. The young generation of politicians at home may perceive them as intruders or competitors. This was the case of Brazilian exiles who fled their country after the 1964 coup and returned home after the Brazilian government was forced, in September 1979, to grant amnesty to its opponents abroad. As a student of Brazilian exiles observed, "it took seven years until the exiles re-integrated into the Brazilian society."[59]

To perpetuate pre-exile loyalties and bolster their position at home, exile groups and leaders must keep in constant touch with the internal opposition and with daily developments at home. They must act with great caution so as not to exacerbate the position of their compatriots by advocating acts of violence. At the same time they must take action that involves risks, so that they appear willing to sacrifice themselves for the cause as much as do their compatriots at home. At least in appearance, they must avoid supporting international enterprises that might alienate their countrymen's nationalist feelings. They must be able to manipulate material and symbolic incentives so as to suppress forces at home that challenge the outside leadership of the exiles' organization.

Italian Exiles Who Failed to Reach the Promised Land

> *The sufferings, the defiance and the rebellion of the exiles may show to the world the indestructible force of Italian civilization.*
> —Carlo Rosselli, 1927

Two cases of Italian exile activity in the nineteenth and twentieth centuries demonstrate the tenuous and fragile nature of the relationship between exiles and an internal opposition. The home regime's ability to suppress internal dissent or to create alternative routes for its expression has important consequences for political exiles in their relationship with their internal compatriots.

Giuseppe Mazzini's Young Italy and Carlo Rosselli's Justice and Liberty bring into sharp relief the interaction between political exiles and home opposition. They demonstrate the exiles' contribution in building a potent internal opposition movement that eventually becomes the center of resistance against the home regime, thus shifting the momentum of the struggle. Mazzini and Rosselli both came to be seen as heroic symbols of the struggle for Italian liberty, though both were prophets who failed to enter the Promised Land.

Mazzini died in Pisa on March 10, 1872, an exile in his own land. He spent his last days in the house of Pellegrino Rosselli, the son-in-law of his old friends the Rossellis, from Leghorn.[60] Sixty-five years later, on June 9, 1937, the grandchildren of the Leghorn Rossellis, Carlo Rosselli, the exiled anti-Fascist leader, and his brother Nello, an anti-Fascist intellectual who lived in Italy, were both assassinated in the forest of Bagnoles-de-l'Orne in Normandy, apparently by Fascist agents dispatched by Mussolini.[61]

In contemporary Italy the names Mazzini and Rosselli have become synonymous with courage and bravery in the struggle for democracy, liberty, and human dignity. Both became legends and sources of inspiration, even before their death, for all who struggled for a liberal republic in Italy.

Mazzini and Rosselli devoted their lives to similar causes. Mazzini fought to overthrow the eight monarchies of Italy and to create a single united republic. He argued that "constitutional monarchy was the most immoral government in the world—an essentially corrupting institution."[62] Carlo Rosselli sought to overthrow Italian Fascism. He and his loyalists held, as Rosengarten has written, "that since the fascist regime owed much of its prestige among the masses of Italians to the cooperation it received from the Monarchy, the monarchical institution itself and in particular the person of King Victor Emmanuel III had to be repudiated."[63] Both Mazzini and Rosselli rejected a monarchical regime, maintaining that freedom could not coexist with monarchy. Both established and led exile organizations that fought to revolutionize the moral, social, and political structure of the Italian nation. Mazzini declared: "There is no such thing as purely political or purely social revolution; every true revolution has its political and social character alike."[64] Rosselli agreed with this. Both considered their own national struggle as part of a greater struggle against tyranny. Mazzini's belief in a federation of "harmonious nationalities" in Europe led him to collaborate with other national liberation movements. He was the founder of Young Switzerland and the leading spirit of Young Europe, a unifying front of Italian, German, and Polish exiles fighting tyrannical European regimes. His own Italian exile loyalists had to swear to devote themselves to "the regeneration of the Father-land" and "to fight in every way inequalities between men."[65]

Rosselli was among the few who in the early 1930s foresaw the war in Europe. He warned the European democracies of a Fascist conspiracy long before Hitler and Mussolini revealed their expansionist nature, and he called on the French and British to initiate a defensive war while it was still possible. His Justice and Liberty was the first of the Italian anti-Fascist exile groups to anticipate the Fascist connection in the Spanish Civil War: "Oggi in Spagna, domani in Italia" (today in Spain, tomorrow in Italy). It was the first group to join the fight beside the Spanish Republicans.

Both Mazzini and the Rosselli brothers learned the importance of equality and freedom in their childhood. Mazzini was taught to worship equality and freedom by parents who were democratic in their relationship with others. For the Rossellis the Mazzinian democratic heritage was central to their education; they belonged to a wealthy Tuscan family nurtured in the tradition of the Risorgimento. Indeed, Nello Rosselli devoted his intellectual life to a study of the Risorgimento and wrote his 1923 dissertation on Mazzini and Bakunin.[66]

In 1828 the young Mazzini publicized his ideas for a unified and independent Italy through a weekly literary paper, *Indicatore Genovese*. The Italian authorities, considering his writings provocative and explosive, arrested and convicted him for instigating the young generation against the government. After five months in jail in Savona, he was forced to flee Italy. He lived the rest of his life as a political exile, returning to Italy only to plan and lead armed insurrections during the 1847–48 revolution. Like many other revolutionary exiles of his generation, he found "a second fatherland" in postrevolutionary France.[67] He established himself at Marseilles, where he founded *La Giovine Italia* (Young Italy). It was, he said, "the first amongst the political associations of our time to comprehend, in its conceptions, all the branches of national activity, and to seek, from a religious point of view, to cause them all to converge towards one object, according to the idea of mission imposed upon man."[68]

Young Italy advocated independence from international support. For them, as Mazzini wrote, it was a fundamental principle that "the Italian revolution might profit by foreign elements, but ought not to choose them as its sole support; . . . it ought to be effected by its own powers."[69] He constantly reminded his exiled followers that assistance from outside sources was acceptable only after the nation was able to prove itself capable of victory without it: "Hope nothing from diplomacy; nothing but ill can come of it; discomfit it, in allowing it no hold upon you: your arms are action and publicity. But know that, provided you rise in the name of a general principle; provided you show yourselves ready to fight and die for all, your cause will become the cause of all."[70] Mazzini believed that the power of the Italian people could defeat their Austrian rulers if they could trust their leaders' commitment to the national cause. "[T]he people love just and useful revolutions," he wrote, "but it does not wish them to be eternal, and it will remain cold and indifferent when it perceives that its chiefs seek, from fear or from bad faith, to hide from it the object in view, or when the object itself is vague and incomplete."[71]

Young Italy's revolutionary call was directed toward Italian youth; members had to be under forty. Only those who were not part of the past would be chosen to fight and die for national independence. Mazzini also regarded the older generation as, in Barr's paraphrase, a "generation of compromisers and diplomatic meddlers."[72]

Young Italy was designed as a central committee in exile, responsible for general strategy in the fight for national liberation to be waged by those at home. To aid the spread of Mazzinian teachings at home, Young Italy published journals in Marseilles and Geneva, where Italian exiles had flocked even before the failure of the 1831 uprisings; these publications were smuggled into Italy. Mazzini's revolutionary call spread throughout Italy and even penetrated the ranks of the Piedmontese Army.[73] In his memoirs Alexander Herzen, known as the intellectual father of nineteenth-century European exiles, described Mazzini's leadership among Italians abroad:

A fanatic and at the same time an organiser, [Mazzini] covered Italy with a network of secret societies connected together and devoted to one object. These societies branched off into arteries that defied detection, split up, grew smaller and smaller, and vanished in the Apennines and the Alps, in the regal *palazzi* of aristocrats and the dark alleys of Italian towns into which no police can penetrate. Village priests, *diligence* guards, the *principi* of Lombardy, smugglers, innkeepers, women, bandits, all were made use of, all were links in the chain that was in contact with him and was subjected to him.[74]

Historians of the Risorgimento agreed that Mazzini, the spiritual leader of Italian unity, failed as a politician. The historian William Roscoe Thayer argues that if Mazzini's own political plans had been adopted by Piedmont, Italy would have had "neither independence nor unity."[75] Although the exiled Mazzini was in close touch in the 1830s and 1840s, Thayer says, by the 1850s he had forgotten what Italy was like and had gradually become a prisoner of his own beliefs of the early 1830s, which by then were no longer suitable.[76] Hans Kohn maintains that the Mazzini of the 1850s had failed to understand Italy's new reality, especially the others who were working for its unity: "He was unjust to the patient efforts of the Italian moderates. He idealized the Italian people, with whom he had no close contact."[77]

Pragmatism in Exile Politics

In November 1926 Mussolini imposed his dictatorship on Italy. He forbade political opposition, forcing many of his adversaries, leaders of socialist parties especially, to flee abroad. These leaders established the Concentrazione antifascista in Paris in April 1927. In its first years the organization was limited in its communication with the clandestine groups inside Italy, and its propaganda warfare was ineffective.[78] In 1929, almost a century after Mazzini established Young Italy, Carlo Rosselli founded Justice and Liberty in Paris.[79] The exile organization was neither the first nor the largest of the Italian anti-Fascist exile groups, but by the early 1930s almost all the other exile groups regarded it as the most effective organization in mobilizing clandestine groups to fight Fascism within Italy.[80] Carlo Rosselli himself earned a reputation as the most dangerous of the Italian anti-Fascists.[81]

Justice and Liberty owed its relative success in mobilizing loyalists inside Italy to its leadership's ability to project personal valor and readiness for self-sacrifice. Its core members in Paris had established their own reputation for heroism a number of years before. Its original nucleus had been formed in 1922 in Italy under the leadership of Piero Gobetti, whose newspaper *Rivoluzione Liberale*, published in Turin, was one of the most "progressive and provocative" anti-Fascist organs in Italy between 1922 and 1924.[82] Carlo Rosselli, Riccardo Bauer, Gaetano Salvemini, Guido de Ruggiero, and others, who later joined Justice and Liberty in exile, had collaborated inside Italy in 1924 in publishing the clandestine anti-Fascist newspaper *Non Mollare!* (Don't Give In!). This newspaper called upon Italians to revive the spirit of the Risorgimento and to boycott the Fascist regime just as their fathers had boycotted the Austrian authorities from 1848 to 1859.[83] Founders of *Non Mollare!* established an underground section in Florence, which advised Florentines to stay at home or leave town on the day of a visit by King Victor Emmanuel, "since the King was no longer the king of the Italians but of the Fascists."[84] The Fascist regime eventually forced many *Non Mollare!* activists to leave Italy.

In September 1927 Rosselli and his friend Ferruccio Parri were sentenced to five years in prison for assisting Filippo Turati to escape abroad. The seventy-year-old Turati, who was parliamentary leader of the right-wing Socialist Party, was kept under house arrest in Milan on charges of anti-Fascist tendencies. Unable to bear the humiliation and persecution of their political teacher, Rosselli and Parri organized his escape; together they navigated a small motor boat from Savona to Corsica, and from there Turati found his way to Paris. In the sensational trial that followed, Rosselli and Parri were convicted as accomplices in the crime of "unauthorized expatriation."[85] They did not deny the charges; on the contrary, they accepted full responsibility for Turati's escape, "not in any hope of clemency, but because they knew their action to have been highly moral."[86] They had followed the Mazzinian code of ethics, placing the duties of man toward humanity above the loyalty of a citizen to his government.

Mazzini believed that without the recognition of a universal law, the law of God, there can be no common rule for man. For "if there be no mind supreme over all human mind, who can save us from the caprice of our fellows?"[87] Like Socrates at his own trial, Rosselli and Parri argued that they owed greater obedience to humanity and morality than to transitory political and legal principles. "Fifty years ago," Rosselli said in his concluding speech at the trial, "my grandmother received into our house the dying Mazzini; could I do otherwise fifty years after than lend assistance to Filippo Turati when in sore need?"[88]

While confined to the island of Lipari, Parri and Rosselli made up their minds to fight Fascism to the bitter end. Rosselli wrote: "The confino is a large cell without walls, a cell composed entirely of sky and sea. The Militia sentries are its walls, walls of flesh and blood rather than of lime and stone. The desire to blow them up becomes an obsession."[89] In his prison diaries Rosselli wrote: "The 'crimes' that sent us here are already of the past. . . . We yearn to commit more. We are not occasional criminals; we are professionals."[90] Rosselli considered the fight against Fascism to be a continuation of Mazzini's fight to unify Italy; he was proud to be a member of a family in the tradition of the Risorgimento. In a letter to a friend he wrote: "I have revised my Socialist beliefs, and have carried them to their last conclusion. In my mind to-day they blend perfectly with the eternal Mazzinian truth."[91]

On July 26, 1929, Rosselli escaped from Lipari with two other anti-Fascist prisoners, Emilio Lussu and Fausto Nitti, nephew of the premier. From the island shore they were daringly rescued by the pilot of Turati's own getaway boat and by Gioacchino Dolci, a former prisoner on Lipari. They went first to nearby Tunisia, then to Paris, where they joined with other Italian anti-Fascists to form Justice and Liberty.[92]

Rosselli followed Mazzini's dictum that "the secret of raising the masses lies in the hands of those who show themselves ready to fight and conquer at their head."[93] From its first days in Paris, Justice and Liberty was designed as a clandestine organization to work inside Italy with headquarters abroad. Remembering Mazzini's experience of losing touch with events and trends at home, Rosselli quickly realized the importance of maintaining connections with events inside Italy.[94]

From the outset, Justice and Liberty concentrated on organizing opposition to Mussolini inside Italy. "The work inside Italy," wrote Salvemini, "could not be dissociated from the work outside, but was to be regarded as more important."[95] Rosselli turned to Young Italy's old methods of internal recruiting, naming his own mobilizing campaign the "Second Italian Risorgimento."[96] Justice and Liberty's program, printed on the first page of the organization's clandestine leaflets, called on Italians "whose dignity has been offended by the present state of servitude" to take active part in the revolt.[97]

By 1930 a nucleus of Justice and Liberty had been established in every Italian urban center, closely monitored by the headquarters in Paris. The role of the internal branches was, as the leaflets said, to educate a "strong and disciplined democratic minority within the frontiers of Italy, who would be ready when the hour for action [came]."[98] Although there were ideological and tactical differences among the individual centers inside Italy, organizational unity was maintained by the guiding principle that Justice and Liberty would be bound to no political party.[99] In contrast to other exile anti-Fascist groups, especially the Italian Communist Party (PCI) and the Italian Socialist Party (PSI), Justice and Liberty sought to attract as many opponents of the regime as possible without insisting on ideological purity. Rosselli tried to remain pragmatic. He knew that, for his Fascist opponents, ideology was a pragmatic tool. The idea that the Fascist ideology should always be adaptable to the necessities of real life became Mussolini's chief political principle. Ideology, Mussolini argued, "must not be a shirt of Nessus clinging to us for all eternity, for tomorrow is something mysterious and unforeseen."[100] Mussolini saw every action as rooted in ideology and vice versa. Justice and Liberty, therefore, could not afford the luxury of ideological dogmatism in the struggle for popular support. To maintain a balance between ideology and pragmatism, Rosselli advocated a political philosophy that combined elements from liberalism, revisionist Marxism, and anarchism. But although the ideological emphasis of Justice and Liberty shifted periodically to meet political developments, it never gave a hint of concessions that would have meant relinquishing basic national democratic and liberal beliefs.[101]

Justice and Liberty's stronghold was in Milan, where Ernesto Rossi, Riccardo Bauer, and Ferruccio Parri established an underground apparatus. Rossi and Bauer, remembering the role of the Milanese in the 1848 insurrection against Austria, hoped to revive the city's revolutionary spirit. In the days of European hope, in 1848, the people of Milan were among the first in Europe to rise. After expelling the Austrian protectorate from their city, in what was later known as "the five days of Milan," they formed a provisional government that invited Mazzini to lead the national revolution. When the exiled leader reached Milan, "the people crowded to see him, kissing him, snatching at his hands, welcoming him with tears of joy. The Provisional Government sent for him. He was obliged to harangue the people from the palace windows."[102]

Both Rossi and Bauer had helped Rosselli publish *Non Mollare!* in 1925; after the newspaper was forced to suspend publication, they resumed clandestine anti-Fascist activities within Italy. They had joined Rosselli and other exiles in Paris on the founding of Justice and Liberty in 1929, while serving as the leaders of the organization at home, setting up close relations with the republicans and radicals of Milan. Together they developed a militant campaign against the Fascist authorities in the northern cities. They maintained their anti-Fascist activities until arrested by the Fascist police in October 1930. The two were sentenced to twenty years and spent thirteen in prison, until set free in 1943 after the fall of Mussolini.[103]

With the arrest of the Milanese leaders in 1930, Turin became the pivot of Justice and Liberty's underground. In that year Aldo Garosci and Mario Andreis organized the Turin chapter of Justice and Liberty. It published a clandestine periodical, *Voci d'officina*. In 1932 Garosci escaped to Paris, where he served with the exile organization as a corresponding secretary.[104] Rosselli and other exiles organized the clandestine distribution of propaganda inside Italy. Articles were scribbled on the walls of villages and on the blackboards of school-rooms and universities, and were posted in factories; some were even printed in advertisements in national newspapers. Italians at home were thus well informed about the despotic nature of the Fascist regime and about events suppressed by official censorship.[105] In the instructions to loyalists at home, the exiles always stressed the importance of maintaining close connections with all other underground groups. In the name of "the real people of Italy," Rosselli urged his home followers, the *Giellisti*, to rise above political disputes and unite their forces against the Fascists' distortion of the national will. Fascism, he said, was more than the illegitimate seizure of power. Max Ascoli, the journalist who was himself an exile and became president of the Mazzinian Society in the United States, has said that Fascism "marked the collapse of the whole moral structure of the Italian people."[106] In a statement published by *Giustivia e Libertà*, the newspaper of Justice and Liberty, in 1932, the organization enumerated the spheres of its duties: the activity of Justice and Liberty in exile was in "response to the command and will of Italians. . . . The struggle for the Italian people is a struggle for all peoples because either freedom is universal or it is a lie for everyone."[107]

Aware of the limitations of propaganda warfare in generating internal resistance, members of Justice and Liberty demonstrated their willingness to take risks through overt opposition. On July 11, 1930, an airplane rented by Justice and Liberty flew from Switzerland over the Piazza del Duomo in Milan and showered the streets in broad daylight with thousands of leaflets denouncing the Fascist dictatorship and urging Italians to resist its rule. The flight had been organized without Swiss cooperation and against the laws of that country; after it was over, the pilot, Giovanni Bassanesi, and seven other exiled members of Justice and Liberty, including Rosselli, were arrested and charged by the Swiss government for "violation of foreign territory by persons resident in Switzerland."[108] Their trial ended with a great victory for Justice and Liberty. Rosselli and his friends openly admitted their guilt; their testimony diverted the public's attention from the original accusation to the exiles' crusade for democracy. It was Mussolini's Fascism that was on the spot. The members of Justice and Liberty won the sympathy of the Swiss press and public. The trial's worldwide coverage captured the imagination of anti-Fascists throughout Italy. In his speech before the Swiss federal tribunal of November 1930, Rosselli described the injustice he personally had experienced under the Fascist regime. He declared: "We will continue to fight. The right to resist has been repeatedly preached in the history of the world. We are prepared to go to prison, but we shall continue the fight as long as we live. By doing so we represent the cause of civilization."[109]

One of the advantages of Justice and Liberty as an exile organization, but paradoxically its greatest weakness, was its lack of a pre-exile organizational structure. On the one hand, this made it possible for Rosselli to appeal to Italians for support as a nonpartisan organization, but it also gave Justice and Liberty no party base and thus no party followers to fall back on. This made the organization particularly vulnerable to dissension and defeatism among its home loyalists. To reduce the pressing threat of internal frustration, Rosselli strove to broaden the organizational base abroad. The question was how to unite with other Italian anti-Fascist exile groups without compromising Justice and Liberty's nonpartisan status. Rosselli rejected the idea of a party, as exemplified by the socialists and communists, as a "totalitarian organism in which all absolute truth was deposited."[110] Justice and Liberty was not bound by any political party. As Rosselli claimed, it was the first anti-Fascist organization in Europe that was not a continuation of pre-Fascist trends.[111]

Justice and Liberty earned a reputation as a revolutionary organization fighting dictatorship for the sake of democracy without necessarily seeking to gain the citadel of political power for itself. The organization's unconditional commitment to the restoration of democracy attracted anti-Fascists at home who differed widely in their ideological beliefs. Intellectuals and persons of the middle class, representatives of the liberals, republicans, and revolutionary socialists, all joined in the early 1930s under the ideological umbrella of Justice and Liberty, without fearing the consequences of betraying their previous ideological affinities. In his plea for anti-Fascist unity, Rosselli maintained: "It is better to promise little and to keep one's promise, than to deceive people by promising them the moon in the well. . . . Our program is not a final one; in a regime of political liberty and universal suffrage, he who has the most thread—i.e., the highest capacity—will weave the most cloth. The day when the Socialists, Communists, Republicans, Democrats and plain anti-Fascists agree to make a great common effort, that day Fascism will fall."[112]

Rosselli was able to avoid severe organizational schisms until 1934. To maintain his organization's appeal, he constantly altered his ideas. Justice and Liberty's ideological formula had become a hybrid of "democratic-liberal socialism."[113] Rosselli foresaw the significance of exile unity for the morale of the opposition at home, so in November 1931 the organization joined an alliance of anti-Fascist exile groups, the Concentrazione antifascista. Within the Concentrazione, Justice and Liberty established itself as the leading authority in directing clandestine operations inside Italy. But although Rosselli promised the other exile groups of the Concentrazione that his organization would merge in the whole, Justice and Liberty remained autonomous.

In January 1932 the organization published a new magazine in Paris and Brussels called *Quaderni di Giustizia e Libertà*, announcing a new "revolutionary program."[114] Under the influence of the organization's Turin section, Rosselli seemed to shift from his original approach of Mazzinian liberalism to a more leftist position. The ideological shift did not reflect a dramatic change in his outlook but, so Delzell believes, served rather to appease the ideological sensibilities of the socialist members of the Concentrazione.[115] The new manifesto continued to support the notion that a liberal state should succeed Fascism. At the same time, Rosselli advocated far-reaching socialist reforms, maintaining his previous *liberalismo socialista* ideological synthesis.[116]

Rosselli's ideological maneuvering and his desire to maintain an exile anti-Fascist alliance without paying the price of coalition could not last. In May 1934 the Concentrazione was dissolved after the exiled leaders of the Socialist Party, Pietro Nenni and Giuseppe Saragat, began to distrust Rosselli's ideological ambiguity. They realized that while Rosselli advocated the continuation of the exile alliance, he was in fact challenging their leadership over Italian labor.[117] Moreover, the rapprochement of the Communist Party toward the socialists in May 1934, and the eagerness of the exiled socialist leaders to establish a Marxist front, resulted in a unity pact in August 1934. Justice and Liberty lost the advantage of the Concentrazione's organizational framework. Even Rosselli's opportunistic "reassessment" of bolshevism in late 1934 could not change the basic fact that Justice and Liberty remained without any operational machinery.[118]

Mussolini's war in Ethiopia drove Justice and Liberty to its organizational nadir. In the spring of 1935 the Fascist police tracked down the organization's branch in Turin. The supporters of Justice and Liberty in Turin included liberals, intellectuals, and workers who were the heirs of the Risorgimento. In May 1935 prominent members of this group were brought before the Fascist authorities and charged with criticizing the government's Ethiopian policy in letters to anti-Fascists abroad.[119] Mussolini was in the midst of his propaganda campaign to mobilize Italians for their "historical mission in Africa" and could not tolerate any opposition. On March 18, 1934, Il Duce had promised Italians that "anti-Fascism [had] ceased to exist."[120] Il Duce "was always right."[121] Meanwhile in Paris Rosselli, accusing Mussolini of bluffing, had predicted that the Fascists would stop short of war. Hoping to take advantage of the Ethiopian situation, Rosselli argued that the crisis was a domestic matter, "a private enterprise of the dictatorship."[122] Rosselli was wrong. Il Duce's intentions in Africa were sincere. From the day he came to power, he wanted to revive the glories of the ancient Roman Empire. Many Italian exiles, among them the historian Gaetano Salvemini, were convinced that Mussolini decided on the war only in August 1935, after becoming convinced that Britain and France would not oppose him. However, as Esmonde Robertson has pointed out, Mussolini's expansionism was not unpredicted, but rather the implementation of an old plan. Fascism needed the glory of victory to avenge the nation's defeat at the hands of Ethiopia in 1896.[123]

Rosselli's ambiguous position during the Ethiopian crisis almost ruined the entire raison d'être of Justice and Liberty. In September a few weeks before the Fascist invasion, Rosselli was still trying to organize in Paris a front of Italian exiles for the International Conference for the Defense of the Ethiopian People.[124] He failed. Il Duce's march on Africa was already underway. On January 7, 1935, the Italian and French governments signed the Rome Agreement, and Mussolini received a green light from France's foreign minister, Pierre Laval, to conquer Ethiopia.[125] By the spring of 1935, Mussolini's intentions in Ethiopia were common knowledge. Mass rallies of Black Shirts in Italian cities in support of Mussolini's African policy indicated that Il Duce was drumming Italy into a real war. On October 2 Italians were summoned into the town squares with bells and sirens to hear Mussolini's announcement, over loudspeakers, that the war against Ethiopia had begun. In the face of the League of Nations' equivocal threat to impose sanctions on Italy, Mussolini proclaimed that the "identity between Italy and Fascism is perfect, absolute, and unchangeable."[126]

It is debatable to what extent the Italian people were enthusiastic about Mussolini's war plans in Africa. Supporters of the Fascist regime have argued that "the idea of occupying and colonizing Ethiopia enjoyed very wide popularity in Italy."[127] Opponents of Mussolini maintained that Italians were primarily hostile to conquering Ethiopia.[128] The undisputed fact among scholars of Fascism, however, is that the unanimous condemnation of Italy by the League of Nations, and especially its policy of economic sanctions, backfired; it provoked the Italian people to a patriotic response, rousing popular nationalist support for Il Duce. Many anti-Fascists, among them political exiles previously opposed to Mussolini's venture, saw in the British-sponsored sanctions an attack on Italy's national pride and prestige. As one opponent remarked, "it has become a matter of Italy's honour to see the Duce through to victory."[129]

Mussolini and Fascist propaganda strove to nourish hatred of the British and to cultivate the patriotic feelings of the masses. On November 16, 1935, the Fascist Grand Council denounced the sanctions "as a vain effort to humiliate the Italian people."[130] December 18, 1935, was declared a "day of faith" or a "wedding ring day"; the regime organized emotional nationwide donation ceremonies in support of the fatherland.

The Ethiopian episode demonstrated further that for communists the dominant motivating force is not national loyalty but ideology. In July 1934, eighteen months after Hitler took power, the Communist International began to reevaluate its dogmatic position against the social democratic parties in Europe. After seven years of an ideologically narrow policy, during which social democracy was condemned as communism's prime enemy and labeled as "social fascism," the Comintern under Stalin's leadership changed its position, influenced by developments in Europe after Hitler assumed power. It now called for a "unity of action [against fascism] between all sections of the working class."[131]

In August 1934 such a new unity of action against Fascists did in fact materialize. The exiled leaders of both the Italian Socialist Party (PSI) and the Italian Communist Party (PCI), for example, signed a "unity of action pact."[132] When, shortly thereafter, the new exile bloc faced the challenge of the Ethiopian war, its leaders hoped that Mussolini's military adventure in Africa would provoke the masses against the Fascist regime. They did everything in their power to sabotage the Fascist war effort. They argued that the Italian people wish to see the "military defeat of the Fascist government," and "urged strikes, prevention of troop departures, fraternization with Ethiopian soldiers, and abandonment of the field of battle."[133] The united socialist-communist community across Europe initiated a meeting of the executive of the Comintern in support of the League of Nations' sanctions against Italy. The Communist International and the European communist parties organized active demonstrations in major cities against the Fascist aggression in Ethiopia. They incited dockworkers in a number of ports to refuse to load ships bound for Italy.[134] The communist revolutionary appeal remained a solitary voice of protest, despite all these activities; it failed to recognize the magnetic force of Fascist nationalism in attracting support for the Ethiopian war.

The socialist and communist exiles had welcomed the League of Nations' sanctions on Italy. Justice and Liberty's response was mild. Carlo Rosselli doubted the ability of the League of Nations to restrain Mussolini's ambitions. He had already perceived the European democracies' impotence in the face of Hitler's rise to power in February 1933 and questioned the desirability of sanctions among the opposition groups at home. As Delzell points out, Rosselli "feared (correctly) that sanctions might simply encourage Italians to rally round the Duce in paroxysms of nationalism and Anglophobia."[135]

On May 16, 1936, Mussolini's successful war in Ethiopia came to an end. The glittering victory of Fascism in the face of the League of Nations' sanctions brought Il Duce's popularity to its zenith. The conquest of Ethiopia seemed to destroy any illusions Justice and Liberty may have had about its foothold among Italian youth. Rosselli admitted his organization's temporary defeat. Trying to infuse hope but without repressing reality, the leader of Justice and Liberty advocated a new strategy of attrition in the fight against Fascism. In the *Giustizia e Libertà* of May 15, 1936, Rosselli wrote:

Fascism has had a complete military victory. Fascism will almost certainly have a victory on the diplomatic field as well. . . . This complete victory does not mean that history stops there. History goes on. One period in Italy has come to an end. Another is beginning. Nothing would be more foolish than to gloss over the enemy's success. We have to admit that in Italy—which is what concerns us most—Fascism has been strengthened and consolidated by this crisis. Many people will now be converted to Fascism. Others will grow resigned to it. Even the economic and financial difficulties are not such as to threaten the regime. No dictatorship has ever fallen for economic and financial reasons. Economic difficulties may cause it to seek war as an outlet. But when the war is won, the crisis is safely past. We must therefore prepare ourselves for a difficult period whose duration will depend on unpredictable factors. The old anti-Fascism is gone for ever. The organizations which drag after them the dead weight of defeat and the chain of obsolete and equivocal positions are empty shells. We of "Giustizia e Libertà" must also review our position.[136]

Max Weber has argued that the ability of a government to provoke massive voluntary submission is a primary indicator of its legitimacy.

Furthermore, the acceptance of the regime's position in times of crisis contributes to the regime's stability and to its leaders' conviction that they deserve power. Many leaders will interpret the subordination of the many as a just fate and will develop some myth of their natural superiority.[137]

Rosselli's acknowledgment of the widespread acceptance of the Fascist regime inside Italy after the victory in Ethiopia confirmed Il Duce's messianic ideal. On May 16, 1936, Mussolini announced in *Il Popolo d'Italia* that Justice and Liberty had proclaimed its defeat.[138] Cut off from political events at home and divorced from other exile groups, which kept their distance from his ideological equivocation, Justice and Liberty's political presence seemed to fail.[139]

With the outbreak of the Spanish Civil War in July a new zone of action opened for Justice and Liberty. Italian political exiles fought side by side with Spanish Republicans against Franco. Confidence in Justice and Liberty once again revived among the organization's followers inside Italy.

Mazzini had introduced and practiced the idea that Italian political exiles should fight for democracy in other countries as part of their own national struggle. After Young Italy had failed to initiate insurrection in Italy in what were known as the First and the Second Savoy Expeditions, Mazzini decided to establish European "associations of the oppressed of all countries against the oppressors of all countries."[140] He joined German and Polish exiles in Bern and signed the pact of Young Europe, and shortly thereafter founded Young Switzerland. The immediate purpose of the two organizations was to inspire the Young Italians on the peninsula who had been discouraged after the fiasco in the Second Savoy Expedition. Although Young Europe was barely active, Mazzini hoped that it would revive the corpse of Young Italy's home loyalists and help "persuade all Italy that nothing is lost."[141] So too, Rosselli abandoned his earlier position that Italy must seek its salvation at home and turned to the international front.

In 1933 Rosselli had visited Spain and sought to obtain the permission of the newly established republic to use Spain as a base for propaganda flights over Italy. The Spanish refused, but Rosselli stayed "on very friendly terms with the regime."[142] With the Spanish coup d'état in the summer of 1936, as soon as it became evident that Franco had secured the support of Mussolini, Rosselli called a special meeting in Paris of all anti-Fascist exile organizations to discuss military intervention. He urged the other Italian exile groups to set up a legion of volunteers to fight beside the Spanish popular militias.[143] Justice and Liberty was the first group to realize the potential of Spain as a base for armed struggle against Mussolini and as an outlet from the operational squeeze imposed on Italian exiles after the war in Ethiopia. In the *Giustizia e Libertà* of August 28, Emilio Lussu, the second in command, wrote: "Our need to go to Spain is greater than the Spanish Republic's need of us. Italian anti-fascism lacks a revolutionary glory. . . . We must recognize that we have not known how to battle against fascism. The small political vanguard of the Italian emigration must generously sacrifice itself in this enterprise. It will acquire experience on the battlefields. It will make its name there. It will become the nucleus that will attract around itself the greater vanguard of tomorrow."[144]

The merged socialists and communists rejected the idea of exile intervention in Spain; they were waiting for instructions from Moscow.[145] Rosselli could not take "no" for an answer. He was about to confront the Fascists directly on the field of battle. In early August Rosselli, with a small column of exile followers, joined the Spanish anarchosyndicalist groups of Catalonia.[146]

In Weber's view, charismatic rulers who claim natural superiority and rely heavily on voluntary compliance must constantly prove their personal strength and demonstrate their ability to perform heroic deeds. When the rulers fail to live up to the standard by which they justify their power, or when some crisis makes the established order appear questionable, then the rulers are likely to become objects of passionate hatred, and their followers may quickly abandon them.[147] Italy's intervention in Spain marked the first crack in Il Duce's authority. The victory in Ethiopia had dazzled him, and his dreams of empire blunted his perception of reality. By backing Franco's coup he saw a chance for Fascism to take over the Mediterranean; he was convinced that the addition of a few transport planes to Franco's forces would make possible a quick and complete victory.[148] The republic's initial victory over the rebels in the face of Italian backing proved him wrong and undermined his prestige. Moreover, the news about the anti-Fascist exiles who fought so valiantly on the other side traveled fast in Italy and helped reinspire the underground opponents of Fascism.[149]

By the end of August, Fascist authorities were drafting Italian "volunteers" against their will to fight in Spain, thereby alienating the Italian military command. At the same time Justice and Liberty's exile column, the Garibaldi Battalion, met a baptism of fire on the road between Huesca and Saragossa. Rosselli sustained minor injuries; the image of his personal bravery was enhanced. On November 13, after a few other initial battles,[150] Rosselli broadcast his famous appeal to fellow Italians over Radio Barcelona: "Today in Spain, tomorrow in Italy." In the name of his comrades-in-arms, Rosselli encouraged Italians to follow Garibaldi and Mazzini and to free their country from Fascist oppression.[151]

The actual participation of Italians alongside the Spanish Republicans did not increase significantly as a result of Rosselli's call.[152] However, the Spanish experience reinforced the anti-Fascists' belief in a final victory. Shortly before he was assassinated with his brother Nello, Rosselli wrote to Salvemini:

> I am sure that if you had lived through the Spanish atmosphere of the first few months, to experience what a people liberating itself is, . . . to touch shoulders with the volunteers, so humane and sympathetic, so friendly and young, you would have felt moved and put aside your reservations for a world which is not any more of this world. Fascism does not allow us to choose. Rather than dreaming of the just milieu . . . it is better to live revolution or to prepare for it as much as possible.[153]

Rosselli's assassination in June 1937, and the events in Europe, led to the decline of Justice and Liberty and the other Italian exile groups in the fight against Fascism. But the seeds of internal resistance were already deeply rooted. The political exiles who constituted Justice and Liberty in Paris continued to collaborate with the internal resistance until Mussolini's fall in July 1943. They laid the foundation for the Action Party, which played an important role in the last stages of World War II and gave Italy its first postwar prime minister, Ferruccio Parri.

CHAPTER SIX

Recognition in the International Community

Exile politicians are forced into a dependent relationship with their hosts and patrons, whose hospitality and generosity may be conditioned and subject to capricious change.
—Tom Lodge, *Third World Quarterly*, 1987

Many exile organizations ascribe vital importance to foreign support for their struggle, and strive to make their case international. They endeavor to generate and cultivate international enmity toward the home regime and to earn recognition for themselves at that regime's expense, so as to undermine and eventually overthrow and replace it. Even when they categorically refuse to accept international assistance that they might otherwise receive, and exclusively direct their energy toward mobilizing their own national community, political exile organizations may still be forced to rely on international aid—at least on the host state from whose territory they try to launch their campaign.

Obviously, a contestant's ability to win power in the nation-state is not simply a matter of sustaining the loyalty of important segments within the national community. Authority in the nation-state also depends on the support of international patrons. In analyzing political exiles' struggle for recognition in the international community, the following questions must be explored: (1) How may international patrons enhance the struggle of political exiles? (2) What determines those patrons' policies in their interaction with exile organizations? (3) What tactics do political exiles employ to encourage international support, and what obstacles are they likely to confront?

Patterns of International Recognition

Two broadly distinguishable segments within the international community periodically extend their support to exile organizations:

1. Governments, including intergovernmental organizations such as the United Nations (UN), the Organization of American States (OAS), or the Organization of African Unity (OAU).

2. Civil society, including (a) transnational nongovernmental organizations such as the Socialist International, the World Council of Churches, the Council of Scientific Unions (ICSU), and Amnesty International; (b) national organizations such as political parties, labor unions, student movements, or even exile groups of other nationalities; (c) public opinion and the media; and (d) private individuals and organizations.

Although these international patrons may often support exile organizations unintentionally and indirectly, for example by denouncing the home regime, my major concern is with direct cases of intentional aid.

International recognition can be granted to exile organizations in the forms of diplomatic and operational aid. Diplomatic recognition ranges from minor declarations of support and symbolic gestures explicitly or implicitly endorsing the exiles' struggle, to fully diplomatic recognition of the exile organization as a government-in-exile. The higher the degree of diplomatic recognition granted to political exile organizations, the more likely it is to be followed by operational aid. Such assistance may include financial and military support, and in extreme cases even direct military intervention by another government in favor of the exile fighting forces. Such was the case of the combined operation of President Julius Nyerere's Tanzanian army and Ugandan exile forces that led to the final collapse of the Amin regime in 1978. Prior to the defeat of Idi Amin Dada, Nyerere played a critical role in bringing together Ugandan exile leaders and organizations that planned to install a transitory government in Uganda until elections could be held.[1]

The degree of diplomatic recognition accorded exile groups does not always, however, reflect commitment by international patrons to subsequent operational needs of these groups. Limited diplomatic recognition may be followed by massive operational assistance, whereas full diplomatic acknowledgment of an exile organization need not always be followed by effective rewards. In fact, diplomatic recognition and operational support of exile organizations are always contingent upon the international patrons' own objectives.

Exile organizations that strive to mobilize international support are often compelled to rest content with vague and tentative gestures on their behalf. Public meetings between exile leaders and heads of states or lower-ranking diplomats, and declarative forms of acknowledgment in corridors of power, become instrumentally important for the political exiles in validating their claims to power. Although the significance of these supportive gestures lies mostly in the very fact that they occur, exile groups tend to present them to their national followers at home and abroad as proof of substantive accomplishments.

Supportive declarations and symbolic gestures can have a vital psychological impact on the exiles' struggle. They can contribute to internal cohesion of the exile organization, enhance its leaders' status among other nonruling aspirants at home and abroad, and strengthen the morale of active or potential supporters. Most of all, declarative recognition can become a catalyst in mobilizing operational support. Obviously, the source and type of political gestures made on behalf of the political exiles are of critical importance in evaluating their impact on the exiles' struggle. Thus we can distinguish between "high-status" and "lesser" international patrons according to their means and the ease with which they may place the exile issue on other nations' agendas or elevate them to a priority status.[2] There is a significant difference, for example, in the potential international impact of the 1985 declaration of support for the African National Congress (ANC) by the Swedish ambassador to Zambia, and the early 1987 meeting in the State Department between Oliver Tambo, the leader of the ANC mission-in-exile, and U.S. Secretary of State George Shultz.

In the absence of operational assistance to promote the political exiles' claims and actions, however, supportive declarations can be seen as mere lip service, as words to foster the exiles' fantasies. As one noted student of African exiles has observed, "the gap between rhetoric and action . . . has contributed to unrealistic expectations [among exile groups] of international action followed by crippling disillusionment."[3] Still, in politics we must remember that declarations have their own dynamics. John L. Austin, the famous British philosopher, observes that "to say something is in the full and normal sense to do something."[4] Words, he goes on, "will often or even normally produce certain consequential effects upon the feelings, thoughts or actions of the audience or of the speaker or of other persons."[5] Robert Jervis, a student of international politics, affirms that Austin's theory of "performative utterance" highlights the essence of recognition in international relations.[6]

Governments-in-Exile

Governments-in-exile are cards, not players.
—A British ambassador during World War II

To be recognized by a sovereign government as a government-in-exile is the highest diplomatic acknowledgment an exile organization can obtain. By such recognition a government acknowledges the exiles' claim to be the legal authority of their home nation's government and/or the "authentic" representatives of the national community.

International law has developed a body of doctrine with criteria for granting, withdrawing, or withholding recognition between governments that also characterize relations between sovereign governments and exile organizations. The variety of theoretical approaches to the practice of recognition reflects ambiguity and arbitrariness.[7] In the first place, international law imposes no obligation on a government to recognize another government "as the international agent of its state."[8] All governments are free to adopt and interpret the concepts and doctrines of recognition in accordance with their own foreign policy objectives and ideologies. The result, or perhaps the cause, of the lack of settled criteria for diplomatic recognition, as also for recognition of exile organizations, is the use of recognition as a political device to support or undermine another government.[9]

Up until the end of World War II, most recognized governments-in-exile were refugee governments deposed by a native or foreign regime. These deposed governments were recognized by governments sympathetic to their cause as the legal and de jure sovereign power of their nation-state. Their officials and representatives were granted the full diplomatic privileges "to which their position and sovereign power entitle[d] them."[10] They were treated "as if they were still ruling the state even though their government has lost effective control."[11] The status of a government-in-exile provided diplomatic immunity to members of deposed governments, control over assets, and limited jurisdiction over fellow nationals in the countries that recognized them. This often included the authority to maintain their own armies. Governments that recognized exile groups as governments-in-exile withheld recognition of the "illegitimate" home regimes.

Governments-in-exile recognized by sovereign governments in the first half of the century included the exiled Republican government of Spain, which lasted until 1977 and was fully recognized by Mexico, and the deposed Provisional Government of Russia, whose ambassadors in France, Italy, and Great Britain were recognized by European countries and the United States in the early 1920s as Russia's official proxy "until the now-defunct Provisional Government was resurrected or replaced by some other non-Bolshevik regime."[12] During World War II the governments deposed by Nazi conquest—those of Belgium, Greece, Czechoslovakia, Luxembourg, the Netherlands, Norway, Poland, and Yugoslavia, all based in London—were recognized by the Allies as the legitimate governments of their countries.

Occasionally, international recognition of a deposed government becomes a significant political and symbolic reminder of the existence of the nation, as for example when governments refuse to acknowledge the annexation of occupied territories and the incorporation of their populations by an occupying nation. According to international law, "military occupation by itself does not confer title or extinguish a nation. Nor does a proclamation of annexation so long as the claims of the occupying Power are effectively challenged and remain unrecognized."[13] When the Baltic republics were incorporated into the Soviet Union in 1940, the United States and other European states refused to recognize the annexation and continued to recognize instead the exiled consular staff as the official representatives of their nations. These exile representatives enjoyed full diplomatic privileges, "not only *de facto* but also *de jure*, on a footing of complete equality with all other foreign representatives."[14] After decades of Soviet domination these diplomatic legations became mere tourist attractions, but they are a reminder of the once independent status of Estonia, Latvia, and Lithuania. The Georgian government-in-exile was recognized by France. After the Soviet occupation of Georgia in the 1920s, the representatives of the stateless Georgian government for a while enjoyed diplomatic immunity and attended diplomatic receptions along with the representatives of their conquerors. "Russia [could] not protest because Georgia was recognized as an independent republic before Russia seized it, and after Russia had recognized that independence herself."[15]

Since World War II, as a result of the growing wave of national liberation in third-world countries, most recognized governments-in-exile have been exile organizations "in the process of establishing a new government in a given territory,"[16] groups intent on national self-determination or decolonization. An archetypical case is that of the Algerian National Liberation Front (FLN), recognized by Morocco and the United Arab Republic. Others include the governments-in-exile in Africa recognized after the founding of the Organization of African Unity (OAU). These groups were recognized as governments-in-exile by African countries that had gained their own independence and "sought to encourage the independence in the remaining colonial territories."[17] Recognition was awarded as an expression of support for the ideal of self-determination, and as an acknowledgment of the authenticity of the exile groups as representatives of the nation to come.

Recognized governments-in-exile, like all exile organizations, are forced into dependency on their patron governments. Recognition by these patrons is conditional and may be subject to unpredictable changes. A government striving to undermine a rival regime, for example, may encourage that regime's exile opponents to form an opposition front that it will eventually recognize as a government-in-exile. President Eisenhower, in the hope of overpowering Castro's communist regime in Cuba, refused to recognize the regime in Havana, and urged exiled Cubans in the United States to select a leader he could recognize as "the head of a government-in-exile."[18] More recently, as part of the struggle against the Soviet-backed government in Kabul, the United States has encouraged Afghan exile groups in Pakistan to unite, with an eye to possible eventual recognition of an Afghan government-in-exile.

On the other hand, a government may withdraw diplomatic recognition from a government-in-exile either because it no longer benefits from the latter's existence and activities, or because the exiles have become an obstacle to new political objectives of its own. A classic example of the instability of a recognized government-in-exile brought about by the new political agenda of their patrons is the Polish government-in-exile abandoned by the Allies after their agreement with the Soviets at Yalta. Britain and the United States transferred recognition from the Polish government-in-exile to the puppet Lublin Committee in Warsaw, which had become the nucleus of the new government. By abandoning the Polish government-in-exile, an American scholar wrote, "England and America betrayed themselves and their concept of justice for which they had struggled since the Magna Carta. These democracies forgot their traditional conscience in the name of Big Three Unity."[19] A more recent example is the withdrawal of recognition by the Organization of African Unity (OAU) from the Angolan revolutionary government-in-exile Govêrno Revolucionário de Angola no Exílio (GRAE) in 1971. The diplomatic recognition granted to GRAE in July 1963 was transferred to the rival Popular Liberation Movement of Angola (Movimento Popular de Libertação de Angola, or MPLA) recognized as the authentic voice of the Angolan people. Only Zaire continued to recognize the GRAE government-in-exile.[20]

Exile organizations that are not recognized as governments-in-exile, or whose recognition has been withdrawn, usually continue to maintain their governmental claims nonetheless, investing considerable energy in symbolic activities that project the strong image of an existing government. Members of the Polish government-in-exile, who today still claim to be the democratically chosen representatives of a free and independent Poland, maintain a governmental structure with various trappings of office. The London office of the Polish government-in-exile issued and renewed Polish passports "for sentimental and morale-raising reasons," and collected and recorded contributions from the old generation of Polish exiles as if they were zlotys.[21] The continued existence of the Polish government-in-exile almost two generations after it was deposed represents a unique fantasy in a world of real politics. Similarly, shortly before the Organization of African Unity extended de jure recognition to the Angolan GRAE as a government-in-exile, exile leaders of the GRAE, "exalted in ministerial titles and stationery, produced a flood of 'governmental' communiqués, sent 'official' telegrams to foreign governments and political organizations, . . . and thrived on protocol and ceremony replete with flag and anthem."[22]

National Exile Committees

Until the end of World War II, exile organizations making governmental claims without reference to previous legal status were not able to obtain full diplomatic recognition as a sovereign authority. At best they could hope to attain the "non-descript status of a National Committee."[23] Governments have been reluctant to confer the title of government-in-exile on an exile group that claims to represent their people authentically but lacks governmental authority before exile. The term "authentic representation" has no legal meaning in international law: " 'peoples' are not a subject of international law and can therefore hardly be legally represented."[24] This was the predicament of de Gaulle's Free French in the early 1940s; de Gaulle was not then recognized by the British government as head of a government-in-exile but rather, as Anthony Eden, secretary of state for war, said, "as leader of all free Frenchmen wherever they may be."[25]

On June 17, 1940, de Gaulle arrived in London with no more than a personal conviction that he had a historic mission to restore his nation's honor. Totally dependent on his British hosts, de Gaulle had to convince the British government that he was capable of bringing the French back to the front line. In the name of the French people he appealed to the British cabinet to authorize the BBC to let him communicate by radio with France. Churchill happened not to be at the cabinet meeting and de Gaulle's request was rejected. The cabinet had decided that de Gaulle had no legal authority to speak on behalf of France; as Bernard Ledwidge stated, there were no grounds to challenge the legitimacy of Pétain's new and legally constituted government, which had diplomatic relations with Britain.[26] But Churchill reversed the decision. Pétain had asked for an armistice, and Churchill needed someone, in Ledwidge's words, who could "[reduce] the shock to British and American opinion [after] the fall of France."[27] On June 18 de Gaulle broadcast his famous appeal to the French to resist the occupation and the Vichy government.

Although de Gaulle enjoyed Churchill's support, the British colonels who were sent by the War Office to address French soldiers in England in the summer of 1940 warned them about the consequences of their participation in the Free French forces: "You are perfectly free to serve under General de Gaulle. But it is our duty to point out to you, speaking as man to man, that if you do so decide you will be rebels against your government."[28] De Gaulle and Churchill, however, had no use personally for legalistic formulae. Although Churchill was able to confer only limited diplomatic status on Free France—as a national committee—that status had little impact on the organization's real status as an embryonic state abroad and on the degree of operational support it received from the Allied governments. Though the Free French was not recognized as a de jure government, Churchill granted its representatives the diplomatic privileges governments enjoy.[29] The Free French—that is, the French Committee of National Liberation—was eventually recognized by the Allied governments as the supreme authority to control the war effort on behalf of France. Indeed, none of the official recognized governments-in-exile were as strong and as independent of their hosts as was de Gaulle's Free French.[30]

In world politics, diplomatic recognition cannot be granted simultaneously to more than one government of the same nation-state. Recognition of one government as the sole representative of the state automatically implies nonrecognition of others claiming to govern the same territory. This is the case regardless of whether the claimant has or lacks effective control inside the nation-state. However, as globalization of domestic politics becomes more common, governments maintaining full diplomatic relations with a home regime may at the same time challenge its rule by openly supporting its exile opposition. Such a situation makes a mockery of international law and renders its conventions meaningless. It results from the growing acknowledgment by governments that the use of nonrecognition as a political weapon to delegitimize opponent regimes may be ineffective or even counterproductive. A critic of the United States's nonrecognition policy in Latin America, Africa, and east Asia has observed that the real victim of the practice "has been the global diplomacy of the United States. When regular channels of official contact are choked off, protection of United States interests and achievement of United States objectives becomes much more difficult."[31] Perhaps the lesson was assimilated; in any case the United States has maintained its recognition of Ortega's Sandinista government while at the same time subsidizing and leading the exile Contra government in its struggle to overthrow the regime in Managua.

As one can see, the type of recognition and the diplomatic status conferred by states on exile groups or home regimes does not always reflect the degree of commitment of these states to either. Considerations as to the legality and legitimacy of the political exiles and the home regime become subordinate to the political objectives of the recognizing governments themselves.

Rationales for Support by Other Nations

International patrons are led to support political exiles by two general and often correlated motivations: ideological and political. Ideological sympathy and humanitarian concerns are primary motivations behind civil society's support, whereas governments generally orient their policies toward exiles to promote their own political objectives.

Exiles seek and find support for their goals in subsystems of the state and international communities that share their goals. Many exile organizations find allies among cultural, humanitarian, and religious organizations, labor unions, political parties, student groups, and their own ideological counterparts abroad. These groups render political and moral sympathy and provide effective aid as an expression of their ideological and moral support. They may distribute funds to the exile organizations as refugee relief agencies, with or without the knowledge that their contributions are being manipulated by exile leaders as tools in their internal rivalries[32] or even being used to procure arms.

The degree and forms of such societal involvement in the activities of exile groups vary dramatically from one country to another. They depend primarily on the country's political system and in particular on the official stance of the government regarding the exiles' conflict with the home regime. In general, the more pluralistic the polity and the greater the variety of legitimate ways available to influence decision makers, the more likely it is that state and society will influence each other in deciding how much and what kind of support to give exile organizations.

Sovereign governments promote their own political objectives through support or nonsupport of political exiles. By and large, exile groups that receive governmental assistance receive it "in recognition of their use as foreign policy instruments in related international rivalries."[33] Governments may use the exile groups as propaganda tools to repudiate opponent regimes, or as bargaining chips in international conflicts, or even as fighting forces in foreign battles. Frequently, pro-exile policies are the direct result of the sponsoring government's animosity toward the home regime, and/or its desire to win the favor of the political exiles in case they eventually gain power. Thus in the last few years various Arab and Western governments who sought to get rid of Qaddafi extended their support to Libyan exile groups, hoping to be remembered by these groups if they should ever come to power.[34] Using a similar rationale, the American administration has been called upon to extend its support to Iranian exile Mujahedeen in their struggle against Khomeini, despite the U.S. State Department's assessment of the Mujahedeen as an "anti-American terrorist group."[35] Clearly, the motivation behind governments' policies to aid exile groups does not always reflect ideological sympathy.

The degree of diplomatic and operational assistance a government may provide to exile organizations obviously varies in accordance with the sponsoring government's own political strength domestically and internationally, and with the way it evaluates the gains and losses of such support. By sponsoring exile invasions in the Caribbean, the U.S. government sought to avoid a direct intervention that would generate political conflict at home or abroad. By utilizing exile forces, a student of Caribbean exiles notes, "Washington has felt that it could play down its direct involvement without sacrificing its desired objective of deposing antagonistic leftist governments."[36]

Relations with the Host State

The critical role in shaping the relations between exile groups and the international community is reserved to the host government, not to the exiles themselves. The host government on whose territory exile groups establish their operational base is striving to enhance its own political objectives. However, for the host state the presence and activity of exile groups are a source of tension and may even pose a security threat.

Exile groups tend to be a constant source of tension between the host government and the home regime, especially when the home regime is under the impression that the host government encourages and aids the exiles' activity. By providing shelter and support, the host state makes itself vulnerable to home regime reprisals, often exposing its own society to violence resulting from the political struggles of others. This danger increases when the host and the home country are bordering states. When a war is being fought between exile groups and the home regime beyond the host's borders, a constant possibility exists that the home regime will bring the war directly to the host territory. This has occurred in recent years when Soviet and Afghan government forces struck Pakistani border villages, and when the Nicaraguan army attacked Contras in their base camps in Honduras. In both cases the host societies have gradually come to question the wisdom of supporting the exiles' struggle.[37]

Yet all exile groups must maintain a territorial base from which to operate. The asylum and aid provided by a host state are usually more critical to their struggle than any other external assistance they may receive.[38] Asylum is a concept associated with refugees who escape violence and persecution in their country of origin in search of freedom and safety. Indeed, this book's definition of political exiles as active opposition from abroad necessarily implies the existence of an operational base. Asylum is a precondition for the existence of political exile organizations. I do not deal with the question of whether or not the political exiles enter their territorial base with the host government's blessing; asylum is simply assumed. Of course it may happen in the course of their struggle that exile groups become asylum seekers searching for new bases of operation. However, for analytical purposes one can distinguish between exile groups searching for a new territorial base as a direct result of their political activities, and refugees searching for sanctuary.

There is often a direct correlation between the host state's policies on asylum and its specific reactions to exile group activity within its territory. Host states may invite refugees to establish themselves as exile groups with the direct intention of aiding and abetting their struggle. This was, in part, the United States's intention in opening its doors to Cuban refugees after the Castro revolution. By granting them hospitality, the American government began to legitimize a plan to employ them later as political exiles who would fight to restore freedom.[39] Similarly, in 1938 Léon Blum's Popular Front government encouraged the SPD anti-Nazi exiles to move their headquarters to Paris, hoping, as one leader put it, that "affording succor to the exiles would build up powerful pro-French anti-Hitler sentiments among the blocs of the German people themselves."[40]

In many other cases asylum does not imply support for the political exiles' activities; on the contrary, many host governments make their hospitality conditional on a pledge not to engage in political actions from their territories. They frequently introduce legalistic limitations so that the political exiles can exist but not function effectively without risk. The host government's attitude toward the political exiles' activities may be a precise indicator of its readiness to grant or deny asylum, but this is beyond the scope of this analysis. The conditions of asylum, however, are an integral part of our concern: what are the degrees and limits of host states' support of exile groups, and what is the rationale behind their policies?

For further examination of the relations between host states and exile organizations, I adopt and elaborate on J. Bower Bell's preliminary classification. In his article "Contemporary Revolutionary Organizations,"[41] Bell suggests a spectrum of host-state responses to the activities of exile groups from their territories. These responses range from "intimate friendship to total opposition."[42] Bell's distinctive categories rarely remain static over periods of time, but typically shift to meet the host state's political interests.

There are five primary identifiable patterns of relationship between the host state and the exile organization.

First, an enthusiastic host state may be dedicated to the exiles' cause ideologically and/or pragmatically. A classic example is the support of the Spanish Republicans by the Mexican government of President Lázaro Cárdenas. Mexican authorities fully identified with the exiled Republicans' moral struggle for democracy, and denied the legitimacy of Franco's regime, despite strong opposition from wide segments of Mexican society—especially the wealthy, the conservatives, and the church—that upheld Franco.[43]

Second, the host state may be ideologically enthusiastic toward the exile organizations but pragmatically reluctant to assume the cost of sponsorship. Such reluctance is due principally to fear of reprisals from the home regime. Apprehension of reprisals varies directly with the geographical proximity of the host state to the home regime, and its relative political weakness. Thus the support of the Mexican government for the Spanish Republicans can be attributed in part to Mexico's geographical removal from the threat of a possible European war, which enabled Mexico to disregard power politics.[44] Hitler's threats against Czechoslovakia's warm hospitality to the exiled SPD, on the other hand, made Edvard Beneš reluctant to let Czechoslovakia continue to shelter the SPD executive; the anti-Nazi exiles were forced to move to Paris in 1938.[45] More recently, since the early 1980s the variety of economic and military pressures applied by Pretoria to its neighboring states—Lesotho, Swaziland, Botswana, Mozambique, and Zimbabwe—left them no other option but to abandon their initial effort to assist ANC diplomatic and military activity. The ANC executive was forced to find new sanctuary states farther to the north in Angola, Zambia, and Tanzania, countries not wholly tied to South Africa's economy and thus less threatened by Pretoria's reprisals.[46]

In the third pattern, the host state may pursue an official policy of impartiality in the political exiles' fight against the home regime. Neutrality, of course, can be measured only by the actual limits imposed by the host state on the political exiles' operational freedom. These include tolerance of the host state toward the aid its civil society extends to exile activities; legalistic restrictions on the exiles' propaganda campaign; and limitations on the exiles' freedom of movement (*assignation à résidence*), especially when the host borders the home country.[47] Another indication of the host's neutrality is its reaction to reprisals by the home regime. Host states may give tacit approval to such reprisals within the host's territory "because of the mutual benefits realized for their foreign intelligence and policing interests."[48]

In the contemporary world all governments are sensitive to internal and external, political and economic issues, and are at least indirectly involved in other nation-states' domestic conflicts. Hence the host state's official impartiality often simply masks a partisan stance, in order to protect the host's own political interests. While maintaining her vaunted reputation as a safe haven for exiles and cultivating an image of impartiality, since the early 1980s France has carefully manipulated her practical policies in the conflict between Iranian exiles in Paris and the Ayatollah Khomeini's regime, keeping her own interests distinct from those of others. In early June 1986, Masood Rajavi, the leader of the Mujahedeen, and many of his exiled followers were forced to flee France, their host country since July 1981. With the growing realization among French officials that their previous judgment of the Mujahedeen as "the best bet to supplant the Khomeini regime,"[49] as journalist Flora Lewis put it, had been a miscalculation, the French government, in an attempt to move closer to Iran, removed its protection of Rajavi on charges that he violated the terms of asylum. Commenting on Rajavi's departure, France's minister of security, Robert Pandraud, declared: "We are favorable to political asylum, but on condition that its beneficiaries show the greatest reserve toward the politics of this country and do not take action from France against their country of origin."[50]

Fourth, the host state may consider the exiles to be its enemies and thus prohibit operations of any kind. This was, for example, the stance of the Daladier government toward the Italian anti-Fascists in 1939 and, to a greater extent, that of Vichy toward the Spanish Republicans. In an attempt to appease Mussolini, Daladier ordered the suspension of the anti-Fascist press in France and took harsh measures to interrupt all organized activity on the part of Italian political exiles. In February 1939 the French government recognized Franco's government. Hoping to keep Spain neutral in the event of a French-German war, Daladier sacrificed the Spanish Republicans as an expression of France's goodwill toward Franco. In close cooperation with Franco's dictatorship, the French made great efforts to convince Republican refugees, who were held in camps in the south of France, to return to Spain. It eagerly complied with Franco's demand for the return of the gold from the Bank of Spain that the Republicans had carried out of the country, and ordered the remnants of the deposed Republican government to abstain from any political activity on French soil. Under Pétain, the alternative was no longer "voluntary" return or remaining in camps; the political leaders of the refugees were prohibited from leaving France, and some were handed over to Franco for execution.[51]

In the fifth and final pattern, the host state may serve, against its will and despite the high cost it has to pay, as a territorial base for political exiles' operations. This may happen when the host government is gradually losing control over part of its state territory on which a well-armed exile organization is establishing a state within the state. The archetypical example is the presence of the Palestine Liberation Organization in southern Lebanon since the early 1970s. Or a "semicoerced" host government dependent on a superpower for financial or military support may be forced to tolerate exile activities on its soil at high cost to its own population and internal stability. For instance Honduras, the poorest country in Central America, almost totally dependent on U.S. aid, has been prompted by the U.S. administration since the early 1980s to offer a base to the Contras, America's surrogate exile army. When they expressed a desire to wash their hands of the Contras and free their country from Sandinista-Contra crossfire, Honduran leaders were rebuked by their powerful ally. Describing the reaction of the White House national security adviser, Robert McFarlane, to the Hondurans' criticism of the Contras, Gen. Walter López, chief of the armed forces in Honduras, re-caled: "He [McFarlane] got kind of mad, and said, okay, you have them here. You're supposed to be our allies. And he got up and was about to leave the table. He said, 'well, you only got two choices, it's either to go to Russia, [or] stay with us,' and that hurt us a lot."[52]

Exile Diplomacy: the Politics of Image

> *Limited and alone though I was, and precisely because I was so, I had to climb to the heights and never then to come down.*
> —Charles de Gaulle, *War Memoirs*, 1955

Since governments operate to satisfy their own political objectives, exiles attempt to convince those governments whose support they perceive as critical that their interests coincide with the exiles' cause. In general, negotiations between political agents are similar to eco-nomic relations in the market: both use cost-benefit analysis as a guideline. In economic relations the commodities exchanged are usu-ally tangible and easily translated into monetary value. But the value of commodities exchanged in political relationships is often not easily identified. The packaging imagery of the commodities plays a critical role for both seller and buyer. Moreover, the commodities so trans-ferred in economic transactions are most usually "cashed in" within a foreseeable term. The political commodities exchanged, on the other hand, often pay dividends only in the long term, if ever. The relatively intangible nature of political exchange is greatly pronounced in the case of political exiles qua sellers. Their assets usually exist only in the realm of their potential and quite possibly will never be realized. Therefore, in order to obtain credit from international actors, political exiles must prove especially good salesmen. Image, in this case, plays a critical role.

One must ask oneself, how do political exiles sell their image so as to convince prospective buyers to act on their behalf without re-linquishing critical aspects of their struggle? Or, in Robert Jervis's terms, how can political exiles "project their image on the cheap?"[53] Jervis observed that there is a limited stock of images that interna-tional actors can project cheaply. Images in general are constrained by the fixed beliefs that both the presenter and the receiver hold in regard to themselves, their goals, and the risks they are willing to run, so the presenter can do little to get others to accept a desired image. Reality, or rather the receiver's beliefs about reality, can be altered only on rare occasions. Yet according to Jervis, there are two condi-tions whereby the limitations on the projector of images can be modified. First, the image to be projected is consistent with the views others already have of it. "In these cases the tendency for observers to perceive what they expect to perceive makes it easier for the actors to project a desired image."[54] Second, the projector is able to approach certain delicate aspects of the receiver's belief system susceptible to change and then influences the receiver's overall perception.[55]

In their campaign to rally the international community, exile organizations operate on two related fronts. They use various techniques to undermine the home regime by provoking the international community to act against it, and they manipulate themselves to gain recognition as a political alternative to the home regime's rule. The questions of to whom exile organizations should appeal for support, how they should portray themselves to their potential supporters, and to what extent they should rely on international aid, are complicated. The campaign in the international community is usually determined by the group's ideological affinities; by the way the political exiles perceive the capability of international patrons to support their aims and actions effectively; by the exiles' resources to mobilize the support of the international community; and by the risks they are willing to take to win outside assistance. All these considerations are subject to change over time in accordance with political developments at home and abroad.

In their quest for international support, exile organizations appeal to three sources: enemies of the home regime, the home regime's allies, and agents perceived as being indifferent to the conflict. When they appeal to all three, the political exiles face an acute difficulty. They have to portray themselves very differently to the home regime's allies on the one hand, and to its enemies on the other.

Naturally, political exiles are more likely to find an attentive ear and easy access among those whose fears and animosity toward the home regime are already well established. In some cases exiles have to invest little energy to gain the support of the home regime's enemies, especially when their prospective patrons have already ascribed to them a role in their own campaign to overthrow the home regime. This is seen in the cooperation between the Cuban exiles and the enthusiastic Central Intelligence Agency in the ill-fated invasion of Cuba in April 1961. A less infamous example is the British-American sponsorship of Albanian exiles' attempt to overthrow Enver Hoxha's communist government in October 1949. Like the Bay of Pigs episode, the Albanian exile invasion resulted in a fiasco. The exiles, "who saw themselves not as British puppets, but as patriots using the British to free their homeland,"[56] were betrayed by Kim Philby, the British double agent serving Stalin's secret service. Philby, appointed by the British to command the operation, revealed it to the Soviet authorities.[57]

Indeed, exile organizations cannot simply count on the initial inclination of friendly governments to recognize and abet their struggle. To improve their prospects for securing the support of the home regime's enemies, they must project certain minimum qualities reflecting strength, organizational unity, undisputed leadership, and popular acceptance among their compatriots. Most of all, political exiles must convince their potential patrons that the latter cannot dispense with the military or political services the exiles offer.[58]

When appealing to the home regime's allies, on the other hand, political exiles are likely to face great difficulty in persuading them of the legitimacy of their agenda and in eventually influencing them to sway their allegiance. Political exiles who try to bring a shift in the policies of the home regime's allies must feign interest in what preoccupies their prospective supporters and redefine their case so as to relate to those preoccupations. Hence many exile organizations tend to be alarmist and use subterfuge; they warn the home regime's allies of the potential dangers that may befall them if they pursue their present policies vis-à-vis the home regime.

In the late 1930s, for example, Central American political exiles launched a plan to undermine the relations between their countries' military dictators and their American allies. They planted rumors in the world press of an alliance between the caudillos of Guatemala, El Salvador, Honduras, and Nicaragua, and the Fascist regimes in Europe. In an attempt to make their home regimes targets of the United States' antifascist phobia, the exiles invented and nourished the myth of the "Dictators' League," linking their home regimes to an alleged fascist conspiracy in the region. The dictators who realized the danger thus posed to their regimes did everything in their power to appease the American administration and public opinion. They even suggested an antifascist pact to satisfy the State Department.[59]

In most cases, exile groups that try to effect a shift in the policies of the home regime's allies must find indirect access to high government authorities who, preferring the status quo, tend to ignore the exiles' pleas. The exiles will try to attain their goals through the manipulation of civil society. They work to attract media attention to the home regime's atrocities, establish contacts with elected representatives and opinion makers, and try to convince cultural and sport associations to boycott international conferences in their home country. This was illustrated in recent years by the campaign of Filipino and South Korean exiles in the United States to influence the

American administration to change its friendly policies toward the Marcos and Chun regimes, respectively. The South Korean and Filipino exiles were received by many senators and representatives, and were influential in Congress's drafting of a resolution, passed unanimously in the House, that urged the regimes in question to move toward democracy. In addition, through the mobilization of their respective diasporas in the United States, South Korean and Filipino exile groups increased the pressure on the American administration to reevaluate its policies toward their countries.[60]

Finally, since the distinction between allies and enemies in world politics is in constant flux, political exiles must exhibit particular sensitivity in making alliances. On the one hand, predominant reliance on a single source of political support involves the risk of fatal disillusionment. On the other hand, in their attempt to secure the support of a great number of international patrons, the exiles must maneuver sensitively between their prospective supporters' conflicting desires. By extending themselves in a number of directions, the exiles cannot entertain much hope of obtaining a strong commitment from any one contributing group. Thus after World War II the exiled Spanish Republicans, while at the same time maintaining warm relations with the Soviets, anticipated the overthrow of Franco's fascist regime by the Western Allies, whose commitment to democracy they had overestimated. The American, British, and French governments had no desire to take decisive action against the Spanish Nationalists. Their plea in March 1946 for the peaceful abolition of the Franco government and the restoration of Republican Spain at the same time voiced their reluctance to interfere in "the internal affairs of Spain,"[61] and was an ominous indication of the future relationship between the Western democracies and Franco's Spain.[62] As Louis Stein has written: "The United States and its allies were preoccupied with political and military planning for a possible war against the Soviet Union. . . . Because of its strategic importance, Franco's Spain became an ideological and military bastion against the Soviet Union."[63]

International Organizations and the Global Mythology

Many exile organizations try to stir world public opinion and obtain international assistance by latching onto issues that the global international community finds symbolically resonant. These issues are usually part of a storehouse of political mythologies widely accepted (at least rhetorically) by the international community as archetypes of legitimacy, especially since World War II. They comprise such messages as human rights, democracy, self-determination, freedom of religion, recognition of sovereignty, and organization of labor. Through direct access to high-status international actors or through indirect avenues to world agendas, the political exiles try to delegitimize the home regime and draw international attention to their struggle.

With the advent of universal organizations, and especially since the formation of the United Nations, international forums have become the mecca for many exile groups that face difficulties in generating governmental support and thus search for alternative routes to the global audience. Despite the fact that the UN and its agencies are ill-equipped to enforce their resolutions on governments without direct support of the organization's stronger members, exile groups still value the UN agencies' ability to offer them symbolic legitimation and to evoke the pressure of public opinion.[64]

As a rule, the UN provides access to the General Assembly or the Security Council and grants diplomatic and material assistance to selective national liberation movements in recognition of their struggle for self-determination and independence, as in the case of the Palestine Liberation Organization (PLO) and the South West Africa People's Organization (SWAPO). Both exile organizations are recognized by the UN as the sole and authentic representatives of their people, and as such have earned the right to participate in the sessions and work of the General Assembly and other UN organs as observers.[65] Exile organizations that seek UN support in their struggle to undermine a native home regime, on the other hand, are forced to establish contact with the organization through its specialized institutions[66] or its nongovernmental agencies.[67] Independent of governments, these bodies are in a position freely and publicly to expose atrocities and violations of human rights by the home regime.[68] Furthermore, since UN organizations are usually reluctant to provide assistance to politically oriented bodies (unless so instructed by the General Assembly[69]), exile organizations appeal for their support by introducing themselves as "functional" as opposed to "political."[70] They supply these international forums with documents and testimonies detailing human-rights violations by the home regime.

Dependency on other governments, of course, entails the risk of compromising the exiles' national credibility among their compatriots. The political exiles become vulnerable to the home regime's counterpropaganda, especially when exiles rely heavily on the support of the regime's enemies. The government at home will portray the political exiles as pawns of foreign conspiracies and hence nationally disloyal. However, the political exiles will fight these charges by presenting themselves as patriots using foreign support to benefit the national cause. They will try to maximize the actual advantage of international assistancae while rhetorically downplaying their dependency.

CHAPTER SEVEN

My Country Right or Wrong
The Exile War Trap

Never is the power of the state greater, and never are the forces of political parties of opposition less effective, than at the outbreak of a war.
　　　　　　　　　　　　　—Robert Michels, *Political Parties*, 1962

The continuous conflict between political exiles and their home regime on the question of national loyalty and representation reaches its extreme when the exiles' native land becomes involved in a war with another country. In wartime the exiles' perpetual dilemma intensifies: to what extent can they cooperate with foreign powers against their home regime without abdicating their claim to being national loyalists? The political exile is "torn between an almost instinctive desire to see his people spared the agony of death, destruction, and defeat and the wish to see the annihilation of the regime which drove him into exile and which to him represented the incarnation of evil."[1] Ideological and tactical differences among political exiles about the nature of the war—whether the war is the home nation's war or the home regime's, and how the exiles should react to it—exacerbate the internal divisions already gnawing at the exile's heart. The result is a wide spectrum of responses stretching from the extreme of reconciliation with the home regime and its acceptance as representing the national interest, to the antithetical extreme of collaboration with the state's present enemy.

One case demonstrates the complications that can arise. In January 1983 Masood Rajavi, the leader of the exiled Mujahedeen National Council of Resistance (NCR), one of the principal forces of opposition to Khomeini's Islamic regime, met in Paris with Iraqi Vice-Premier Tariq Aziz. The two issued a joint call for peace between their countries. The declaration caused a setback for the NCR and provoked a rupture between its leader, Rajavi, and the exiled former Iranian president Bani-Sadr, because the meeting and the joint communiqué made it easy for the Iranian regime to discredit the Mujahedeen opposition as nationally disloyal and to label the NCR as "Iraqi pawns and collaborators." Bani-Sadr, who realized the negative effect of Rajavi's move on the exiles' struggle, criticized him publicly and divorced himself from the NCR's activities. He argued that, "while all exiles agree that the war helps keep Khomeini in power, most do not want to be identified with the Iraqis in any way."[2] On June 7, 1986, Rajavi and his exile loyalists were forced to flee France (as part of the French government's attempted rapprochement with the Iranian regime) and were welcomed with great honors in Iraq. The alliance with the Iraqi hosts further damaged the Mujahedeen's credibility. The organization, which claims to enjoy "complete freedom of movement in Iraq,"[3] was seen by Iranians as being "dependent on the national enemy," and Rajavi was dubbed as a "man who sold his soul to foreigners."[4]

In the era of nationalism, military service and participation in a country's war effort are broadly considered direct manifestations of national loyalty.[5] External war is a magnetic force mobilizing the members of a nation-state around a home regime. The vast majority of citizens equivocally loyal to their regime are transformed into patriots who give passionate obedience to the national "call of duty." Gustave Hervé, the French socialist prophet of antipatriotism and antimilitarism, who prior to World War I advocated a workers' revolt against their countries' war effort, was compelled after the war to acknowledge the appeal of nationalism: "People who would not take one step to render a service to their neighbors . . . march hundreds of miles in order to get killed" for their nation-state.[6]

The famous declaration by Stephen Decatur, the American naval commander, "My country right or wrong," expressing the ultimate commitment of the passionate nationalist to the nation-state, long ago became a guiding principle for those many nationalists who join their country's war effort despite objections to its rulers. Nationalists support their country in war even if they are convinced that the existing regime "overrides any consideration of [national and] international morality."[7] Under these circumstances opposition groups—especially political exiles—are pushed into a defensive posture. Their constant attempt to maintain a dichotomy between the home regime as a malignant force without popular support and the true home nation, is grievously assaulted. During the Falklands/Malvinas crisis in April–June 1982, the Galtieri government in Argentina managed to confuse and shatter its Peronista opposition, which was forced to support the Argentinian government in the conflict with the British.

The antigovernment feeling that the Peronistas had generated before the war had to be shelved at the outbreak of the crisis. The Peronista leader, Miguel Unamuno, was forced to admit that his party stood (at least partially) behind the regime's claim that it represented the overall national interest: "We support them on Las Malvinas and nothing more."[8] The confusion of loyalty prompted by the Malvinas conflict also exacerbated the internal debate among Argentinian exile groups in Europe and Latin America. The exiles were pressed to determine whether their return would benefit their fellow countrymen at home, or whether it would be "a useless self-immolation."[9]

When the cannons are thundering, the political exiles' argument that tendencies toward "inertness"[10] among their compatriots at home are latent manifestations of opposition to the home regime, is weakened. Their compatriots' willingness to support the war effort solidifies the regime's claim that it represents the people's will. The anxieties of war enable the home regime to stress the distinction between the "insiders" who share the national burden, and the "outsiders," parasites who oppose the country's war efforts for their own selfish interests.[11] The home regime that tries to exploit the uncertainties and insecurities inherent in times of external warfare thus tends to manipulate the symbolic nature of the nation-state as an emotionally laden and resonant entity.[12] On the outbreak of war, exiles who have been projecting their image as national loyalists now face the further predicament of having to ward off the home regime's attempts to discredit them as "disloyal." As two students of postrevolutionary Iranian exiles have observed: "War does mobilise patriotic feelings, when too much has been suffered and lost to allow the devaluation of the process, and it became politically almost naive to argue support for the 'people' while disavowing the 'nation.' "[13]

Political exiles, being less able than the regime's domestic opponents to exert control over wartime developments,[14] must now conduct their activities with extra care. First, their persistent ideological and political opposition to the internal war effort may alienate the exiles' potential allies at home. Second, such continual opposition may supply unintended fuel for the home regime's propaganda, which already portrays the political exiles as conspirators against the national interest. Yet support of the war effort can be interpreted as affirmation of an exile group's defeat and acceptance of the home regime's claim to be authentic representatives of the national interest.

The exiles' conflicting loyalties are further tested when a war involves the exiles' host country and their native land. The host government naturally expects full gratitude for its hospitality from the exiles; it may even demand that exiles become auxiliary units of its army. The political exiles for their part will try to avoid direct collaboration, which could damage their credibility among compatriots at home or abroad and make them appear as traitors. Exiles who take up arms against their own country justify their participation in their host country's war effort as a national mission to save their people from "false" representatives at home. Thus a French exile who in 1792 fought alongside the Prussian army under the flag of the Bourbons against revolutionary France was, as Margery Weiner put it, a "soldier armed not against France but [for France] against the felons of the Revolution."[15]

Political exiles whose host country engages in a war with their home nation are very likely to find themselves in a political limbo. Both belligerent parties will always remain suspicious of the exiles' motives and loyalties; loyalty to either side compromises the exiles' credibility in the eyes of the other. In the host country, the exiles will find it hard to rid themselves of the stigma of their national origin. Even if fully committed to their host's war effort, they are often regarded as "enemy aliens, secret representatives of an odious regime, whilst their erstwhile supporters at home could too easily see them as cowards or traitors."[16]

Such confusions of loyalty lead many exile groups and their leaders to hold their activities in abeyance in wartime. Until the political picture is clarified, they often mute their expressions of opposition and avoid clear declarations in support of one side or the other. Yet indecisiveness in wartime risks making the exiles politically marginal and eventually irrelevant. In attempting to escape the risks associated with a wait-and-see attitude and with ideological uncertainties, exile leaders typically refocus their energies on strengthening their organizations' cohesiveness. Nevertheless, ideological indecisiveness and lack of political determination on the part of exile leaders in wartime may accelerate feelings of isolation and despair among loyalists both at home and abroad. Exile leaders who stall pending developments in wartime thus risk losing the support of their followers.[17]

The complexities of loyalty and the variety of responses on the part of political exiles in times of war have historically taken many forms, as manifested by exiled communists like Lenin during the Russo-Japanese conflict and World War I; Italian communists during Mussolini's Ethiopian war of the 1930s; exiled German communists in Moscow before and after Hitler's invasion of 1941; and exiled German Social Democrats and Russians during World War II. The exiles' wartime behavior is affected by such influences as the degree of their independence from the host government (if indeed any independence is possible); their relationship with the host government and the home country; their need to maintain a reputation as loyalists despite the awkwardness of residing in the host nation; and the ambivalence of genuine concern for their compatriots on the war front combined with a desire to defeat the home regime.

Both Britain and Russia used exile groups to enhance their own political goals, but the degree of exploitation differed drastically. Britain allowed freedom to German exile groups on its territory even while imprisoning German refugees. The German communists in Moscow, on the other hand, were compelled to follow Soviet goals absolutely.

The Government's Defeat Is the Nation's Victory

> *The least evil would be the defeat of the Tsarist monarchy and its armies.*
> —Lenin, *Seven Theses on the War*

The idea that the government's defeat is the nation's victory was introduced by Lenin during the Russo-Japanese conflict. While millions of Russian citizens were called by the czarist government in February 1904 to fight and perhaps to die in the Far East, Lenin, the leader of the Bolsheviks in exile, firmly supported the Japanese. According to Lenin, Japan served the cause of Russian liberty. Georgi Plekhanov, Lenin's close collaborator in exile, joined hands at the International Socialist Congress at Amsterdam in 1904 with Sen Katayama, the Japanese socialist leader, in a demonstration of international working-class solidarity in the midst of a war between their governments.[18] In January 1905, when the Japanese had finally won at Port Arthur, Lenin declared: "The proletariat has every reason to rejoice. The military goal of Japan is in the main attained. . . . The Russian people has won by the defeat of absolutism. The capitulation of Port Arthur is the prologue to the capitulation of Tsarism. . . . It brings us nearer to the moment of a great new war, the people's war against absolutism."[19]

Lenin's 1904 antiwar posture continued to influence Russia's future ruler throughout World War I. While the Mensheviks, Lenin's perennial rivals in exile, split into two factions—supporters and opponents of czarist war efforts—Lenin persisted in willing his country's defeat. He urged his Bolshevik followers in the Russian Duma to declare that, from the standpoint of the Russian working class and the toiling masses of all Russia, defeat would be the "lesser catastrophe, because Tsarism is a hundred times worse [even] than Kaiserism."[20] He dismissed the czarists' attempts to present themselves as the sole representatives of the Russian nation. He regarded the monarchy's idea of national obligation to the motherland as an "unconscionable bourgeois lie."[21] He called on soldiers to desert.

Lenin's idea of converting the "imperialist war" into many civil wars met with a hostile reception from most of the European antiwar socialist groups assembling in September 1915 at the Zimmerwald conference in Switzerland. Delegates of socialist groups from all over Europe warned against Lenin's antinational approach. They maintained that socialists who followed Lenin's call for desertion "would face a death penalty as traitors when they returned to their homes, while Lenin himself remained safely in neutral Switzerland."[22] Against the Bolsheviks' insistence on a more militant resolution, the European delegates at Zimmerwald adopted a moderate position calling for peace and the right to national self-determination.[23]

Aware of the power of nationalist sentiment the war had evoked, Lenin himself did not avoid incorporating nationalist symbols and slogans into his "internationalist" position. He justified his support of the monarchy's defeat, for example, as an authentic expression of his national commitment and deep attachment to his Russian homeland: "We love our language and our motherland. . . . We are full of a sense of national pride and for that reason we *particularly* hate *our* slave past . . . and our slave present when the same landlords, allies of the capitalists, lead us into war in order to strangle [other nations]."[24]

Lenin's hope that the working class would transform what he regarded as bourgeois imperialist and dynastic wars into a civil war against the czarist regime became a revolutionary rallying cry for exiled European communists in future international conflicts in the 1920s and 1930s. Their adherence to a Marxist-Leninist position made it easier for them to deride their respective home regimes' war efforts and join forces with other states to achieve their own country's defeat. Lenin's exiled party had adopted its revolutionary opposition to the czarist regime independently; exiled communists in Europe after the Russian civil war, on the other hand, were following Lenin's formula. A student of German exiles, Anthony Glees, has described them as "the mouthpiece of Moscow and wholly subservient to the Soviet Union."[25]

Ironically, the anti-Bolshevik exile movement in Europe during World War II adopted Lenin's teaching that the government's defeat is the nation's victory. A remarkable manifestation of this pattern of exile behavior came in the activities of the Vlasov movement, which included Russian prisoners of war in Germany, soldiers and citizens who had changed sides in the first few months of the invasion, and a small group of Russian political exiles from the 1917 revolution. They all supported the cause of Nazi Germany in order to free Russia from what they called the Bolshevik yoke. The war offered these exiled Russians a new opportunity, after more than twenty years of frustration, and rekindled the dream of return. The political exiles now faced the most critical decision of their lives—what role to play in this attack on the motherland. "The Soviet struggle compelled 'Russia Abroad' to reexamine its fundamental views of the Russian people and, in particular, of its government."[26]

The anti-Bolsheviks, as Robert Johnston, a student of Russian exiles, has written, were split among those who favored reconciliation, those who sat on the fence, and those who collaborated with the Nazis.[27] The group that adopted a conciliatory approach toward the Soviet Union included political exiles of all political persuasions. Leaders of the right-wing monarchists joined exile leaders of the Liberals and Mensheviks in a call to serve the "motherland in danger." Many were members of the second generation of Russians abroad who saw in the war against the Nazis an opportunity to regain their national pride.

The fence-sitters were exiles who opposed both Nazis and Bolsheviks but refrained from adopting any definite position. Unconvinced by Soviet attempts to project a new image of political moderation, but at the same time sympathetic to their brothers and sisters suffering at home, they continued to maintain a clearcut distinction between the Russian people and its government.

Among those who chose collaboration with the Nazis, either as Wehrmacht auxiliaries or as an independent military force fighting alongside the Nazis, were both the older and the second generation of exiled monarchists then living in Germany. Many, previously loyalists of Grand Duke Cyril, the self-proclaimed czar, converted completely to Nazism. A few were monarchists from the Parisian community who were tempted by the hope of overthrowing the Stalin regime with German assistance.

When on June 22, 1941, German troops crossed the Soviet frontier without a declaration of war, the monarchists, like other anti-Soviet exile groups, anticipated a quick defeat of the Bolsheviks. Indeed, in December 1941 Alexander Kerensky proclaimed from exile in the United States "a new 'program of restoration' in which the émigrés must play their rightful part, already underway."[28] However, unlike other Russian exiles who were struggling to come to terms with their loyalty, a large number of monarchists determined to fight the Red army alongside or as part of the German fighting forces. Firm in their conviction of Stalin's wickedness, they regarded those who called for reconciliation with the Soviets as "deep-dyed reds or Stalinist agents."[29]

The old monarchical belief that the Soviet regime would dissolve from within had been destroyed by Stalin's consolidation of his regime by suppressing internal opposition. To the older monarchists, therefore, it became clear that only a German victory could ensure the abolition of Stalin's regime. They saw no moral dilemma. The conflict of allegiance and the possible consequences of cooperation with the home nation's new enemy paled in significance beside the actual possibility of destroying the Soviets. In a letter to the Russian exile newspaper in Paris, an old monarchist wrote, "I do absolutely nothing against my conscience. . . . This war is not terrible for us, Russian patriots, but only joyous; for the Bolshevik yoke over our motherland will be ended."[30]

Andrei Andreyevitch Vlasov, a former general in the Red army and heroic defender of Moscow, and a member of the Communist Party with anti-Stalinist tendencies, offered the exiled monarchists both moral justification and an actual opportunity to fight Stalin along with the Nazis, "without being contaminated with Nazism."[31] General Vlasov was taken prisoner by the Germans in the summer of 1942.[32] He was recruited by Wilfried Strik-Strikfeldt, a Russian German in charge of the main camp of Soviet prisoners of war at Dabendorf, to join the Nazi war effort against Kremlin leaders. According to Strik-Strikfeldt, the plan offered to Vlasov by the Wehrmacht included a German promise to remove SS control over the Russians in the German occupied zone and to improve conditions in the prisoner-of-war camps.[33] Vlasov agreed to collaborate with the Nazis only as a leader of an independent Russian army and refused to become a mercenary or quisling against his country. He considered himself a "Russian loyalist."

In December 1942 the Nazis authorized Vlasov to establish the Russian Army of Liberation—a semiindependent Russian military force. In March 1943 Vlasov published an open letter, "Why I Took Up Arms against Bolshevism," in which he appealed to his fellow prisoners of war, to Russian citizens under German occupation, and to old Russian exiles to join him in an attempt to destroy the Bolshevik system. "It became clear to me," he said, "that Bolshevism has involved our people in a war on behalf of interests that are not our people's. . . . Is not Bolshevism—and Stalin himself in particular—the main enemy of the Russian nation? Is it not the first, and sacred, duty of every honor-loving Russian to take up arms against Stalin and his gang?"[34]

Vlasov received more than a million offers of voluntary enlistment.[35] Most of the Russians who came forward probably did so to escape death at the hands of the Nazis and not out of ideological conviction. But for the old Russian exiles Vlasov was a true redeemer, even though Vlasov himself advocated democracy for a future Russia. Vlasov made any participation of the political exiles conditional on their giving up a czarist restoration. Nevertheless, the old monarchists enthusiastically welcomed the idea of a Russian Army of Liberation and on July 24, 1943, six thousand Russian exiles assembled in Paris to listen to General V. F. Malyshkin, a former Soviet general who represented Vlasov. After two decades of absence and isolation, their homesickness and desire to fight Bolshevism had not diminished.[36]

Like many other political exiles who stubbornly refuse to acknowledge defeat, Russian exiles disregarded the painful fact that, as of late 1942, the Soviet armed forces had not revolted against Stalin. The massive military defections in the first months of the invasion, seeming to give the lie to the Soviet myth of the "monolithic solidarity of Soviet society,"[37] were not repeated. The Politburo had already appealed to love for Mother Russia to retain military support and reinforce loyalties to Stalin. Moreover, the Nazis' cruelty to Soviet prisoners of war and to Russian citizens in the conquered areas engendered new loyalty—"Stalin and the people were one."[38]

The Vlasov movement demonstrated that the rationale that national loyalty and patriotism could be expressed by fighting one's own country was repugnant to all sides in the war. Hitler was always suspicious of Vlasov's loyalty and therefore permitted his military action only at the very end of the war, when the Nazis were desperate; he believed that Russian political exiles remained loyal to their country and its regime.[39] For the Soviets as well as the Western Allies, however, Vlasov and his exile followers were mere traitors.

In May 1945 Vlasov was captured by the American army near Prague and turned over to the Russians. He was accused of "treason and espionage and terrorist activities against the USSR as an agent of the German espionage service."[40] He was executed by the Soviets in August 1946, taking to his grave the last hope of an exile return. Vlasov had claimed, apparently, that he cooperated with Hitler in the same way that Churchill and Roosevelt cooperated with the Kremlin.[41]

In Defense of a Home People, Not a Home Regime
I have never given up Germany—the other Germany.
—Willy Brandt, In Exile, 1971

The ways in which the exiled leaders of the German Social Democratic Party (SPD) dealt with the question of national loyalty during World War II cogently exemplifies the complexity of the "exile war trap." From the first days of the war, shortly after Germany invaded Poland, until the final defeat of Hitler, SPD leaders in exile tried to shape their political activities and convictions so as to satisfy the Allied governments without compromising their future claim for representation in postwar Germany. As the war progressed, it became increasingly clear to them that the only prospect for democracy in Germany would be the total defeat of the Nazis. As a last resort they sided with the Allies, thus making themselves vulnerable to the accusation that they were indeed traitors, as Nazi propaganda had already charged.[42]

The proper amount of involvement in the Allied war effort posed a serious dilemma for the SPD leadership. The first preference of the party's executive abroad was to provoke a rebellion within Germany against the Nazis. Throughout their years abroad, the exiled leaders of the SPD agitated against the Nazis but not against Germany itself. They argued that liberation and a national cleansing were more likely to result from a popular insurrection against Hitler than from the total defeat of the German nation by "foreign bayonets."[43] Hans Vogel, the SPD leader in exile, stated: "We have always said that war is not the best means of getting rid of Hitler."[44] While in Paris, shortly before the Nazis invaded France, the SPD leaders repeatedly called upon the German people to oppose the war and topple Hitler. Their public messages warned the Germans against active or passive cooperation with the Nazis and their atrocities, which might contaminate the entire nation: "Take every means of making opposition to this criminal war. . . . Hitler must die so that Germany may live."[45] But their call to overthrow Hitler from within fell on deaf ears. Most of the German people lined up behind Hitler or, even if opposed to the repressive regime, nonetheless chose passivity. The exiled SPD vigorously resisted the notion of collective guilt that had gained acceptance among the Western Allies. Stubbornly presenting themselves as representatives of the "other Germany," the real Germans, they refused to accept the equation of German with Nazi.[46]

The SPD's prolonged attempts to distinguish between Nazis and the German people undercut their reliability in the eyes of the British, who were their hosts during much of the war. Their former chief advocate within the British Labour Party, William Gillies, as well as leaders of the Tory-led government, came to adopt a hostile stance toward the SPD exile executive. They withdrew support from them and in the end abandoned them. The British could not tolerate the exile leaders' persistence in maintaining their independent, "other Germany" policy. Their refusal to permit their followers to participate in combat units alongside the British provoked suspicion and led to charges of collaboration with the Nazis.[47] Even within the SPD, calls were heard against the leadership's stubborn refusal to accept some notion of "collective guilt"; Hans Vogel and Erich Ollenhauer, the senior SPD leaders, were denounced by their fellow exiles as "anti-democratic" and "rabid nationalists."[48]

The conflicting needs of the SPD, on the one hand to persuade the Allies—the presumed future arbitrators of postwar Germany—of their unequivocal opposition to the Nazis, and on the other hand to establish their credibility as loyal Germans, compelled the SPD leaders to try to maneuver their "other Germany" policy with sensitivity to both imperatives. The stronger the notion of collective guilt grew among the Western Allies, the weaker became the exiles' claims in the name of the entire German people. Sometimes they claimed to represent only the opposition minority of the German people whom Hitler had forced to fight with Britain.[49] On other occasions they insisted on being treated as the voice of the future Germany.[50] As the war drew near to an end, the Allies and especially the British lost interest in any coordination of operations with the SPD exile leadership. They were convinced that it was pointless to work with the exiled SPD, likely to be regarded by the Germans at home as "traitors in enemy pay" and therefore without support for the rebuilding of postwar Germany.[51] In this analysis the Allies were mistaken.

The SPD's old leadership found itself in a political limbo. Not only had it failed to maintain its credibility among the Western powers, but it also had to cope with a new threat to its political future in the form of the Soviet-backed National Committee for Free Germany.[52] Factions, desertions, and loss of faith among the exiles left the SPD's senior leadership isolated and disheartened about its own political destiny. Recognizing its political irrelevance until the fighting ceased, the SPD leadership sought desperately to preserve the party abroad. After the guns at last had fallen silent, the leaders hoped to reestablish their organization as the leading socialist party inside Germany.

Like many exile leaders Hans Vogel, who for thirteen years had shouldered the burden of holding the exiled SPD executive together, died before his party realized its dream. He did not live to see Hitler's defeat and the SPD's return to its homeland to reemerge as the major mass party of the German working class in the Federal Republic. It took several years for the SPD to solidify its reputation inside Germany as nationally loyal. Under the occupying powers in West Germany, and against the threat of communism in East Germany, the SPD executive committee in exile, together with members who had survived the war inside Germany, battled the old accusations of having failed to put Germany's interest first. To prove their national loyalty, the postwar SPD leaders vehemently opposed the Soviet occupation and control of East Germany; in West Germany it "would only cooperate with the Western allies on the basis of equality—and then only if German national interests were not sacrificed."[53]

The German communist exiles in Moscow during World War II, on the other hand, exemplified the impotence of exiles who are politically and ideologically subordinate to their host government. On August 23, 1939, the Soviet Union and Germany stunned the world by announcing the signing of a nonaggression pact. For European communists, especially Germans and Italians in exile, the pact caused confusion and consternation. It utterly defied rationalization, even for minds accustomed to the subtleties and contradictions of Marxist dialectics. In their years of submission to Stalin, nothing had prepared the European communists for this. Rationalization became irrelevant. The word "fascism"—like the rest of the principles, theories, and previous resolutions of the Communist International—suddenly vanished from their lexicon. The arch enemy suddenly had become the major ally.

Hitler continued to terrorize members of the German Communist Party (KPD) inside Germany despite the pact, which meanwhile neutralized the KPD leaders in Moscow. Subordinated to Stalin's dictates, the exiled KPD, Günther Nollau writes, "did not deviate one inch from the [Soviet] line."[54] Indeed, when Hitler invaded Poland, the exiled KPD leaders took up the stance adopted by the Communist International, blaming the Western Powers and not the Third Reich for the war. They leveled not a word of criticism against the Nazi regime but rather, as in the past, against the new-old enemy of the workers, the exiled SPD leaders in Paris. Now the Social Democrats were condemned for cooperating with the French and the British in the so-called "imperialist war" against Germany. A joint declaration by the central committee of the German, Austrian, and Czech Communist Parties maintained: "The former leaders of the Social Democracy . . . have enlisted in the service of the British and French imperialists. . . . They are covering up facilitating the swindling lies of the Anglo-French imperialists pretending to be carrying on an anti-Fascist war against the Hitler regime."[55] Hitler's propagandists themselves could not have asked for more.

The German invasion of Russia in June 1941 was welcomed with relief by the KPD in Moscow. For the first time in two years, the word "fascism" reechoed on Moscow radio.[56] At last the exiles could agitate against Hitler in accordance with Lenin's original teachings. With a pragmatic need to reassure the Allies in the West, on May 15, 1943, Stalin dissolved the Communist International. After twenty-four years of monolithic control over the various national communist parties, the leader of the Kremlin tried to convince his new allies that these parties were not mere puppets of the Russians. Two months later, on July 12, the Soviets formed the National Committee for Free Germany, presenting it to the Western world as an authentic, independent exile organization representing all divergent tendencies among Germans opposed to Hitler, "a coalition of Communists, Social Democrats, bourgeois, and *Wehrmacht* opponents of Hitler."[57] As before, however, the exiled KPD in Moscow were mere pawns of the Russians, used for Soviet propaganda purposes and held in political reserve for Stalin's postwar aspirations.

In a firsthand account Wolfgang Leonhard, then a KPD member, has described the activities of the National Committee for Free Germany. In what were known as Institutions 99 and 205, Moscow members of the exiled KPD worked under the supervision of their host government. They published exile newspapers and made radio broadcasts into Germany.[58] Unlike in Britain, where collective guilt was accepted, the Soviet official policy distinguished for propaganda purposes between the German people and Hitler, in order to encourage internal rebellion. The KPD publications and broadcasts urged Germans to overthrow the Nazis before the notion of collective guilt could prevail. The exiles campaigned among high-ranking German prisoners of war in Soviet hands to call on Germans in Germany to rise up against Hitler. In a dramatic appeal fifty German generals, including General Field-Marshal von Paulus, the former supreme commander at Stalingrad, joined in this call to the Germans to depose Hitler and end the war: "The war is lost for Germany. This is the situation to which Germany has been brought by the political and military leadership of Adolf Hitler, despite the heroism of her army and the entire people. . . . Germans! restore the honour of the German name in the eyes of the world by an act of courage."[59]

The terror and persecution inflicted by Stalin on his potential Russian opponents "was brought to bear even more viciously against the emigrés [Austrian, German and Eastern Europeans in Russia] than against the helpless Russians."[60] The exiled KPD in Moscow had no choice but to assert commitment to Stalin's communism. The younger German exiles of Leonhard's generation, he reports, had already been so "Russified" that even their German nationalist attachments were undermined.[61]

With the end of the war in Europe, on April 30, 1945, a first group of KPD exiles, led by Walter Ulbricht (later leader of the German Democratic Republic until 1971), was flown from Moscow to the Soviet occupation zone to reestablish their party. Within that zone Russian occupation forces coopted or eliminated the KPD's potential rivals. The returned exiles were used to support Soviet policy. Until Stalin's death "the party leadership functioned as an executive organ of the Soviet Military Administration (SMA); it could develop no initiative on its own."[62] Unlike the SPD, the KPD never confronted the loyalty dilemma so characteristic of exiles generally in times of war. The KPD supported Stalin, whatever his policies toward Germany.[63] Furthermore, the KPD did not have to contend with the demand of German compatriots at home to prove their national loyalty, as the SPD was required to do.

In times of war, when questions of national identity and loyalty are at stake, those who oppose a regime are frequently confronted by a dilemma. To continue the struggle against the regime may threaten the credibility of the opposition, yet to suspend activities may be interpreted as an affirmation of defeat and an acceptance of the existing authorities' claims to be the sole representatives of the national interest. For many who are dissatisfied with the regime but who have been afraid to make a clean break, external war establishes a personal excuse for submission.

Maintaining a prewar revolutionary spirit among the regime's old opponents and instilling it in new recruits becomes critical for exile organizations and leaders who are remote from the day-to-day realities of their homelands. In the face of national solidarity at home, when the regime's calls for national loyalty overpower other ideologies, it becomes more difficult for political exiles to recruit new loyalists and maintain existing underground collaborators. Outsiders become prime targets for charges of disloyalty and cowardice. The political exiles often find themselves in a trap; temporarily suspended from the battle over the direction their nation will take, they face an agonizing choice. They must either support the home regime or their nation's present enemy and thereby appear to be traitors. Their third option is, of course, to remain neutral, but such a passive stance rarely captures hearts abroad or at home.

CHAPTER EIGHT

Counterexile Strategies by the Home Regime

> Citizenship is man's basic right for it is nothing less than the right
> to have rights. Remove this priceless possession and there remains
> a stateless person, disgraced and degraded in the eyes of his coun-
> trymen. He has no lawful claim to protection from any nation, and
> no nation may assert rights on his behalf. His very existence is at
> the sufferance of the state within whose borders he happens to be.
> —Perez v. Brownell 356 U.S. 64 (1957)

The ability of political exiles to engender loyalty and recognition for
their cause is significantly affected by a home regime's countercampaigns against them. Regimes use their monopoly over the legal use
of violence and manipulate nationalism as a major weapon in sustaining their rule at the expense of nonruling aspirants. The repertoire of responses employed by different home regimes to suppress
the challenge posed by political exiles is extensive. The point here is
not to address the question: what is the likelihood that regime Q will
employ various means, X, Y, Z, during time T, to accomplish A.
Rather, it is to provide a systematic approach to the study of counterexile measures. I will propose some provisional typologies for more
exhaustive case-by-case studies of individual regimes.

The activities of exile groups have long been a source of concern
for many governments. Regimes usually confident of their ability to
suppress domestic subversion are often frustrated, even obsessed, by
an inability to control political exiles seeking to undermine their
power from abroad. In the midnineteenth century, for example, Napoleon III was constantly terrified by the possibility of French exile
plots against his life. In 1850 the Bonapartist dictatorship established
a French Political Police to suppress subversive acts against the regime said to be provoked by political exiles in England. Napoleon
himself declared that "until the [exile] problem was solved, it would
never be safe in France 'to relax the present system' of authoritarian

government."[1] Similarly the czarist government feared Russian exile groups in Western Europe and moved to suppress them. From the revolutionary days of Alexander Herzen until Lenin's victorious homecoming in 1917, czarist police agents strove to break the connection between domestic opponents of the regime and exiled revolutionaries, and used a variety of means to infiltrate and eliminate the latter.[2]

Operating outside their nation-state and often under the shelter of sympathetic governments, exile groups may have a better opportunity than internally based opposition to carry on a forceful campaign against the home regime. Indeed, in some cases the exiles' campaigns are the only indication of an active opposition to the home regime— indisputable proof of the falseness of that regime's claim that the nation is unified behind its leadership. Mussolini, for example, was constantly troubled that the attacks on his regime by the Italian anti-Fascist press abroad "could create the impression of a divided nation in which Fascism faced strong opposition." Thus "it was necessary," he was convinced, "to criticize behavior [of] Italian renegades and to insist on almost unanimous—I stress unanimous—support of the Italian people for the Fascist Regime."[3]

Because they have held a position of power at home, political exiles may maintain or acquire international recognition and even diplomatic immunity. By utilizing personal connections, they may gain easy access to international political, industrial, and financial quarters, and to social and scientific organizations, through which they may contest the legitimacy of the home regime. Thus home regimes, dependent in many ways on foreign diplomatic, economic, and military support, are often extremely vulnerable to international criticism and pressure, especially if their rule is despotic or tyrannical. They often perceive a threat in the exiles' ability to foster international animosity and channel it toward them.[4]

In response to this perceived threat, home regimes may employ a wide range of symbolic and coercive measures at home and abroad to discredit political exiles as illegitimate and destroy them as a political force. At home, regimes employ massive propaganda campaigns to slander the exiles as nationally disloyal and subject to foreign interests. This propaganda warfare is often accompanied by confiscation of exiles' property, by withdrawal of academic awards, by persecution of exiles' friends, families, and supporters, and most of all by isolation from their potential loyalists inside the country. To demolish the exiles' status and power base abroad, home regimes manipulate legal and diplomatic, provocative and violent means. The most common measures are the withdrawal of citizenship, spies, and the use of agents provocateurs to infiltrate the exile ranks, inflame dissension, incriminate political exiles in their host country, expose their supporters at home, and induce division in their ranks. Other antiexile strategies include agreements with host governments and other international agents to disrupt exile operations; nonviolent and violent measures, to discourage members of the national diaspora from engaging in antigovernment activities; and kidnapping and political assassination.[5] In 1979 the counsel of the Senate Committee on Governmental Affairs wrote in a classified report: "The C.I.A. became aware in October 1973 that the Philippine government had become increasingly concerned that President Marcos's enemies in the U.S. might be developing, or had already, an influence that would adversely affect the Philippine government." He added that Gen. Fabian Ver, Marcos's chief of staff and intelligence, had been sending his military agents to the United States "for the purpose of infiltrating, monitoring and possibly counteracting the threat of anti-Marcos groups."[6]

Denationalization and Statelessness

The home regime may impair exiles' operational activities and undermine their claim to political legitimacy by branding them as disloyal and in effect no longer citizens. In the modern concept of citizenship, which took hold particularly after the American and French revolutions, citizenship is acquired by birth or by some process of naturalization. In the age of the nation-state it became one of the most critical identifications of an individual. Often used synonymously with "nationality," "citizenship" implies a sense of national community and patriotism.[7] It is a source of the individual's national pride and a primary symbol of solidarity with and obligation to a wider community with which the individual shares cultural and political existence.[8] Moreover, citizenship defines one's national loyalty in interaction with members of other nation-states and denotes which government is responsible for the individual's security. The loss of citizenship is thus often interpreted as a loss of national identity.[9] Citizenship is a benefit that the nation-state's government provides to the state's members. The authorities of a nation-state, without regard to the government in power, acknowledge an obligation to grant security to their citizens at home and abroad. In return, the state authorities "expect gratitude from the citizens they protect"[10]—that is, behavior in accordance with the government's criteria of national loyalty. Thus all governments decide who deserves to be protected and when citizenship should be revoked; they order their citizens to fulfill their national duty (as defined by the government), regardless of their place of residence abroad.[11] Failure to do so can be very costly. It may result in charges of treason that can lead in turn to loss of citizenship and national exclusion. For example, article 2 in the Nazi law of citizenship stated that "members of the Reich who are resident abroad may have their German citizenship declared null and void if it is considered that they have harmed German interests by offending against their duty to remain loyal to Reich and *Volk*."[12] Similarly the Decree on Public Safety, issued by Mussolini in November 1926, permitted the Fascist government "to denationalize opponents abroad even if they committed no crime; all that was needed was that, in the view of the government, they had injured Italian interests or brought Italy into disrepute."[13]

At least since the Roman Empire, exile and loss of citizenship have been employed as punishments. However, citizenship in the ancient world was profoundly different from nationality in the modern epoch. Although banishment did not mean the loss of nationality before our days,[14] the identity crisis suffered by exiles in the absence of citizenship already existed in prerevolutionary France.

A generation before the French Revolution Jean-Jacques Rousseau, an exile from his native city-state, Geneva, whose citizenship had been revoked, acknowledged the difficulty of maintaining a national identity in the absence of citizenship. Rousseau continued to feel himself a patriot. But like many other exiles of his time, he soon realized that his love for his country became meaningless without actual participation with his fellow citizens in some sort of public activity. For Rousseau, citizenship was the work of the rational will: "commitment stems not from what we naturally are but from what we rationally chose to be . . . [the] readiness to match public utterances with public deeds."[15]

Withdrawal of citizenship (denaturalization or denationalization) was commonly adopted as a weapon against political exiles during and after World War I. "Such grounds as disloyalty or disaffection, acts prejudicial to the state or its interests, collaboration with the enemy, advocacy of subversive activities, etc."[16] were frequently stipulated as causes for deprivation of citizenship. By stripping exiled opponents of one of their critical national possessions—their citizenship—regimes have tried to undermine the very foundation of the exiles' national identity. The act of denaturalization aims to create a symbolic—and actual—rupture between the *Rechtsgemeinschaft*, the community under law that deserves protection, and the outsiders, the outlaws abroad.[17] Retraction of citizenship is often followed by massive propaganda campaigns against the "treasonable activities" of the exiles, and derogatory terms are frequently used to repudiate the exiles as nationally disloyal. The Italian Fascists, for example, reintroduced the medieval terms *fuoruscito* and *fuoruscitismo*, implying that anti-Fascists abroad were a band of self-interested outlaws.[18] In the 1940s and 1950s the Caribbean dictators used to discredit their exiled opponents as "mercenaries, adventurers and arms traffickers."[19]

Fidel Castro, who following the Cuban revolution encouraged emigration as a primary means of removing internal dissent, nevertheless contemptuously labeled the émigrés *gusanos* (worms). In 1965 Castro declared: "In this country, when we say to someone, 'If you want to leave we aren't going to stop you; you are free to leave,' this country doesn't lose a citizen. Why? Because that citizen could never be considered—from our revolutionary point of view, from our Marxist point of view—a citizen of this country."[20]

Ironically (but not at all surprisingly), many home regimes that use denaturalization as a weapon against political exiles regard the modern concept of citizenship (i.e., a body of citizens seeking their autonomy and identity in a secure nation-state) as inadequate for defining the national membership, solidarity, and community.[21] Ardent nationalist governments, on the one hand, have established their basis for national belonging on allegedly unimpeachable criteria such as *Volk* or tribe identity, which seemingly "guarantee a certain and irrevocable citizenship to those with the correct identity,"[22] irrespective of their location. Internationalist regimes, on the other hand, deny the idea of national unity and purport to represent crossnational interests such as class or religion. However, both types of governments recognize the central importance of territorial boundaries and national symbols and appreciate the exiles' need to maintain political identity abroad. Furthermore, they understand the propaganda effect of denationalization at home, and most of all the direct damage to the exiles' political operation in the absence of official documents (e.g., passports). Therefore they tend to redefine the concept of citizenship in accordance with their practical policies.

The Bolsheviks, who regarded national citizenship as a "bourgeois fiction,"[23] were nonetheless the first in this century to employ massive denaturalization measures against opponents of the regime abroad. On October 28, 1921, the Soviets issued a decree depriving of Russian citizenship all former subjects of the Russian Empire abroad (about two million people) who had been involved in "counter-revolutionary" activities against the Soviet regime, or "were considered as being opposed to it."[24] Moreover, under the Nazi's racial or *Volk* definition of nationality, "Germans cannot lose, non-Germans cannot acquire Germanhood."[25] Hence German Jews and other minorities were automatically denationalized.[26] They were declared "undesirable," or "objective enemies of the regime."[27] However, the Nazi authorities then inconsistently employed denaturalization as a primary weapon against all varieties of German opponents abroad, regardless of their racial origin.[28]

Home regimes have tended to manipulate citizenship as a stick-and-carrot mechanism. Naturalization and denaturalization are not always final acts; "all patriots are potential traitors,"[29] and vice versa. On the one hand, political exiles are deprived of their citizenship and labeled as traitors. On the other hand, home regimes have often made conciliatory gestures and, using various means of propaganda, have tried to convince the less determined opposition and exiled intellectuals, who may have developed second thoughts about their struggle, to return home and cooperate with the existing power for the "benefit of the nation." Thus Italian anti-Fascists abroad who decided to act in "harmony" with their country's "national interest" during the Ethiopian war could return home and regain their citizenship.[30] The Bolsheviks granted amnesty and reconferred citizenship upon exiles who changed their attitude about the regime and were willing to return "to work with the whole people for the reconstruction of the country."[31] The amnesty, which was proclaimed by the Soviet government almost simultaneously with the decree of denaturalization, led about 180,000 Russian refugees to return home.[32] Spain under Franco proclaimed broad amnesty and restoration of citizenship to exiled Republicans on October 9, 1945. In the middle of the Republican exiles' campaign to persuade the postwar Allied governments to overthrow Franco and grant recognition to their government-in-exile, Franco opened the gates as part of his attempt to wipe away the stain of fascism from his international image.[33] More recently, Cuban exiles who met with Castro in 1978, in what became known as the "diálogo," ceased to be regarded as "traitors" and became "members of the Cuban community abroad."[34]

The twofold policy of citizenship withdrawal and restoration is employed principally for propaganda purposes at home and in the national community abroad. The exiles' so-called "regret" is used by home regimes to forge the image of unity between the regime and the entire nation. But most important, by persuading significant segments within the exile diaspora to return to their country, the home regimes attempt both to undermine the political exiles' claim on the loyalty of the national community abroad, and to challenge the exiles' reputation at home. As a result, the exiles' self-confidence may suffer a psychological setback, their militancy may decrease, and their bitterness and internal divisiveness may grow more intense. The Nicaraguan dictator, Anastasio Somoza García, who usually refrained from coercive measures against his opponents abroad, used to encourage his exile opponents to return home in order to negotiate a political compromise. Somoza's "open door" policy toward the Nicaraguan exiles weakened and fragmented the opposition abroad, leaving political exiles with virtually no ties and little support at home. After Somoza's assassination in 1956, the Nicaraguan exiles proved incapable of preventing the smooth transition of power to Somoza's sons.[35] His policies of weakening the opposition abroad were in part responsible.

By depriving the political exiles of state protection and casting them out as traitors, regimes confer upon themselves the legitimacy to use all "necessary" means to put an end to the exiles' subversive acts. The employment of denaturalization against political exiles is often followed, therefore, by confiscation of property, cancellation of academic awards, and both indirect and direct persecutions abroad.

The breakup of the modern world into self-sufficient nation-states, and the closing of the frontiers especially in times of international crisis, often create a legal limbo for those who have lost their citizenship. For example, during the rule of Gen. Ernesto Geisel (1974–78), the Brazilian government launched a massive campaign against its exile opposition, which was discrediting the dictatorship abroad. "The Brazilian government denied passports to all exiles and their children, as well as refusing them any type of assistance or protection in their countries of residence. In some cases the [Brazilian] political police extended their persecution across the frontier, openly acting against members of the Brazilian opposition . . . in Chile."[36]

In official international usage, citizenship generally means holding a national passport. It enables a citizen "to enjoy abroad the diplomatic protection which is granted to the nationals of the issuing country."[37] Without a national passport a person becomes stateless. As wanderers searching for political protection, the stateless are subject to the mercy or caprice of the state they find themselves residing in at the time of their loss of citizenship. As the Cains of the modern world, they are often forced to change their country of residence a number of times. They are restricted in their human rights in times of peace and are often treated as the "scum of earth"[38] in times of war.

Like the mark of protection God is said to have conferred on Cain, the documents issued by the League of Nations in 1922, known as "Nansen passports," aimed to provide the stateless with basic human rights and a means of livelihood.[39] They prohibited host governments from harassing stateless refugees who lacked national passports. Nonetheless, even Nansen's special documents, recognized by the majority of European governments throughout the 1920s as proof of identity and a laissez-passer, lost their value in the 1930s. With mounting numbers of refugees and consequently a growing demand for identification papers, the Nansen passports—although theoretically recognized—became suspect and were no longer sufficient.[40] "Holding a Nansen passport, recalled Nabokov [who had one], was like being a criminal on parole or a child born out of wedlock."[41]

The condition of statelessness is especially grave for political exiles committed to effecting a return from abroad. Unlike most refugees, who seek to establish themselves (even if temporarily) in their host country, or to return home regardless of the regime in power, militant political exiles try to avoid any emotional, professional, or official connections with what they conceive as their temporary residence. Yet like many other refugees, active exiles often find themselves thousands of miles from home in places where their militancy can barely be maintained. Like many of their potential followers within the refugee community, they may be compelled to give primary attention to economic and social problems created by their refugee status. Even in their own households they sometimes face great difficulties in preventing the cultural and psychological denationalization of their children.

Political exiles' difficulty in maintaining and rejuvenating the revolutionary energy of their fellow refugees is exacerbated when the host country offers their compatriots new citizenship. Many refugees who see their dream of quick return receding pursue the possibility of acquiring their host country's citizenship in order to lead a more normal life. For example, when on January 23, 1940, the Mexican government offered Spanish refugees the right to Mexican citizenship, leading them to reconsider their identity as "loyal Spaniards," the vast majority accepted the offer, but the most active political exiles refused. Patricia Fagen points out that, "committed to the idea of returning to their homeland as soon as possible . . . [they] considered it a moral obligation to retain their Spanish passports, and not to accept the citizenship of any other country."[42] However, as Alicja Iwańska observes in her study of the Polish and Spanish diasporas, militant exiles who insisted on holding ineffectual passports issued by their unrecognized governments-in-exile respectively, suffered severely in their freedom of movement.[43]

For militant political exiles, possession of foreign citizenship can become the kiss of death compromising credibility among other active exiles or with the inside opposition to the home regime: it may be interpreted as a confession to the home regime's charges of national betrayal. When they acquire new citizenship, the severity of the political exiles' condemnation either by the home regime or by its opposition depends in many cases on how the exile's new country of nationality is perceived by both sides—either as "enemy nation" or as "friendly host." Thus Ebrahim Yazdi, a key figure in the Islamic antishah movement abroad and Khomeini's representative among the opposition forces in the United States, after the revolution became the constant target of fundamentalists who accused him of being an American agent. Yazdi's opponents based their claim on the fact that during his long stay in the United States he had acquired American citizenship. To counter these charges Yazdi requested and received a formal letter from Khomeini declaring him to be a man "of Iranian origin and a [loyal] Muslim."[44]

Thus many political exiles refrain from acquiring new national identity. The few exile activists who accept foreign citizenship will try to minimize the perception of this as renunciation of their former national commitment. Emphasizing their opposition activities as the highest manifestation of their national loyalty, these political exiles justify their foreign citizenship as an important stratagem in promoting their ultimate goal of overthrowing the rival regime. Willy Brandt, who took Norwegian citizenship after the Nazis stripped him of his German citizenship, later wrote:

Norway gave me citizenship when others had made me stateless. Despite this my Norwegian friends did not think ill of me when I remained in Berlin in 1947 to give my best in the work of reconstructing my own country. . . . Even in the hour of its deepest distress I could not cut myself off from the true Germany. . . . I have [always] worked to the limit of my ability to make my own modest contribution to the struggle against the forces of enslavement.[45]

Divisions and Splinters Within Exile Organizations

Ideological, tactical, and personal divisions within the exile organizations often debilitate and exhaust the political exiles' revolutionary energy. Such divisions undermine the exiles' ability to generate loyalty and international recognition for their cause, and weaken their claim to represent the authentic nation. (See chapter 3.) Political exiles often engender their own internal splinters. But home regimes, while encouraging the exiles' factionalism, usually do not rely on it. They actively promote destructive feuding among exile groups.

To exacerbate ideological and tactical divisions and promote personal rivalries, home regimes charge that the exiles slavishly tie themselves to foreign powers and thereby abdicate their claim to be national patriots. More directly, home regimes may seek to trigger internal strife among the exiles through the use of infiltrators and agents provacateurs who join the exile organizations in the guise of persecuted victims of the home regime. Such agents strive to deepen the splits between already existing camps, to promote dissatisfaction with exile leaders among the rank and file, and to induce suspicion and fear within and between exile groups. Hence, for example, "the ever-present fear of the Gestapo and its spies reportedly promoted the various [German] exile groups to denounce one another as Nazi agents to the authorities of their haven countries."[46] Mussolini's agents provocateurs also sought to split the anti-Fascist exile movement and promoted dissatisfaction among its leaders in France. They pretended to be victims of Fascism, published a manifesto castigating the exiles' leadership as incompetent, and called for its replacement because of its failure "to restore liberty to Italy."[47] They even employed bribery, offering "five hundred francs to each anti-Fascist who would sign the manifesto, and promised further material aid in [the] future—a great temptation when it is remembered that many of these refugees had lost home, profession, family, savings and [were] on the borderline of destitution."[48]

One of the more famous stories of an agent provocateur who penetrated an exile organization to foster factionalism and discredit its members is the case of Roman Malinovsky and the anti-czarist opposition abroad. A former criminal in czarist Russia, Malinovsky was recruited through blackmail by the secret police, the Okhrana, for espionage missions abroad. Malinovsky, who managed to penetrate the Bolsheviks' exile circles, then penetrated the inner ranks and soon became Lenin's intimate friend. He was chosen a member of the Bolsheviks' Central Committee, and represented the organization in the Duma before leaving to join the exile forces in 1914. While abroad, Malinovsky, a well-paid secret agent, became known for his dedication to Lenin's "splitting mania."[49] As Lenin's biographer, Louis Fischer, notes, he was "always on the side of extremism, of splits with the Mensheviks and liquidators,"[50] trying to weaken the subversive opposition to the czar. The Okhrana, seeking to enhance the divisions between communist factions at home and abroad, used Malinovsky's reports to arrest Mensheviks and Bolsheviks in Russia who opposed splits and urged unity. Malinovsky himself had earned Lenin's confidence to such a degree that, when the Bolshevik leader was warned by his closest advocates that Malinovsky was suspected of spying, Lenin dismissed the charges and blamed the Mensheviks for being "unscrupulous as to the means they employed in the struggle against the Bolsheviks."[51]

"It is no surprise," writes Alan Dowty, "that the Bolsheviks, having themselves operated as an exile group, would after seizing power become extremely leery of émigré communities."[52] The Soviets' fear of the outside world and especially of Russians abroad led them to develop counterexile machinery unprecedented in its efficiency and brutality. In the early 1920s the Soviet secret police, the G.P.U., established its own "exile" organization, the Trust, as part of its activities to destroy the monarchists' opposition inside and outside Russia. The G.P.U.'s pseudoexile organization successfully penetrated White exile circles. It managed to destroy the exiles' operational foundation and compromise many monarchist leaders in the eyes of the West.[53]

The Trust's principal tactic was to provoke internal divisions within the monarchists' ranks by discrediting the sterility of their activity and the helplessness of their leaders: "They only squabble— they never get anything done."[54] Presenting themselves in the exile community in Paris as "guerrilla fighters" of the supposed monarchist underground in the Soviet Union, Trust members attacked the exile opposition as pathetic and outdated, calling upon the exile ranks to reject "unrealistic acts" of anti-Soviet "terrorism and subversion activities" that would jeopardize the entire operation of the mythical opposition at home.[55] The G.P.U. agents offered the Russian exiles access to the Trust's connections and encouraged them to go back to Russia to join forces with the alleged opposition at home.[56]

Diplomatic Pressures on the Host Government

Home regimes that seek to eliminate their opposition abroad have been perennially aware of the importance of host governments in determining the exiles' operational effectiveness. They often try to manipulate their diplomatic, economic, and military links, employing provocative measures to encourage host governments to suppress exiles' activity or at least reduce the warmth of their "hospitality." (See chapter 6.) This approach reduces the home regime's need to employ more drastic means like agents provocateurs and death squads, which are costly, demand complicated operational skills, and are often very risky in the international arena.

On the diplomatic level, home regimes try to urge or compel host governments to renounce their support of the exiles for the host country's benefit. They maintain that by protecting and assisting the political exiles—"an insignificant non-representative minority which had conspired against the national interest"—the hosts are endangering their diplomatic relations, even risking charges of complicity with the home regime's national enemies. On the level of direct provocation, home regimes try to discredit political exiles in the eyes of their host governments by incriminating the exiles in illegal conspiracies and misuse of the right of asylum.

In the early 1850s, for example, France under Napoleon III made its exiled opposition in London a key issue in Franco-British relations. It protested against the British tolerance of anti-French activities and insisted futilely that the British suppress the exiles' alleged plots to assassinate the emperor.[57] So also, almost a century later in the mid-1930s, the Nazis, who associated international criticism with "lies" spread by German exiles,[58] used their diplomatic officials in London to try to convince British authorities to expel "or at least to threaten with expulsion" anti-German exiles who had a "bad effect on Anglo-German relations."[59] Just a few months before the Munich agreement, Hitler was threatening Czechoslovakia for harboring the enemies of Germany,[60] and in early 1938 the German SPD in Prague had been asked by Edvard Beneš to leave Czechoslovakia.

In the late 1920s Mussolini's agents provoked a series of attempts on the lives of Italian diplomats and representatives in Europe. In response to an apparent anti-Fascist "world campaign of terrorism" by exiles, abetted by incriminating evidence supplied by Italian authorities, French, Belgian, and Swiss police arrested key anti-Fascist leaders. However, the investigation of these governments did not produce the results Mussolini wanted. An official Swiss communiqué concluded that "no motives to warrant expulsion" were discovered and the exiles were set free.[61] The Fascist plot was discovered and official protests were delivered to Rome.[62]

In early 1941 Franco, in a meeting with Marshal Pétain, protested to French authorities against the protection given to Republican exiles in Vichy, France, under a joint agreement between Vichy and Mexico. He demanded that those responsible for resistance to his regime be returned to Spain.[63] Vichy responded at once. Following a list of Spanish delinquents prepared by the Spanish ambassador in Paris, it arrested exile leaders and handed them over to Franco for execution.[64] After World War II, when Franco had emerged in Allied eyes as an anticommunist, and when he gradually relaxed his dictatorship, Franco no longer considered the Republican exiles a threat to his regime but persecuted them all the same. In 1961, during the Algerian war, Franco made military assistance to the French government conditional upon cancellation of the exiled Republicans' diplomatic credentials and the eviction of the Spanish government-in-exile from its Paris headquarters. As before, the French complied.[65]

Rafael Trujillo, who ruled the Dominican Republic for more than a quarter of a century, gaining a reputation for arbitrary "nonideological" terror and violation of human rights at home, mercilessly hounded his opponents abroad. He terrorized exiles' relatives who were still living in the Dominican Republic and employed physical violence and propaganda, as well as diplomatic measures, to suppress exile activities abroad. In the international sphere, he pressed Venezuela and Guatemala to renounce their support of anti-Trujillo exiles based in Cuba. He denounced the Cuban government for violation of treaty obligations to block subversive activities within its borders against a sister republic. In July 1947, Trujillo even threatened Cuba with war. As a devoted ally of the United States, he called upon the Americans to order the Cuban government of Ramón Grau San Martín to cease support for the Dominican exile "liberation army" in Cuba. He condemned the exiled Dominican Revolutionary Party (PRD) as "mercenaries" bringing communism to the Caribbean and, through pressure on the U.S. government, kept Cuba from helping Dominican exiles formulate and execute plans for invasion.[66]

In a more recent case, on August 13, 1984, King Hassan II of Morocco signed a treaty of union with Libya after years of bitter and violent relations between the two countries. Muammar al-Qaddafi's conciliatory policies toward Hassan were conditioned on the king's willingness to turn over exile leaders and members of the National Front of the Salvation of Libya (NFSL) who had operated since 1980 to overthrow his regime. The Moroccans subsequently handed over several members of the NFSL to the Libyan authorities, presumably to be executed.[67]

Assassinations and Kidnappings of Key Leaders

In this century, assassination and kidnapping of key leaders, ideologues, and front-line activists in exile have gradually been adopted by despotic regimes as a key strategy for suppressing exile groups. Political exiles who use modern communications to provoke the overthrow of their home regime from abroad can operate beyond the reach of the regime and therefore pose a serious threat. As a consequence, many secret police forces maintain agents in their foreign embassies.

"While they may be called 'attachés' or some such title, their real job is to keep track of the exiles"[68] and if necessary to liquidate them. A number of home regimes routinely use their agents abroad to abduct and liquidate political exiles.

The G.P.U. under Stalin established special divisions to operate from the Soviet embassies in Europe to control political exiles.[69] With ample resources they were able to mount a systematic and remarkably successful campaign against anti-Soviet exiles: first against the leaders of the White Russians,[70] then the Trotskyites, and after World War II the Ukrainian exiles.[71]

For Stalin, the "fact" that revolutionary groups were constantly plotting from abroad against the Soviet national interest became an *idée fixe*, serving to justify domestic terror. For thirty years of Stalin's rule every political trial implicated the Russian émigrés directly or indirectly in anti-Soviet plots.[72] Moscow frequently announced new discoveries and liquidations of exile conspiracies to overthrow the regime, said to be led and supported by "imperialistic headquarters" abroad.[73] With no substantial activities in the monarchist camp in the late 1920s, Stalin found it necessary, Hugh Hessell Tiltman has said, to "invent plots abroad and to import them into Russia."[74]

Leon Trotsky's banishment in February 1929, and the stigma he bore as the revolution's number-one enemy, set the tone for the 1930s purges. The label "Trotskyites" became a derogatory term, and the ranks of Trotsky's supporters at home were depleted. Despite the arrest in the Soviet Union and death by torture of his young son, Sergei, who was charged with attempting on his father's orders to poison factory workers,[75] Trotsky nevertheless believed that Stalin's evil deeds were only a transitory phenomenon: "History has to be taken as she is and when she allows herself such extraordinary and filthy outrages one must fight her back with one's fists."[76]

Even after the poisoning of his elder son, Lyova, by G.P.U. agents in Paris, and even after the Munich agreement, the Nazi-Soviet pact, and the outbreak of World War II, which was a negation of his political predictions, Trotsky remained an orthodox Marxist. He remained stubbornly loyal to the mythology of a Soviet workers' state until, on August 8, 1940, he was assassinated in exile in Mexico by Frank Jakson, Stalin's G.P.U. agent.[77]

So too, the agents of Mussolini's Organization of Volunteers of the Repression of Anti-Fascism (OVRA) operated under the direct orders of the Italian embassy in Paris, and in close cooperation with the government in Rome, to liquidate Italian anti-Fascists in France,[78] their major achievement being the assassination of the most active anti-Fascist exile, Carlo Rosselli, and his brother Nello. The Gestapo agents, working with the German diplomatic service in Europe, sent out murderers to liquidate anti-Nazi exiles in Czechoslovakia, France, and England.[79] In April 1965 the bludgeoned body of Humberto Delgado, the leading figure of the exiled opposition to the Portuguese ruler Antonio Salazar, was found near the Spanish frontier town of Badajoz. A former air-force general who had led the domestic opposition in the fraudulent elections of 1958 and the abortive exile-initiated coup of 1962, he was probably assassinated by agents of Salazar's secret police (PIDE). The investigations of the case after the 1974 coup in Lisbon implicated the PIDE but did not produce conclusive results.[80] More recently, a few Yugoslavs and Croatians opposed to Tito have been kidnapped or murdered by Yugoslav secret police (UDBA) in Europe.[81]

In Asia, since the early 1970s, agents of the Korean Central Intelligence Agency (KCIA) have been active in silencing exile opponents of the regime. "Highlights of this plan were the abduction of Kim Dae Jung from Japan and the disappearance of the fomrer KCIA director, Kim Hyung Wook, in Paris during 1979. Kim Hyung Wook is widely believed to have been killed by South Korean agents."[82]

In the Middle East, liquidation of exile opponents has long been an integral component of political intrigue. Col. Adib Shishakli was assassinated in Brazil in September 1964 by the Syrian Ba'th ten years after he was overthrown as Syria's strongman.[83] Iraqi security agents assassinated exiled communists who sought to discredit the Ba'th regime abroad, either directly or through Soviet-supported states.[84] In October 1965, Mahdi Ben Barka, leader of the National Union of Popular Forces (Union Nationale des Forces Populaires, or UNFP) in Morocco, who had been persecuted by Hassan II for alleged complicity in the plot against the king's life, disappeared during a stay in Paris. French authorities concluded that he was abducted by agents of Gen. Mohammed Oufkir, the Moroccan minister of the interior; France issued international warrants for Oufkir's arrest. In 1966 Oufkir was sentenced in absentia by a French court to life imprisonment. The Ben Barka affair led to a serious rift between France and Morocco, and Hassan's regime faced severe domestic and international criticism because of it.[85]

In 1976, in Paris, the shah's SAVAK hired a gunman to assassinate Sadeq Qotbzadeh, the leading organizer of antishah student movements in exile, but the hired assassin surrendered to French police, and "a minor scandal ensued."[86] Iranian agents sent by the Ayatollah Khomeini were less conscientious. In the streets of Paris, in 1979 and 1980, they murdered the nephew of the exiled shah and the former military governor of Teheran. Unsuccessful attempts were made also on the lives of former Prime Minister Shahpour Bakhtiar, a leader of the exiled Iranian monarchists, and the former first president of the Islamic revolution, Abolhassan Bani-Sadr, who with Masood Rajavi led the Council of National Resistance in exile. In 1984 a French Senate committee on terrorism accused the Iranian government of sponsoring "an army of believers," as the *Los Angeles Times* called it, throughout Europe to battle Khomeini's opponents; it prompted the French government to expel Iranian diplomats and close down the Iranian Cultural Center in Paris.[87]

Muammar al-Qaddafi, who became known for his fear of opposition groups abroad, established a special unit attached to Libya's Foreign Liaison Bureau to kidnap and assassinate Libyan exiles. This unit was responsible for the disappearance and liquidation of many Libyans abroad identified by the Libyan General People's Congress (GPC) as "enemies of the Libyan revolution."[88]

In Latin America, from the late 1930s through the 1950s Trujillo "maintained an efficient espionage system and used the Dominican diplomatic and consular service to harass and . . . liquidate his enemies in the exile community." His massive and brutal campaign to destroy his exiled opponents reached all corners of the Americas; it was described by Charles Ameringer as "one of the most sensational criminal mysteries of recent times."[89]

In Chile, after the overthrow of Allende in 1973, the Dirección de Inteligencia Nacional (DINA), Pinochet's Chilean secret police, was granted broad powers to eliminate the regime's opponents in exile. The DINA was responsible for some of the most sensational and vicious assassinations of exiles abroad. It arranged the murder of Gen. Carlos Prats Gonzáles and his wife in Buenos Aires; the car bomb that killed Orlando Letelier, the former Chilean ambassador in Washington; and the attempt on the life of Bernardo Leighton, the Chilean democratic exile leader in Rome, and his wife. The assassinations abroad, especially the brazen murder of Letelier in Washington, exposed Pinochet's government to heavy criticism and pressure from the Carter administration and some European democracies. Pinochet was forced to extradite Letelier's murderers to the United States, dissolve the DINA, and restrain coercive measures against critics abroad.[90]

Likelihood of the Use of Antiexile Measures

In his study "Totalitarian and Authoritarian Regimes," Juan Linz refrains from including terror as a crucial variable in distinguishing between these two types of regime. He argues that, "while terror acquired a unique importance in totalitarian systems, many of its manifestations are not absent in regimes that lack many of the characteristics used by most authors to characterize totalitarianism, and we can conceive of a particularly stabilized system with all the characteristics of totalitarianism except widespread and all-pervasive terror."[91] There are cases, Linz maintains, where it is hard to determine whether the form and scale of coercive measures employed by regimes against their opposition result from the nature of the regime or from the personalities of their rulers. By the same line of reasoning, I have avoided distinguishing here between different types of home regimes on the basis of their employment of counterexile measures, especially since "the degree of control of exiles depends in part on the degree of paranoia and insecurity on the part of the controlling authorities."[92] I have concluded, however, that a systematic framework of typologies can be proposed to gauge the likelihood of a regime's using counterexile measures.

To provide such a systematic analysis, one must take into account the following interrelated variables: (1) the home regime's perception (objective, subjective, or self-serving) of the exiles' threat; (2) the regime's available options and skills for suppressing the exiles' threat through coercion; and (3) the regime's cost-benefit calculation of such coercive activities.

The home regime's perception of the exiles' threat is influenced by its own internal stability, its character; by the line it draws between insignificant and dangerous opposition; and the actual or perceived ability of the exiles to engender loyalty to their cause within the national community at home and abroad, and their ability to provoke international support.

The options a regime has for suppressing the exile opposition depend on where the exiles are and what kind of organization they have; whether the regime can isolate the exiles from potential supporters at home; what kind of direct or indirect relations the regime has with the exiles' host government, and its capacity to provoke the host state against the exiles; and what range of skills the regime can muster to implement violence and other antiexile sanctions abroad, as for example the ability to track down and dispose of its exile opponents through use of spies, agents provocateurs, kidnappers, and killers.

Finally, a home regime's cost-benefit calculation in employing counterexile measures abroad will be determined in accordance with that regime's vulnerability to outside criticism, its dependence on international support (economic, diplomatic, and military), and the effect or likely effect of antiexile measures abroad on the national community at home.

We can construct a range of classifications that anticipate the behavior of a home regime toward its political exiles. Such behavior is usually multidimensional. The following hypotheses can be drawn:

1. The more tolerant the home regime is toward its internal opposition, the less likely it is to employ extreme means against its opposition abroad.

2. The greater the ideological component in the exile-regime conflict, the more likely the regime is to use systematized, organized, sophisticated, broad measures to suppress exile opponents.

3. The more ambiguous the ideological component in the exile-regime conflict, the less likely the regime is to wage total war against its exile opponents.

4. The more personalized the home regime, and the more its rulers fear external attempts on their lives, the more likely the regime is to use extreme means to liquidate its exile rivals.

5. The more dependent the home regime is on international support, and the greater its vulnerability to outside criticism, the more likely it is to restrain its antiexile measures.

Conclusion

[E]xiles have always challenged conventional boundaries and limits.
—Randolph Starn, *Contrary Commonwealth*, 1982

The Moving Frontier of National Loyalty

In this study of exile political activity, I have examined:

1. Inter- and intra-exile organizational relations.
2. Exiles' attempts to mobilize their compatriots abroad (that is, in the diaspora).
3. Exiles' mobilization efforts inside their country—in particular, their relations with the internal opposition to the home regime.
4. Interaction between political exiles and the international community.
5. Home regimes' responses to the challenge that political exiles represent.

I have concentrated, for purposes of theory, on the activities of exile groups that try to gain power in the state at the expense of their native regime. Patterns of exile political behavior have also been identified and illustrated by studying exile groups seeking "self-determination" and "decolonization," as well as groups struggling to regain their country's independence from foreign occupation. The wide range of case studies used serves as a prism through which to view exile political activity as a whole. These stories, taken together, form a composite picture of political phenomena that illuminate the larger context of relations between governments and oppositions in the nation-state.

I have examined the dynamics of the conflict among these contestants for power as a process of building "loyalty" and "recognition." In this process each contestant tries to generate and sustain loyalists to his cause (empowerment) at the expense of the loyalty shown to others who aspire to power. Aspirants may be either a ruling government or nonruling contestants seeking power. Neither has absolute loyalty or absolute recognition. I have distinguished between "loyalty" and "recognition," one as a national and the other as an international manifestation of support, and have identified "national loyalty" as a political weapon to manipulate the attitudes and behavior of relevant constituencies. Contestants for power exploit national loyalty not only to maintain and broaden their constituency of loyalists, but also to discredit rivals. This examination of the struggle between political exiles and other power seekers, especially the home regime, has sought to enrich our understanding of the effectiveness, the elasticity, and the limits of national loyalty as a political device.

As we have seen, political exiles often find themselves in a uniquely difficult posture, because they are removed from the domestic political order from which they must draw their loyalists, and also because they are vulnerable to charges of disloyalty. An important part of the exiles' struggle is therefore to challenge the home regime's attempts to impose its own interpretation of national loyalty both at home and abroad. In Albert Hirschman's schema, the home regime maintains that "exit" from the national soil, especially when followed by "voice" against the existing authorities in the state, is an expression of national "disloyalty." Exiles contest this view, maintaining that their "exit" was not an alternative to internal "voice" (opposition) against the regime, but indeed a sine qua non for the exercise of "voice."

The home regime's exploitation of national loyalty as a political weapon, backed by its monopoly over the state's means of violence (a sign of commanding the loyalty of the armed forces), has frequently proved highly effective in undermining a regime's opposition abroad. Regimes, particularly those of an authoritarian character, may create a rupture between their domestic and external opponents. They tend to qualify the limited tolerance of their domestic opponents by restricting the latter's cooperation with exiles, whom they label as subjects of foreign manipulation and therefore nationally disloyal. Moreover, when the home regime deprives political exiles of citizenship, it undercuts exiles' mobilizing efforts by making them stateless, and pushes them to defend their claims to national loyalty. Home regimes frequently force exiles to calculate carefully the consequences of foreign alliances; in many cases the exiles hesitate to enter into such alliances, especially at times when notions of national loyalty are in dispute, as above all in time of war.

Once national loyalty is contested outside the nation-state borders, it is subject to the vagaries of the international arena. Some potential allies can enhance, and others impede, contestants' claims to be "authentic representatives of the national interest." When exiles work to generate international support for their cause among nations regarded by the home regime as allies, the exiles find themselves in a good position to challenge their home regime's interpretation of national loyalty. The home regime will be hard pressed to label exiles' cultivation of such foreign contacts as acts of treason.

The use of national loyalty for political ends beyond the state's territorial boundaries is an essential part of exiles' inter- and intra-organizational debates. It serves to justify their position and their tactics of struggle, and also to discredit other competing exile groups as "nonrepresentative." Examination of the struggle for the support of the national community abroad demonstrates even further how flexible is the concept of "national belonging," when used for political purposes. It enables us to arrive at a political understanding of a diaspora.

A home regime's distinction between insiders and outsiders as an indication of national loyalty or disloyalty serves the regime's political ends. But the regime's demarcation between "us" and "them" does not necessarily stop at the borders of the state. It alters with the regime's changing definition of the national interest and of the behavioral criteria it prescribes for national loyalty. Thus people who have left their country (for whatever reasons) to reside abroad are sometimes included in, and at other times excluded from, the regime's definition of the national community. The regime's interpretation of what is "nationally beneficial" or "nationally disloyal" behavior abroad fluctuates. Its attempt to manipulate "us" and "them" beyond the nation-state's frontiers aims to expand, within the national community abroad, its psychological and actual control over the distinction between national loyalty and treason. In so doing, the home regime seeks to deter members of the nation who reside abroad from aligning themselves with "disloyal" aspirants or the state's foreign enemies. Manipulation of the concept of disloyalty abroad is one of the reasons why people who flee their native country often refrain from attacking it abroad, despite hatred of the home regime.

In political science it is generally accepted as a methodological convention that theoretical concepts have to be empirically verifiable or falsifiable. But "legitimacy," one of the most popular concepts in political science and indeed in the social sciences in general, has lacked this empirical rigor and hence has been subject to ambiguity. Although there is an abundance of theoretical literature on legitimacy, Ekkart Zimmermann maintains that, "in terms of systematic empirical evidence, however, almost the reverse is true."[1] From the celebrated typologies of Max Weber to contemporary scholarship, students of legitimacy have failed to establish a clear-cut distinction between a "legitimate" and an "illegitimate" regime, especially in nondemocratic systems. The question of when a regime is legitimated has remained unresolved. Attempts at answers have usually been trapped in a vicious circle.[2] By adopting the approach that regimes are legitimate "to the extent that their citizens regard them as proper and deserving of support,"[3] social scientists have been unable to free their empirical investigations of the Weberian tautology: "every domination always entails some successful claim for legitimacy,"[4] or alternatively, "a ruler, regime or governmental process . . . that is not widely perceived as clothed in legitimacy is not able to function authoritatively."[5] As Adam Przeworsky correctly observed, Weber himself was not at ease with the empirical slipperiness of legitimacy.[6] According to Weber:

It is by no means true that every case of submissiveness to persons in positions of power is primarily (or even at all) oriented to this belief [in the authority's right to rule]. Loyalty may be hypocritically simulated by individuals or by whole groups on purely opportunistic grounds, or carried out in practice for reasons of material self-interest. Or people may submit from individual weakness and helplessness because there is no acceptable alternative.[7]

Moreover, Weber and other social scientists who have constructed theories of legitimacy around existing forms of government have paid little attention to the "degree of legitimacy" of nonruling aspirants.[8]

"Legitimacy," like "national loyalty," is a political (ideological/rhetorical) concept used by aspirants to power in the nation-state and by those in the national and international arenas who endorse their claims. Because of its ideological character, legitimacy has been misleading as an analytical device for understanding the dynamics of power in the state, especially issues of transition and maintenance of power. Because the concept of legitimacy suffers from a lack of empirical validity, it has failed to give an account of the actual processes by which power is gained, maintained, or lost. To guard against such conceptual abstraction, I have suggested "loyalty" and "recognition" as empirical measures for analyzing the power struggle in the nation-state, and as a potential means for circumventing the obscurity implicit in the concept of legitimacy.

The challenge of exile politics is to chart a successful course within the constellation of domestic and international forces. Therefore one needs to understand what constitutes success or failure. Success has an entirely different character when measured by the goals of exile politics, rather than by the exiles' ability to return home and seize power.

Success in exile is measured by an organizational ability to generate and maintain loyalty and recognition at the expense of the home regime. As we have observed, the degree of loyalty and recognition won by political exiles may vary dramatically over time, and its effectiveness is often ambiguous; exile leaders, loyal constituencies, the home regime, and outside observers may all see it differently. Evaluation of success or failure, therefore, requires caution. For, like evaluation of the effectiveness of other forms of opposition, "[r]eal success must be distinguished from symbolic reassurances, and short-term gains may perhaps be judged long-term losses,"[9] as we have seen in comparing the early international recognition of the exiled Russians and the Spanish Republicans, both of whom later succumbed to inertia and stagnation as their home regimes consolidated power.

Naturally, effective exile mobilization is only one factor in determining a victorious homecoming. Other developments, domestic and international, are generally more critical to the ultimate goal of attaining political power at home. Thus international pressure (political and economic) on the home regime, or the home state's defeat in war followed by temporary occupation, or civil war, a coup d'état, guerrilla warfare, the death of a dictator, or a peaceful transition toward democracy, as well as other shifts of loyalty and recognition, will all play a significant part. Exiles may benefit from such developments by a fortuitous turn of circumstances or by default, as illustrated in the dramatic homecoming of Constantine Karamanlis, Greece's exiled former premier, hailed as the savior of Greek democracy after the Junta's failure in Cyprus.[10] Another instance is the German SPD's successful return to its homeland and its reemergence as the major mass party of the German working class in the Federal Republic. The SPD's position was brought about by foreign occupation without its having had a hand in it at all.

Whether exiles will come to play a dominant role in and indeed become the future rulers of their society, or remain mere marginal actors, is also in many cases a result of accidents. Political exiles must be poised and ready to enjoy the potential benefits of events. Thus, despite the SPD's failure to create an internal resistance to Hitler and to undermine the Nazi regime from abroad, its exile politics can be regarded as successful. Anthony Glees notes that the SPD's "success in exile had more to do with sheer survival than whether the German people listened to the SPD's exhortations to overthrow their Fuehrer. . . . Exile was less about continuity or change than it was about staying in the business of politics."[11]

While one might argue that such dependency upon external factors reduces political exiles' actions to marginality, inconsequentiality, or total dependence on circumstance, many political exiles may in fact be significantly instrumental in initiating and advocating events. Classic examples of our time are the establishment of the Fourth Republic after de Gaulle's triumphant return to France; the activities of Khomeini and the exile opposition to the shah; the Acción Democrática struggle for democracy in Venezuela; and Perón's eighteen years of manipulation of the Argentine polity from abroad, which led to his victorious return. These examples and others in this study form a panorama of exile political activity that has animated much of recent history. The exiles' ontological status as a political opposition is thus integral in affecting the composition of many a nation-state in the twentieth century.

Notes

INTRODUCTION

1. 1 Kings 11–13.
2. Aristotle, *Politics* 1284b4.
3. For a discussion of ostracism in ancient Greece, see John V. A. Fine, *The Ancient Greeks: A Critical History* (Cambridge, Mass.: Harvard University Press, 1983), 239–40, 291–92.
4. Quentin Skinner, *The Foundation of Modern Political Thought*, vol. 1, *The Renaissance* (London: Cambridge University Press, 1978), 26.
5. On the place of exiles in medieval and Renaissance Italy, see the excellent study by Randolph Starn, *Contrary Commonwealth: The Theme of Exile in Medieval and Renaissance Italy* (Berkeley: University of California Press, 1982).
6. For the complete story of the Marian exiles, see Christina H. Garrett, *The Marian Exiles: A Study in the Origins of Elizabethan Puritanism* (Cambridge: Cambridge University Press, 1938).
7. Michael Walzer, *The Revolution of the Saints: A Study in the Origins of Radical Politics* (Cambridge, Mass.: Harvard University Press, 1965), 113.
8. Gianfranco Poggi, *The Development of the Modern State: A Sociological Introduction* (Stanford: Stanford University Press, 1978), 97.
9. Margery Weiner, *The French Exiles, 1789–1815* (London: John Murray, 1960), 28.
10. Ibid., 43–44.
11. James H. Billington, *Fire in the Minds of Men: Origins of the Revolutionary Faith* (New York: Basic Books, 1980), 149.
12. Hugh Thomas, *Cuba: The Pursuit of Freedom* (New York: Harper & Row, 1971), 293–309.
13. Nicholas P. Cusher, *Spain in the Philippines: From Conquest to Revolution* (Quezon City: Institute of Philippine Culture, 1971), 222–27.
14. Martin A. Miller, *The Russian Revolutionary Emigres, 1825–1870* (Baltimore: Johns Hopkins University Press, 1986), 12–15.
15. Ibid., 16.
16. Benedict Anderson, *Imagined Communities: Reflections on the Origin and Spread of Nationalism* (London: Verso, 1983), 145.
17. See John A. Marcum, "The Exile Condition and Revolutionary Effective-

ness: Southern African Liberation Movements," in Christian P. Potholm and Richard Dale, eds., *Southern Africa in Perspective* (New York: Free Press, 1972), 262–75.

18. See Donald L. Horowitz, *Ethnic Groups in Conflict* (Berkeley: University of California Press, 1985), 4–5.

19. Ernest Gellner, *Nations and Nationalism* (Ithaca: Cornell University Press, 1983), 1.

20. Among the studies that take a comparative and more theoretical approach to the study of exile politics, those especially worth noting are the work of Paul H. Lewis, on the Febrerista Party of Paraguay, Alicja Iwańska's essay on the Spanish and Polish governments-in-exile, Robert D. Tomasek's study on exile invasions in the Caribbean, and John A. Marcum's article on the activities of Southern African exile liberation movements. These works played an important role in shaping the direction of my thoughts. See Paul H. Lewis, *The Politics of Exile: Paraguay's Febrerista Party* (Chapel Hill: University of North Carolina Press, 1968); Alicja Iwańska, *Exiled Governments: Spanish and Polish* (Cambridge, Mass.: Schenkman Publishing Company, 1981); Robert D. Tomasek, "Caribbean Exile Invasions: A Special Regional Type of Conflict," *Orbis* 17 (1974): 1354–1938; John A. Marcum, "The Exile Condition and Revolutionary Effectiveness," 262–75.

21. Two exceptions would be George Fischer's work on the opposition to Stalin during World War II and Charles Ameringer's book on the opposition to the dictatorships in the Caribbean. See George Fischer, *Soviet Opposition to Stalin: A Case Study in World War II* (Cambridge, Mass.: Harvard University Press, 1952); and Charles D. Ameringer, *The Democratic Left in Exiles: The Antidictatorial Struggle in the Caribbean, 1945–1959* (Coral Gables, Fla.: University of Miami Press, 1974).

22. Henry P. Fairchild, ed., *Immigrant Backgrounds* (New York: Wiley, 1927).

23. See William Petersen, "A General Typology of Migration," *American Sociological Review* 25 (June 1958): 256–66; Jacob Eichenbaum, "A Matrix of Human Movement," *International Migration Review* 13 (1975): 21–41; Egon F. Kunz, "The Refugee in Flight: Kinetic Models and Forms of Displacement," *International Migration Review* 7 (1973): 125–46; Egon F. Kunz, "Part II: The Analytic Framework Exile and Resettlement: Refugee Theory," *International Migration Review* 15 (1981): 42–51.

24. Petersen, "A General Typology of Migration," 258.

25. Art Hansen and Anthony Oliver-Smith, eds., *Involuntary Migration and Resettlement: The Problems and Responses of Dislocated People* (Boulder, Colo.: Westview Press, 1982), preface.

26. Kunz, "The Refugee in Flight," 130–31.

27. Petersen, "A General Typology of Migration," 261.

28. Kunz, "The Refugee in Flight," 135.

29. Barry N. Stein, "The Refugee Experience: Defining the Parameters of a Field of Study," *International Migration Review* 15 (1981): 322.

30. Eugene F. Provenzo, Jr., and Concepción Garcia, "Exiled Teachers and the Cuban Revolution," *Cuban Studies* 13 (1983): 2.
31. Stein, "The Refugee Experience," 322.
32. Lewis A. Coser, *Refugee Scholars in America: Their Impact and Their Experiences* (New Haven: Yale University Press, 1984), 1.
33. Ibid., 6.
34. Hans Speier, *Social Order and the Risks of War: Papers in Political Sociology* (New York: G. W. Stewart, 1952), 92.
35. Kunz, "Part II: The Analytic Framework," 48.
36. See Tom Rees, "The United Kingdom: Migration Policies of an Empire," in Daniel Kubát, ed., *The Politics of Migration Policies: The First World in the 1970s* (New York: Center for Migration Studies, 1979), 69–91.
37. C. A. Smith, "Spain's Forgotten Men Disclose the Story of Their Exile," *Labour: The TUC Magazine*, revised series, May 1951, 301–302.
38. Lewis J. Edinger, *German Exile Politics: The Social Democratic Executive Committee in the Nazi Era* (Berkeley: University of California Press, 1956), vii.
39. Kunz, "The Refugee in Flight," 133.
40. Edward W. Said, "The Mind of Winter: Reflections on Life in Exile," *Harper's*, September 1984, 49–56.
41. Peter I. Rose, "Thoughts about Refugees and Descendants of Theseus," *International Migration Review* 15 (1981): 9.
42. Kunz, "Part II: The Analytic Framework," 44.
43. Coser, *Refugee Scholars in America*, 244.
44. Ibid., 189–91.
45. Stein, "The Refugee Experience," 326.
46. J. Donald Cohon, Jr., "Psychological Adaptation and Dysfunction among Refugees," *International Migration Review* 15 (1981): 25–63.
47. Kunz, "Part II: The Analytic Framework," 43.
48. Ibid., 45.
49. Cited in Guy S. Goodwin-Gill, *The Refugee in International Law* (Oxford: Clarendon Press, 1983), 5–6.
50. Ibid., 17–18.   51. Ibid., 18.
52. Göran Melander, "Refugee and International Cooperation," *International Migration Review* 15 (1981): 36.
53. Gilbert Jaeger, "Refugee Asylum Policy and Legislative Developments," *International Migration Review* 15 (1981): 53.
54. Starn, *Contrary Commonwealth*, 159.
55. Goodwin-Gill, *The Refugee in International Law*, 19.
56. Herbert C. Kelman, "A Social-Psychological Model of Political Legitimacy and Its Relevance to Black and White Student Protest Movements," *Psychiatry* 33 (1970): 231.
57. Starn, *Contrary Commonwealth*, 6–11.
58. Paul Tabori, *The Anatomy of Exile: A Semantic and Historical Study* (London: Harrap, 1972), 26.
59. Ibid., 37.   60. Ibid., 37–38.

61. Miller, *The Russian Revolutionary Emigres*, 6–8.
62. The distinction between reform and revolutionary organizations is borrowed from the literature on social movements. See Robert R. Evans, ed., *Social Movements: A Reader and Source Book* (Chicago: Rand McNally & Co., 1973).
63. See Jack Calhoun, "The Exiles' Role in War Resistance," *Monthly Review* 30 (March 1979): 27–42.
64. See Robert A. Dahl, "Patterns of Opposition," in Robert A. Dahl, ed., *Political Opposition in Western Democracies* (New Haven: Yale University Press, 1966), 332–47.
65. *New York Times*, 14 May 1986.

CHAPTER ONE: *Who Represents the Nation's Will?*

1. Hereafter I will distinguish between "nonloyal" and "antiloyal" as behavioral descriptions and "disloyal" as a value judgment.
2. Harold S. Guetzkow, *Multiple Loyalties: Theoretical Approach to a Problem in International Organization* (Princeton: The Center for Research on World Political Institution, Woodrow Wilson School of Public and International Affairs, Princeton University Press, 1955), 30.
3. Cited in Ekkart Zimmermann, *Political Violence, Crises, and Revolutions: Theories and Research* (Boston: G. K. Hall & Co., 1983), 315.
4. Morton Grodzins, *The Loyal and the Disloyal: Social Boundaries of Patriotism and Treason* (Chicago: University of Chicago Press, 1956), 25.
5. Harold D. Lasswell and Abraham Kaplan, *Power and Society: A Framework of Political Inquiry* (New Haven: Yale University Press, 1950), 267.
6. Ernest Gellner, *Nations and Nationalism* (Ithaca: Cornell University Press, 1983), 1.
7. The assumptions that undergird the concept of "national interest" are "(1) there exists an objectively determinable collective interest which all individual members within a given national society share equally, and (2) this collective interest transcends any interest that a particular subset of those individuals may share with individuals in other national societies." See J. Martin Rochester, "The 'National Interest' and Contemporary World Politics," *The Review of Politics* 40 (1978): 79.
8. Juan J. Linz and Alfred Stepan, eds., *The Breakdown of Democratic Regimes* (Baltimore: Johns Hopkins University Press, 1978), 61.
9. Albert O. Hirschman, *Exit, Voice, and Loyalty: Responses to Decline in Firms, Organizations, and States* (Cambridge, Mass.: Harvard University Press, 1970), 96.
10. The problem of subjectivity inherent in the concept of national interest has bewildered critics who sought to use it as an analytic tool. Arnold Wolfers writes: "When political formulas such as 'national interest' or 'national security' gain popularity they need to be scrutinized with particular care. They may not mean the same thing to different people. They may not have

any precise meaning at all. Thus, while appearing to offer guidance and a basis for broad consensus, they may be permitting everyone to label whatever policy he favors with an attractive and possibly deceptive name." Cited in Rochester, ibid., 78.

11. George K. Young, *Who is My Liege: A Study of Loyalty and Betrayal in Our Time* (London: Gentry Books, 1972), 25.

12. Samuel P. Huntington, *Political Order in Changing Societies* (New Haven: Yale University Press, 1968), 461.

13. Michael A. Ledeen, *Universal Fascism: The Theory and Practice of the Fascist International, 1928–1936* (New York: Howard Pertig, 1972), 54.

14. See Anthony D. Smith, *Nationalism in the Twentieth Century* (New York: New York University Press, 1979), 13.

15. Cited in Grodzins, *The Loyal and the Disloyal*, 63.

16. Shaul Bakhash, *The Reign of the Ayatollahs: Iran and the Islamic Revolution* (New York: Basic Books, 1984), 40.

17. Grodzins, *The Loyal and the Disloyal*, 54.

18. John H. Schaar, "Loyalty," in David L. Sills, ed., *International Encyclopedia of the Social Sciences*, vol. 9 (New York: Macmillan and Free Press, 1968), 484.

19. Paul H. Lewis, *The Politics of Exile: Paraguay's Febrerista Party* (Chapel Hill: University of North Carolina Press, 1968), 191.

20. Andrew Graham-Yooll, *A Matter of Fear: Portrait of an Argentinian Exile* (Westport, Conn.: Lawrence Hill & Co., 1981), 6–7.

21. Lewis J. Edinger, *German Exile Politics: The Social Democratic Executive Committee in the Nazi Era* (Berkeley: University of California Press, 1956), viii.

22. Hirschman, *Exit, Voice, and Loyalty*, 60.

23. Ibid., 78.   24. Ibid.   25. Ibid., 82.

26. A. H. Birch, "Economic Models in Political Science: The Case of 'Exit, Voice, and Loyalty,' " *British Journal of Political Science* 5 (1975): 79; also Brian Barry, "Review Article: 'Exit, Voice, and Loyalty,' " *British Journal of Political Science* 4 (1974): 92.

27. Alan Dowty, *Closed Borders: The Contemporary Assault on Freedom of Movement* (New Haven: Yale University Press, 1987), 4.

28. John Somerville, "Patriotism and War," *Ethics* 91 (July 1981): 568.

29. Roger Neville Williams, *The New Exiles: American War Resisters in Canada* (New York: Liveright Publishers, 1971), xi–xii.

30. Juan J. Linz, "Opposition to and under an Authoritarian Regime: The Case of Spain," in Robert A. Dahl, ed., *Regimes and Oppositions* (New Haven: Yale University Press, 1973), 237.

31. Theodore Draper, *Castro's Revolution: Myths and Realities* (Fredrick A. Praeger Publisher, 1962), 92.

32. In what may seem a contradiction in his model, Hirschman uses as an example of "loyal behavior" the story of a public official who resigns his public post in order to be free to criticize from outside the policies of a system he perceives as antithetical to the public good: "[The] exit will now mean

to resign under protest and, in general, to denounce and fight the organization from without instead of working for change from within. In other words, the alternative is now not so much between voice and exit as between voice from within and voice from without (after exit)" (104). The possibility of raising "voice" from without, which destroys the exit/voice dichotomy, suggests that Hirschman's concept of exit can be interpreted as a sequence of transitions within the system itself, in Stein Rokkan's term, "part-exits." See Stein Rokkan, "Entries, Voices, Exits: Toward a Possible Generalization of the Hirschman's Model," *Social Science Information* 13 (1974): 40.

CHAPTER TWO: *Exile Organizations*

1. "Targets of mobilization" are defined by Gamson as "those individuals or groups whose resources and energy the group seeks in carrying out its efforts at change." See William A. Gamson, *The Strategy of Social Protest* (Homewood, Ill.: Dorsey Press, 1975), 14–15.

2. Alicja Iwańska, *Exiled Governments: Spanish and Polish* (Cambridge, Mass.: Schenkman Publishing Co., 1981), 59–103.

3. See Nicholas Shakespeare, *The Men Who Would Be King: A Look at Royalty in Exile* (London: Sidgwick & Jackson, 1984).

4. William Chapin Huntington, *The Homesick Million: Russia-out-of-Russia* (Boston: Stratford Co., 1933), 181.

5. Howard C. Payne and Henry Grosshans, "The Exiled Revolutionaries and the French Political Police in the 1850s," *American Historical Review* 68 (July 1963): 962.

6. Peter Wyden, *Bay of Pigs: The Untold Story* (New York: Touchstone Books, 1979), 119.

7. See Theodore Draper, *Castro's Revolution: Myths and Realities* (New York: Fredrick A. Praeger Publisher, 1962), 59–103.

8. Iwańska, *Exiled Governments*, 59–60.

9. Eva Hoffman, "The Government of Memory," *Atlantic Monthly*, February, 1986, 20.

10. Patricia W. Fagen, *Exiles and Citizens: Spanish Republicans in Mexico* (Austin: University of Texas Press, 1973), 35.

11. Hans Habe, "Washington, Mecca of Lost Nations," *American Mercury*, January–June 1943, 407–15.

12. Charles F. Delzell, *Mussolini's Enemies: The Italian Anti-Fascist Resistance* (Princeton: Princeton University Press, 1961), 62.

13. See John D. Martz, "Latin America's Exile Politics," *Latin American Research Review* 10 (1975): 193–201; also Manuel Antonio Garretón, "The Political Processes in an Authoritarian Regime: The Dynamics of Institutionalization and Opposition in Chile, 1973–1980," in J. Samuel Valenzuela and Arturo Valenzuela, eds., *Military Rule in Chile: Dictatorship and Oppositions* (Baltimore: Johns Hopkins University Press, 1986), 166–71.

14. Huntington, *The Homesick Million*, 238–39.

15. See Fagen, *Exiles and Citizens*, 106–107.

16. Egon F. Kunz, "Part II: The Analytic Framework Exile and Resettlement: Refugee Theory," *International Migration Review* 15 (1981): 46.
17. Shakespeare, *The Men Who Would Be King*, xvii.
18. Arturo Valenzuela and J. Samuel Valenzuela, "Party Oppositions under the Chilean Regime," in Valenzuela and Valenzuela, eds., *Military Rule in Chile*, 210–11.
19. Hoffman, "The Government of Memory," 22.
20. Paul H. Lewis, *The Politics of Exile: Paraguay's Febrerista Party* (Chapel Hill: University of North Carolina Press, 1968), 106–13.
21. Franz Michael, "Survival of a Culture: Tibetan Refugees in India," *Asian Survey* 25 (July 1985): 738, 744.
22. Juan J. Linz, "Time and Regime Change," unpublished essay, Yale University, 1986, 8. For an Italian version see "Il fattore tempo nei mutamenti di regime," *Teoria Politica* 2 (1986): 3–47.
23. Bertram D. Wolfe, *Three Who Made a Revolution: A Biographical History*, 3rd ed. (New York: Dial Press, 1961), 481.
24. Anthony Glees, *Exile Politics during the Second World War: The German Social Democrats in Britain* (Oxford: Clarendon Press, 1982), 226–47. Also see Werner Link, "German Political Refugees in the United States During the Second World War," in Anthony Nicholls and Erich Matthias, eds., *German Democracy and the Triumph of Hitler* (London: George Allen and Unwin, 1971), 246–260.
25. Tom Lodge, "State of Exile: The African National Congress of South Africa, 1976–86," *Third World Quarterly* 9 (January 1987): 26–27.
26. Ibid.
27. Robert J. Alexander, *The Tragedy of Chile* (Westport, Conn.: Greenwood Press, 1978), 359.
28. J. W. Brugel, review of *Die Deutschen Sozialistischen Exilgruppen in Grossbritannien, 1940–1945*, by Werner Röder, *International Affairs* 46 (1970): 326.
29. Nadia Tongour, "Diplomacy in Exile: Russian Emigrés in Paris, 1918–1925," Ph.D. diss., Stanford University, 1979, 2.
30. See Charles D. Ameringer, *The Democratic Left in Exile: The Antidictatorial Struggle in the Caribbean, 1945–1959* (Coral Gables, Fla.: University of Miami Press, 1974), 194.
31. Max Nomad, "Underground Europe," *Current History*, February 1938, 38.
32. Delzell, *Mussolini's Enemies*, 63.
33. Ameringer, *The Democratic Left in Exile*, 23–32.
34. Cited in Silvia Pedraza-Bailey, *Political and Economic Migrants in America: Cubans and Mexicans* (Austin: University of Texas Press, 1985), 21–23.

CHAPTER THREE: *The Politics of Schism*

1. For further discussion of exile splinters, see Paul H. Lewis, *The Politics of Exile: Paraguay's Febrerista Party* (Chapel Hill: University of North Carolina Press, 1968), xiv–xv, 188–89.

2. Stanley Meisler, "Sharply Divided Factions: Thousands of Iran Exiles Wait, Hope, Plot in Paris," *Los Angeles Times*, 5 August 1984.

3. James Q. Wilson, *Political Organizations* (New York: Basic Books, 1973), 10.

4. Ibid., 259.

5. Bertram D. Wolfe, *Three Who Made a Revolution: A Biographical History*, 3rd ed. (New York: Dial Press, 1961), 518.

6. Louis Fischer, *The Life of Lenin* (New York: Harper & Row, 1964), 39.

7. Cited in Wolfe, *Three Who Made a Revolution*, 468.

8. Alicja Iwańska, *Exiled Governments: Spanish and Polish* (Cambridge, Mass.: Schenkman Publishing Co., 1981), 36–38.

9. Robert H. Johnston, "The Great Patriotic War and the Russian Exiles in France," *Russian Review* 35 (1976): 309.

10. "Exiles from Eastern Europe," editorial, *The Economist*, 22 November 1952, 551–52.

11. Louis Stein, *Beyond Death and Exile: The Spanish Republicans in France, 1939–1955* (Cambridge, Mass.: Harvard University Press, 1979), 181–99.

12. Wilson, *Political Organizations*, 270.

13. Charles D. Ameringer, *The Democratic Left in Exile: The Antidictatorial Struggle in the Caribbean, 1945–1959* (Coral Gables, Fla.: University of Miami Press, 1974), 166.

14. Charles F. Delzell, "The Italian Anti-Fascist Emigration, 1922–1943," *Journal of Central Europe Affairs* 12 (April 1952): 26–35.

15. This term is borrowed from Martin Seliger, who distinguishes between fundamental principles, which determine the ultimate goals of political organizations, and "operative ideology," which serves to justify the policies actually devised or executed by a group. Martin Seliger, *Ideology and Politics* (London: George Allen & Unwin, 1976), 175.

16. Lewis, *The Politics of Exiles*, 188.

17. "Italy Against Fascism," in *The Voice of Freedom*, pamphlet (New York: Quaderni Italiani, n.d.), 6.

18. See Es'kia Mphahlclc, "Africa in Exile," *Daedalus* 111 (Spring 1982): 33.

19. Lewis, *The Politics of Exile*, 189.

20. Patricia W. Fagen, *Exiles and Citizens: Spanish Republicans in Mexico* (Austin: University of Texas Press, 1973), 132.

21. St. J. Paprocki, "Political Organization of the Ukrainian Exiles after the Second World War," *Eastern Quarterly* (January/April 1952): 41–50.

22. Theodore Draper, *Castro's Revolution: Myths and Realities* (New York: Fredrick A. Praeger Publisher, 1962), 132.

23. John A. Marcum, "The Exile Condition and Revolutionary Effectiveness: Southern African Liberation Movements," in Christian P. Potholm and Richard Dale, eds., *Southern Africa in Perspective* (New York: Free Press, 1972), 267.

24. Cited in Warren Rogers, Jr., *The Floating Revolution* (New York: McGraw-Hill, 1962), 209. For two conflicting interpretations of the Santa Maria incident, see Henrique Galvão, *My Crusade for Portugal* (London: Weidenfeld

& Nicolson, 1961) and *The Memoirs of General Delgado* (London: Cassell, 1964), 185–99.

25. António de Figueiredo, a Portuguese anti-Fascist, argued that the exiles' hijacking of the Santa Maria had a critical impact on the eruption of the revolt in Angola in February 1961. See Tom Gallagher, *Portugal: A Twentieth-Century Interpretation* (Manchester: Manchester University Press, 1983), 150.

26. Rogers, *The Floating Revolution*, 209.

27. Cited in John A. Marcum, *The Angolan Revolution* vol. 2, *Exile Politics and Guerrilla Warfare (1962–1976)* (Cambridge, Mass.: MIT Press, 1978), 12.

28. Ibid., 180.

29. Gen. Baron Peter N. Wrangel, *Always With Honour* (New York: Robert Speller & Sons, 1957), 347.

CHAPTER FOUR: *Political Exiles and the Diaspora*

1. Francis Honti, "Atlantic Defence and Our Standpoint," *Eastern Quarterly* (July 1951): 10.

2. Philip V. Cannistraro and Gianfausto Rosoli, "Fascist Emigration Policy in the 1920s: An Interpretive Framework," *International Migration Review* 13 (1979): 686–87.

3. Cited in Gianfranco Cresciani, *Fascism, Anti-Fascism and Italians in Australia: 1922–1945* (Canberra: Australian National University Press, 1980), 100.

4. Ronald C. Newton, "Indifferent Sanctuary: German-Speaking Refugees and Exiles in Argentina, 1933–1945," *Journal of Interamerican Studies and World Affairs* 24 (November 1982): 395–420.

5. See Michael Parks, "Peking vs. Taiwan: Chinese—2 Sides Tug at Old Roots," *Los Angeles Times*, 15 March 1984.

6. In Iwańska's classification, "the term 'diaspora' written with capital 'D' may stand for all actual and potential members" in the exile organization. The word diaspora with minuscule "d" is used to describe all national members abroad who are "non-active" and "non-proved." See Alicja Iwańska, *Exiled Governments: Spanish and Polish* (Cambridge, Mass.: Schenkman Publishing Co., 1981), 43–44.

7. See Steve Psinakis, *Two "Terrorists" Meet* (San Francisco: Alchemy Books, 1981), 27, 240–44; for the Marcoses' campaign in Filipino diaspora see also Fred Poole and Max Vanzi, "Hounding Philippine Exiles: Marcos's Secret War in America," *The Nation*, 12 May 1984, 577–79.

8. See Tolchin Martin, "High Profile for South Korean 'Embassy in Exile,'" *New York Times*, 10 October 1986.

9. Lee Shin-Bom, "South Korea: Dissent from Abroad," *Third World Quarterly* 9 (January 1987): 130–47.

10. Martin A. Miller, *The Russian Revolutionary Emigres, 1825–1870* (Baltimore: Johns Hopkins University Press, 1986), 112–15.

11. Ibid., 202. Also see Alfred Erich Senn, *The Russian Revolution in Switzerland, 1914–1917* (Madison: University of Wisconsin Press, 1971), 3–8.
12. Seymour M. Lipset and Philip G. Altbach, eds., *Students in Revolt* (Boston: Houghton Mifflin, 1969), xv–xxiv.
13. Houchang E. Chehabi, "Modernist Shi'ism and Politics: The Liberation Movement of Iran," Ph.D. diss., Yale University, 1986, vol. 1, 369–78.
14. Shaul Bakhash, *The Reign of the Ayatollahs: Iran and the Islamic Revolution* (New York: Basic Books, 1984), 40.
15. Ibid.   16. Ibid.
17. See Silvia Pedraza-Bailey, *Political and Economic Migrants in America: Cubans and Mexicans* (Austin: University of Texas Press, 1985), 148–49.
18. See Alan Angell and Susan Carstairs, "The Exile Question in Chilean Politics," *Third World Quarterly* 9 (January 1987); 155–56; Shirley Christian, "Most Chilean Exiles Still Keeping Their Distance," *New York Times*, 4 May 1986; Malcolm Coad, "Gen. Pinochet Says Exiles Can Return," *Washington Post*, 1 January 1987.
19. Alan Dowty, *Closed Borders: The Contemporary Assault on Freedom of Movement* (New Haven: Yale University Press, 1987), 13.
20. Editorial, "The Exiles: A Clutch of Feverish Factions . . . And A Coolly Neutral Monarch," *Newsweek*, 19 January 1970, 36–37.
21. John P. Fox, "Nazi Germany and German Emigration to Great Britain," in Gerhard Hirschfeld, ed., *Exile in Great Britain: Refugees from Hitler's Germany* (Atlantic Highlands, N.J.: Humanities Press, 1984), 30.
22. Pedraza-Bailey, *Political and Economic Migrants in America*, 18–29.
23. P. A. M. Nikolaieff, "Russia beyond the Border," *The Independent* (Boston), 9 July 1927, 40.
24. Daniel Katz and Robert L. Kahn, *The Social Psychology of Organizations*, 2nd ed. (New York: John Wiley & Sons, 1978), 284.
25. James Q. Wilson, *Political Organizations* (New York: Basic Books, 1973), 32.
26. See F. E. Oppenheimer, "Governments and Authorities in Exile," *American Journal of International Law* 36 (1942), 584.
27. On the activity of Omega 7 see Joan Didion, *Miami* (New York: Pocket Books, 1987), 99–115; also Henry W. Degenhardt, *Political Dissent: An International Guide to Dissident, Extra-Parliamentary, Guerilla and Illegal Political Movements* (London: Longman, 1983), 349–50.
28. Aristide R. Zolberg, Astri Suhrke, and Sergio Aguayo, "International Factors in the Formation of Refugee Movements," *International Migration Review* 20 (1986), 165–66.
29. Ibid.
30. Patricia W. Fagen, *Exiles and Citizens: Spanish Republicans in Mexico* (Austin: University of Texas Press, 1973), 106–107.
31. Brian Lapping, "Unromantic Exiles," *New Society*, 24 July 1965, 121–22.
32. Gen. Baron Peter N. Wrangel, *Always With Honour* (New York: Robert Speller & Sons, 1957), 344.
33. The National Committee for a Free Europe, Inc., "Political Trends among

Russian Exiles," in George Fischer, ed., *Russian Emigré Politics*, limited ed. (New York: Free Russia Fund, 1951), 63.

34. Robert D. Tomasek, "Caribbean Exile Invasions: A Special Regional Type of Conflict," *Orbis* 17 (1974): 1361.

35. Morton Grodzins, *The Loyal and the Disloyal: Social Boundaries of Patriotism and Treason* (Chicago: University of Chicago Press, 1956), 61.

36. Charles D. Ameringer, *The Democratic Left in Exile: The Antidictatorial Struggle in the Caribbean, 1945–1959* (Coral Gables, Fla.: University of Miami Press, 1974), 180.

37. See *Iran Liberation*, a publication of the Union of Moslem Iranian Students Societies outside Iran, supporters of the People's MOJAHEDIN Organisation of Iran, 13 July 1984.

38. Paul H. Lewis, *The Politics of Exile: Paraguay's Febrerista Party* (Chapel Hill: University of North Carolina Press, 1968), 196.

39. William Chapin Huntington, *The Homesick Million: Russia-out-of-Russia* (Boston: Stratford Company, 1933), 175–76.

40. Grodzins, *The Loyal and the Disloyal*, 155–56.

41. See Iwańska, *Exiled Governments*, 103–107.

42. Ryszard Wraga, "Russian Emigration after Thirty Years' Exile," in George Fischer, ed., *Russian Emigré Politics*, 23.

43. Samuel Cahan, "Russia's Former Ruling Class at Home and in Exile," *Current History*, November 1927, 195.

44. Robert C. Williams, *Culture in Exile: Russian Emigrés in Germany, 1881–1941* (Ithaca: Cornell University Press, 1972), 235–36.

45. *New York Times*, 3 March 1927.

46. Ibid.   47. Ibid.

48. Huntington, *The Homesick Million*, 180.

49. Ibid.

50. See Boleslaw Szczesniak, ed. and trans., *The Russian Revolution and Religion, 1917–1925* (Notre Dame: University of Notre Dame Press, 1959), 12.

51. See Williams, *Culture in Exile*, 118, 202.

52. Ibid.

53. The Council of Russian Ambassadors was founded in Paris at the end of 1917 by the ambassadors of the former Russian Provisional Government in France, Italy, Great Britain, and the United States, "to defend Russia's national interests and gain for itself allied acknowledgment of its role as Russia's official proxy until the now-defunct Provisional Government was resurrected or replaced by some other non-Bolshevik regime." To achieve its goals, the Council had to satisfy the leftist tendencies prevailing in France. The French government held the key to blocking Western recognition of the Bolshevik regime. Rightist zealotry would only have offended the French desire to see a "unified and democratic regime" in Russia. See Nadia Tongour, "Diplomacy in Exile: Russian Emigrés in Paris, 1918–1925," Ph.D. diss., Stanford University, 1979, Introduction.

54. Cyril Vladimirovich, Grand Duke of Russia, *My Life in Russia's Service—Then and Now* (London: Selwyn & Blount, 1939), 246–48.

55. Nicholas's actual contribution to the Russian war effort was controversial among the Russians in exile. His adversaries regarded him as a "crackpot," while his exile followers called him a "military idol of pre-Soviet Russia." An editorial in the *New York Times* summarized the debate as follows: "It is a fashion to call Grand Duke Nicholas a great soldier, but while he was a first-class fighting man he was victor on few fields." *New York Times*, 8 January 1929.
56. *New York Times*, 11 October 1925, sec. 2, p. 2.
57. John J. Stephan, *The Russian Fascists: Tragedy and Farce in Exile, 1925–1945* (New York: Harper & Row, 1978), 11.
58. For the complete study of Cyril's life, see Princess Marthe Bibesco, "The Shadow Emperor of All the Russias," *Philadelphia Saturday Evening Post*, 25 May 1929, 46–70.
59. Stephan, *The Russian Fascists*, 12.
60. See John D. Bergamini, *The Tragic Dynasty: A History of the Romanovs* (New York: G. P. Putnam's Sons, 1969), 465. Also see Paul Bolygin, *The Murder of the Romanovs* (London: Hutchinson & Co., 1935), 88–89.
61. Gen. Baron Peter N. Wrangel, *Always With Honour* (New York: Robert Speller & Sons, 1957), 346.
62. Dimitry V. Lehovich, *White Against Red: The Life of General Anton Denkin* (New York: W. W. Norton & Co., 1974), 423.
63. *New York Times*, 15 April 1925.
64. "The Russian Future as Nicholas Sees It," *New York Times*, editorial, 31 May 1925, sec. 2, p. 1.
65. Alfred Knox, "Grand Duke Nicholas," *The Slavonic and East European Review* 7 (June 1928–March 1929): 539.
66. *New York Times*, 7 April 1926.
67. Ibid.
68. "Personal Glimpses—A Grand Duke Whose Soldiers Loved Him," *Literary Digest*, editorial, 2 February, 1929, 39–42.
69. One of the reasons for Cyril's unpopularity among the monarchists in exile was his affiliation with Colonel Balasheff, whom many exiles distrusted for having entered the service of the Bolsheviks after the abdication of Nicholas II. Balasheff appeared in Paris in 1923 and argued that he had deserted the Bolshevik cause to devote himself to the restoration of the monarchy. Although many Russians insisted that he was a Bolshevik agent, Cyril made Balasheff one of his confidants and advisers. See *New York Times*, 2 November 1924.
70. Marie, Grand Duchess of Russia, *A Princess in Exile* (New York: Viking Press, 1932), 237–38.
71. Cited in Fredrick Cunliffe-Owen, "Not All Plain Sailing for Cyril," *New York Times*, 2 November 1924.
72. Ibid.
73. *New York Times*, 25 August 1925.
74. *New York Times*, 2 November 1924.
75. Stephan, *The Russian Fascists*, 13.

76. Gleb Botkin, "The Czar of Shadowland," *North American Review,* May 1930, 537.

77. *New York Times,* 5 January 1925, p. 25; see also Williams, *Culture in Exile,* 215.

78. Cyril, *My Life in Russia's Service,* 248.

79. *New York Times,* 25 August 1925.

80. Charles Sarolea, "The Case for the Russian Monarchists," *The Outlook,* 10 June 1925, 217.

81. Ibid.

82. "Personal Glimpses," *Literary Digest,* 2 February 1929, 40.

83. *New York Times,* 11 December 1924.

84. *New York Times,* 3 May 1925, sec. 2.

85. Ibid.

86. The letter of appointment read as follows: "Monseigneur: The Russian Congress, which unites all the patriots aspiring to the re-establishment of the Russian nation, who come from all over the world, acclaims in the person of your Imperial Highness the foreordained representative of the nationalist ideas as well as the glorious supreme chief of the army and defender of the fatherland since the days of our calvary.

   "The Congress is unanimous in sharing the patriotic hope of the masses within and without Russia. It expresses its full confidence in your wisdom as a statesman and your valor as supreme military chief. The Congress is firmly convinced that upon the issuance of your appeal all Russians without exception will take up unhesitatingly the glorious task of liberating the fatherland. May the most High sustain you in supreme labor of resurrecting the fatherland." *New York Times,* 7 April 1926.

87. Ibid.

88. *New York Times,* 12 April 1926.

89. *New York Times,* 10 April 1926.

90. *New York Times,* 12 April 1926.

91. Cited in *Literary Digest,* 2 February 1929, 39.

92. Lehovich, *White Against Red,* 429.

93. Pierre Van Paassen, "Anti-Soviet Concentration in Paris," *The Nation,* 2 December 1931, 602–603.

94. Ibid.

95. Louis Stein, *Beyond Death and Exile: The Spanish Republicans in France, 1939–1955* (Cambridge, Mass.: Harvard University Press, 1979), 234–63.

96. Cited in ibid., 192.

97. Hugh Thomas, *The Spanish Civil War* (New York: Harper & Row, 1965), 770–71.

98. Vincent Sheean, "Spain: The Aftermath of Defeat," *New Republic,* 6 September 1939, 126–27.

99. Lois E. Smith, *Mexico and the Spanish Republicans* (Berkeley: University of California Press, 1955), 199.

100. Isabel de Palencia, *Smouldering Freedom: The Story of the Spanish Republicans in Mexico* (New York: Longmans, Green and Co., 1945), 230.

101. Fagen, *Exiles and Citizens*, 108.
102. Juan Negrín, "Spain's Hour Is Near," *The Nation*, 16 August 1941, 139.
103. Stein, *Beyond Death and Exile*, 88.
104. Fagen, *Exiles and Citizens*, 107.
105. Ibid., 110.
106. Negrín, "Spain's Hour Is Near," 139.
107. Ibid.
108. Julio Alvarez del Vayo, "Free Spain Fights On," *The Nation*, 16 September 1944, 320.
109. Fagen, *Exiles and Citizens*, 109.
110. Stein, *Beyond Death and Exile*, 87.
111. Palencia, *Smouldering Freedom*, 228–29.
112. Del Vayo, "Free Spain Fights On," 320.
113. Smith, *Mexico and the Spanish Republicans*, 282.
114. Juan Negrín, "Future of the Spanish Republic," *The Nation*, 6 January 1945, 4–6.
115. See Stein, *Beyond Death and Exile*, 183.
116. Palencia, *Smouldering Freedom*, 238–39.
117. Editorial, *The New Republic*, 5 February 1945, 165.
118. Freda Kirchwey, "If Negrín Comes to Mexico," *The Nation*, 27 January 1945, 90–91.
119. *The New Republic*, 5 February 1945, 165.
120. See Smith, *Mexico and the Spanish Republicans*, 283.
121. Palencia, *Smouldering Freedom*, 241.
122. Cited in Stein, *Beyond Death and Exile*, 201.
123. For the complete statement, see *New York Times*, 5 March 1946.
124. Fagen, *Exiles and Citizens*, 201.
125. Smith, *Mexico and the Spanish Republicans*, 285.
126. Fagen, *Exiles and Citizens*, 113.
127. Julio Alvarez del Vayo, *Give Me Combat* (Boston: Little, Brown and Co., 1973), 192.
128. Juan J. Linz, "Opposition to and under an Authoritarian Regime: The Case of Spain," in Robert A. Dahl, ed., *Regimes and Oppositions* (New Haven: Yale University Press, 1973), 35.
129. Stein, *Beyond Death and Exile*, 191.

CHAPTER FIVE: *Political Exiles and the Domestic Opposition*

1. See Arturo Valenzuela and J. Samuel Valenzuela, "Party Opposition under the Authoritarian Regime," in J. Samuel Valenzuela and Arturo Valenzuela, eds., *Military Rule in Chile: Dictatorship and Oppositions* (Baltimore: Johns Hopkins University Press, 1986), 210–12; also Alan Angell and Susan Carstairs, "The Exile Question in Chilean Politics," *Third World Quarterly* 9 (January 1987): 159–66.
2. Robert J. Alexander, *Juan Domingo Perón: A History* (Boulder, Colo.: Westview Press, 1979), 119.
3. Ibid., 119, 127.

4. Martin Tolchin, "High Profile for South Korea 'Embassy in Exile,' " *New York Times*, 10 October 1986.

5. Anthony Glees, *Exile Politics during the Second World War: The German Social Democrats in Britain* (Oxford: Clarendon Press, 1982), 19.

6. Jose Maravall, *Dictatorship and Political Dissent: Workers and Students in Franco's Spain* (New York: St. Martin's Press, 1979), 23.

7. Patricia W. Fagen, *Exiles and Citizens: Spanish Republicans in Mexico* (Austin: University of Texas Press, 1973), 130–35.

8. Julio Alvarez del Vayo, "Free Spain Fights On," *The Nation*, 16 September 1944, 319.

9. Juan J. Linz, "Opposition to and under an Authoritarian Regime: The Case of Spain," in Robert A. Dahl, ed., *Regimes and Oppositions* (New Haven: Yale University Press, 1973), 232.

10. Steven Mufson, "Who is the A.N.C.?," *New Republic*, 25 August 1986, 20.

11. Tom Lodge, "State of Exile: The African National Congress of South Africa, 1976–1986," *Third World Quarterly* 9 (January 1987): 2–3.

12. Alicja Iwańska, *Exiled Governments: Spanish and Polish* (Cambridge, Mass.: Schenkman Publishing Co., 1981), 56.

13. Ibid.

14. Cited in Lewis J. Edinger, *German Exile Politics: The Social Democratic Executive Committee in the Nazi Era* (Berkeley: University of California Press, 1956), 88–89.

15. Ibid., 76.

16. See Werner Link, "German Political Refugees in the United States During the Second World War," in Anthony Nicholls and Erich Matthias, eds., *German Democracy and the Triumph of Hitler* (London: George Allen and Unwin, 1971), 241–60.

17. Edinger, *German Exile Politics*, 257.

18. See Michael J. Coppedge, "Strong Parties and Lame Ducks: A Study of the Quality and Stability of Venezuelan Democracy," Ph.D. diss., Yale University, December 1988, 225–27.

19. Paul H. Lewis, *The Politics of Exile: Paraguay's Febrerista Party* (Chapel Hill: University of North Carolina Press, 1968), 113.

20. Valenzuela and Valenzuela, eds., *Military Rule in Chile*, 212.

21. Mark R. Thompson, "The Role of the Exiles in Democratic Transition: The Case of the Philippines," unpublished paper, Yale University, March 1988, 14–15.

22. Charles F. Delzell, "The Italian Anti-Fascist Emigration, 1922–1943," *Journal of Central Europe Affairs* 12 (1952): 53.

23. *The Voice of Freedom*, pamphlet (New York: Quaderni Italiani, n.d.), 6.

24. Valenzuela and Valenzuela, eds., 212.

25. Suzy S. Salazar, "Chilean Exiles," unpublished paper,.Yale University, December, 1986, 13.

26. Lewis, *The Politics of Exile*, 195.

27. For analytical purposes I have adopted Robert Dahl's ideal type classification of political systems. In accordance with the opportunities they pro-

vide to potential internal opposition, Dahl developed a continuum of regimes stretching from "pure hegemony" to "pure egalitarian democracy" or "polyarchy." Under hegemony, "organized dissent and opposition are prohibited in any form." Polyarchies are political systems that impose the "fewest restraints" on potential opponents of the government. Between these two extremes there are numerous variations of "mixed regimes, which alternatively approach hegemonies or polyarchies." See Dahl, ed., *Regimes and Oppositions*, 3.

28. See Ronald Gaucher, *Opposition in the U.S.S.R., 1917–1967*, trans. Charles L. Markmann (New York: Funk & Wagnalls, 1969).

29. Charles D. Ameringer, *The Democratic Left in Exile: The Antidictatorial Struggle in the Caribbean, 1945–1959* (Coral Gables, Fla.: University of Miami Press, 1974), 46.

30. *Washington Post*, 7 September 1986.

31. *New York Times*, 13 September 1984, sec. 2, p. 11.

32. Ameringer, *The Democratic Left in Exile*, 159.

33. Lillian Craig Harris, "Libya's Exiles: Fear and Frustration," *Washington Post*, 30 November 1986, sec. 3, p. 2.

34. Guy S. Goodwin-Gill, *The Refugee in International Law* (Oxford: Clarendon Press, 1983), 31.

35. Dahl, ed., *Regimes and Oppositions*, 16.

36. Linz, "Opposition," in ibid., 171–259.

37. Ibid., 211.

38. Juan J. Linz, "Totalitarian and Authoritarian Regimes," in Fred I. Greenstein and Nelson W. Polsby, eds., *Handbook of Political Science*, vol. 3 (Reading, Mass.: Addison-Wesley Publishing Co., 1975), 273.

39. Daniel H. Levine, *Conflict and Political Change in Venezuela* (Princeton: Princeton University Press, 1973), 42–43.

40. On the role of civil society in democratic transition, see Alfred Stepan, *Rethinking Military Politics: Brazil and the Southern Cone* (Princeton: Princeton University Press, 1988), 3–10, 128–33.

41. Levine, *Conflict and Political Change in Venezuela*, 44–45n.

42. Linz, "Opposition," in Dahl, ed., *Regimes and Oppositions*, 237.

43. Cited in Adam B. Ulam, *Lenin and the Bolsheviks: The Intellectual and Political History of the Triumph of Communism in Russia* (London: Secker & Varburg, 1965), 250.

44. Cited in Bertram D. Wolfe, *Three Who Made a Revolution: A Biographical History*, 3rd ed. (New York: Dial Press, 1961), 481.

45. Ulam, *Lenin and the Bolsheviks*, 259.

46. The Mensheviks empowered their representatives in the Duma "to decide matters of policy and technique in their day-to-day activities without continuous dictation and instruction by the émigré underground executive committee. Lenin, however, . . . felt that it should instruct the Social Democratic Deputies on all matters large and small, review and pass on all their speeches, motions, interpellations, projects of 'law.' " Wolfe, *Three Who Made a Revolution*, 523.

47. Linz, "Opposition," in Dahl, ed., *Regimes and Oppositions*, 208.
48. Robert L. Youngblood, "The Philippines in 1982: Marcos Gets Tough with Domestic Critics," *Asian Survey* 23 (February 1983): 215n.
49. Guillermo O'Donnell and Philippe C. Schmitter, *Transitions from Authoritarian Rule: Tentative Conclusions about Uncertain Democracies* (Baltimore: Johns Hopkins University Press, 1986), 23.
50. Thomas E. Skidmore, *Politics in Brazil, 1930–1964: An Experiment in Democracy* (New York: Oxford University Press, 1967), 25.
51. John W. F. Dulles, *Vargas of Brazil: A Political Biography* (Austin: University of Texas Press, 1967), 192.
52. Cited in Skidmore, *Politics in Brazil*, 58.
53. Ibid., 39.
54. Karl Loewenstein, *Brazil under Vargas* (New York: Macmillan, 1942), 257.
55. Marvine Howe, "South Koreans in the U.S. Are Going Home," *New York Times*, 19 July 1987.
56. See Arturo Valenzuela and Pamela Constable, "Plebiscite in Chile: End of the Pinochet Era?," *Current History*, January 1988, 32; also Alfred Stepan, "The Last Days of Pinochet?," *New York Review of Books*, 2 June 1988, 34.
57. See Ekkart Zimmermann, "Political Violence and Other Strategies of Opposition Movements: A Look at Some Recent Evidence," *Journal of International Affairs* 40 (1987): 344–45.
58. Ulam, *Lenin and the Bolsheviks*, 314.
59. Herbert D'Souza, "Return Ticket to Brazil," *Third World Quarterly* 9 (January 1987): 208.
60. Bolton King, *The Life of Mazzini* (London: J. M. Dent & Sons, 1912), 217–21.
61. For the story of the assassination see Gaetano Salvemini, "The Rosselli Murders," *The New Republic*, August 1937, 94–95. Also see "The Stiletto Murders," *Current History*, August 1937, 94–95.
62. Cited in Luigi Salvatorelli, "Unification Spurred by Mazzinianism," in Charles F. Delzell, ed., *The Unification of Italy, 1859–1861: Cavour, Mazzini or Garibaldi?* (New York: Holt, Rinehart & Winston, 1965), 30.
63. Frank Rosengarten, *The Italian Anti-Fascist Press (1919–1945): From the Legal Opposition Press to the Underground Newspapers of World War II* (Cleveland: Case Western Reserve University, 1968), 68.
64. Cited in King, *Life of Mazzini*, 283.
65. Cited in Harry Hearder, *Italy in the Age of the Risorgimento, 1790–1870* (London: Longman, 1983), 186.
66. Gaetano Salvemini, *Carlo and Nello Rosselli: A Memoir* (London: For Intellectual Liberty, 1937), 35–36.
67. Hans Kohn, *Prophets and People: Studies in Nineteenth Century Nationalism* (New York: Macmillan, 1957), 80.
68. Joseph Mazzini, "Letters on the State of Prospects of Italy: No. IV," *The Monthly Chronicle*, vol. 4, July–December 1839, 226–237.
69. Ibid.　　70. Ibid.
71. Ibid.

72. Stringfellow Barr, *Mazzini: Portrait of an Exile* (New York: Henry Holt and Co., 1935), 39.
73. Ibid., 48.
74. Alexander Herzen, *My Past and Thoughts*, abridged by Dwight Macdonald (Berkeley and Los Angeles: University of California Press, 1982), 366.
75. William R. Thayer, *The Life and Times of Cavour*, vol. 2 (Boston: Houghton Mifflin, 1911), 431–32.
76. Ibid.
77. Kohn, *Prophets and People*, 100.
78. See Delzell, "The Italian Anti-Fascist Emigration, 1922–1943," 34.
79. The name "Justice and Liberty" was taken from a poem by Carducci, the great nineteenth-century poet who described the Risorgimento as a "modern epic." See Serge Hughes, *The Fall and Rise of Modern Italy* (New York: Macmillan, 1967), 181.
80. Ibid., 33–34.
81. Denis Mack Smith, *Mussolini* (London: Weidenfeld & Nicolson, 1981), 211.
82. Delzell, *Mussolini's Enemies: The Italian Anti-Fascist Resistance* (Princeton: Princeton University Press, 1961), 27–29.
83. Max Gallo, *Mussolini's Italy: Twenty Years of the Fascist Era*, trans. Charles Markmann (New York: Macmillan, 1973), 159.
84. Salvemini, *Carlo and Nello Rosselli*, 14.
85. See "Two men who will never learn what ruling means," a letter from an Italian to the Editor of the *Manchester Guardian*; cited in *Bernard Shaw and Fascism*, pamphlet (London, 1928), 27–29.
86. Ibid.
87. Cited in King, *Life of Mazzini*, 249–50.
88. Cited in *Bernard Shaw and Fascism*, 40.
89. Cited in Gallo, *Mussolini's Italy*, 238.
90. Cited in Salvemini, *Carlo and Nello Rosselli*, 29.
91. "Letter from Carlo Rosselli, from Prison to a Friend," in *Bernard Shaw and Fascism*, 42–43.
92. On the escape from Lipari, see Francesco Fausto Nitti, *Escape* (New York: Putnam, 1930), 206–67; also Emilio Lussu, *Road to Exile*, trans. Graham Rawson (New York: Covici Friede Publishers, 1936), 226–38.
93. Mazzini, cited in Kohn, *Prophets and People*, 84.
94. Carlo Sforza, *Contemporary Italy: Its Intellectual and Moral Origins*, trans. Drake and Denise De Kay (New York: E. P. Dutton & Co., 1949), 321.
95. Salvemini, *Carlo and Nello Rosselli*, 51.
96. Cited in H. Hessell Tiltman, *The Terror in Europe* (New York: Fredrick A. Stokes Co., 1931), 321.
97. Ibid.
98. Ibid.
99. Hughes, *The Fall and Rise of Modern Italy*, 182.
100. Cited in Zeev Sternhell, "Fascist Ideology," in Walter Laqueur, ed., *Fas-*

cism: A Reader's Guide (Berkeley: University of California Press, 1976),
319.

101. Delzell, *Mussolini's Enemies*, 62–63.

102. See William J. Linton, *European Republicans: Recollections of Mazzini and His Friends* (London: Lawrence and Bullen, 1892), 65–95.

103. See Philip V. Cannistraro, ed., *Historical Dictionary of Fascist Italy* (Westport, Conn.: Greenwood Press, 1982), 64, 468–69, 472; also Rosengarten, *The Italian Anti-Fascist Press*, 66–68.

104. Cannistraro, *Historical Dictionary of Fascist Italy*, 240–41.

105. See William Ebenstein, *Fascist Italy* (New York: American Book Co., 1939), 77–85.

106. Max Ascoli, "The Rosselli Brothers," *The Nation*, 3 July 1937, 11.

107. Cited in Rosengarten, *The Italian Anti-Fascist Press*, 68n.

108. Cited in Tiltman, *The Terror in Europe*, 320; on Bassanesi's flight, see also Delzell, *Mussolini's Enemies*, 66–67.

109. Cited in Tiltman, *The Terror in Europe*, 299.

110. Cited in Enrico Decleva, "Le delusioni di una democrazia: Carlo Rosselli e la Francia 1919–1937," *Nuova Rivista Storica* 43 (1979): 583.

111. Max Ascoli, "The Rosselli Brothers," 11.

112. Cited in Salvemini, *Carlo and Nello Rosselli*, 50.

113. Max Nomad, "Underground Europe," *Current History*, February 1938, 35–38.

114. Delzell, *Mussolini's Enemies*, 78–79.

115. Ibid., 80.

116. According to Ernst Nolte, Justice and Liberty's Manifesto is a typical example of the way Fascist rhetoric forced adversaries to adopt enigmatic ideologies. Rosselli's new program, Nolte maintains, reveals many striking similarities, even in its style, to Mussolini's rhetoric of the early 1920s. See Ernst Nolte, *Three Faces of Fascism: Action Française, Italian Fascism, National Socialism*, trans. Leila Vennewitz (New York: Holt, Rinehart & Winston, 1966), 464n.14.

117. Hughes, *The Fall and Rise of Modern Italy*, 184.

118. Delzell, *Mussolini's Enemies*, 134.

119. See Anne O'Hare McCormick, "Masses Are Silent on Italian Drive," *New York Times*, 15 September 1935.

120. Cited in Charles F. Delzell, ed., *Mediterranean Fascism, 1919–1945* (New York: Walker and Co., 1971), 189.

121. The notion that Duce is always right was part of the "Ten Commandments of the Fascist Fight." See Christopher Leeds, *Italy Under Mussolini* (London: Wayland, 1972), 102.

122. Cited in Delzell, *Mussolini's Enemies*, 139.

123. Esmonde M. Robertson, *Mussolini as Empire-Builder: Europe and Africa, 1932–36* (London: Macmillan, 1977), 193.

124. See Delzell, *Mussolini's Enemies*, 139.

125. In the Rome Agreement, France signed over to Italy her economic interests in Ethiopia. In a private meeting with Mussolini Laval used the term

"free hand," which was interpreted by the Duce as a tacit agreement for an Italian invasion. In a letter to Mussolini on 23 January 1936 Laval rejected this interpretation: "I have never given my approval to the war which you subsequently believed yourself obliged to undertake." For the exchange of letters on Ethiopia between Laval and Mussolini, see Anthony P. Adamthwaite, *The Making of the Second World War,* 2nd ed. (London: George Allen & Unwin, 1979), 149–57.

126. Cited in Delzell, *Mediterranean Fascism,* 193.
127. Lugi Villari, *Italian Foreign Policy under Mussolini* (New York: Devin-Adair Co., 1956), 141.
128. Gaetano Salvemini, *Prelude to World War II* (London: Victor Gollancz, 1953), 471.
129. Cited in ibid., 473.
130. Cited in Delzell, *Mediterranean Fascism,* 197.
131. Cited in John M. Cammett, "Communist Theories of Fascism, 1920–1935," *Science and Society* 31 (1967): 155.
132. See Delzell, *Mussolini's Enemies,* 131.
133. Ibid., 138.
134. See A. I. Sobolev, et al., *Outline History of the Communist International,* trans. Bernard Isaacs (Moscow: Progress Publishers, 1971), 404–407.
135. Delzell, *Mussolini's Enemies,* 141.
136. Cited in Salvemini, *Carlo and Nello Rosselli,* 56–57.
137. Reinhard Bendix, *Max Weber: An Intellectual Portrait* (Berkeley: University of California Press, 1977), 297.
138. See Salvemini, *Carlo and Nello Rosselli,* 57.
139. In a letter to Rosselli, Salvemini wrote: "the Ethiopian war, and the coming of Blum to power in France, put a lid on any hope for better times." Nothing remained but "to vegetate waiting for death." Cited in Decleva, "Le delusioni di una democrazia," 601.
140. See Barr, *Mazzini,* 78.
141. Cited in ibid., 80.
142. Hughes, *The Fall and Rise of Modern Italy,* 186.
143. Delzell, *Mussolini's Enemies,* 147.
144. Cited in E. J. Hobsbawm, *Revolutionaries: Contemporary Essays* (New York: New American Library, 1973), 34n.
145. Until the end of September 1936, the Central Committee of the PCI in exile paid little attention to Spain although its cells at home were longing for action. Only more than a month after Justice and Liberty joined the actual fighting the Committee met in Paris in the presence of Codovilla, the senior Comintern representative of the Spanish Party, and decided that "a column larger than that of Rosselli" should be organized from Italian anti-Fascists to go to Spain. See Hugh Thomas, *The Spanish Civil War* (New York: Harper & Row, 1965), 452–53; Hobsbawm, *Revolutionaries,* 39.
146. Hughes, *The Fall and Rise of Modern Italy,* 186.
147. Max Weber, *Economy and Society: An Outline of Interpretive Sociology,*

vol. 3, Guenther Roth and Claus Wittich, eds., trans. Ephraim Fischolf, et al. (New York: Bedminster Press, 1968), 1114–15.

148. Mack Smith, *Mussolini*, 207.

149. Hobsbawm, *Revolutionaries*, 39; Salvemini, *Carlo and Nello Rosselli*, 59–60.

150. On the battles of Rosselli's exile column in the Spanish Civil War, see Thomas, *The Spanish Civil War*, 366–67, 381.

151. Rosengarten, *The Italian Anti-Fascist Press*, 71.

152. Approximately 5,000 Italian anti-Fascists fought in the civil war in Spain, 500 of whom died. Most of the Italian volunteers came from the exiled community in Europe, the rest from Italy. See *The Voice of Freedom*, 5–6; Hobsbawm, *Revolutionaries*, 34–35; Salvemini, "The Rosselli Murders," 94–95.

153. Cited in Decleva, "Le delusioni di una democrazia," 601.

CHAPTER SIX: *Recognition in the International Community*

1. See Robert H. Jackson and Carl G. Rosberg, *Personal Rule in Black Africa: Prince, Autocrat, Prophet, Tyrant* (Berkeley: University of California Press, 1982), 263–64.

2. See Richard W. Mansbach and John A. Vasquez, *In Search of Theory: A New Paradigm for Global Politics* (New York: Columbia University Press, 1981), 96.

3. John A. Marcum, "The Exile Condition and Revolutionary Effectiveness: Southern African Liberation Movements," in Christian P. Potholm and Richard Dale, eds., *Southern Africa in Perspective* (New York: Free Press, 1972), 275.

4. John L. Austin, *How To Do Things with Words* (Cambridge, Mass.: Harvard University Press, 1962), 94.

5. Ibid., 101.

6. Robert Jervis, *The Logic of Images in International Relations* (Princeton: Princeton University Press, 1970), 37.

7. L. Thomas Galloway, *Recognizing Foreign Governments: The Practice of the United States* (Washington, D.C.: American Enterprise Institute for Public Policy Research, 1978), 5–12.

8. M. J. Peterson, "Political Use of Recognition: The Influence of the International System," *World Politics* 34 (1982): 325.

9. Galloway, *Recognizing Foreign Governments*, 5–12.

10. F. E. Oppenheimer, "Governments and Authorities in Exile," *American Journal of International Law* 36 (1942): 576.

11. Peterson, "Political Use of Recognition," 332.

12. Nadia Tongour, "Diplomacy in Exile: Russian Emigrés in Paris, 1918–1925," Ph.D. diss., Stanford University, 1979, 2.

13. Philip M. Brown, "Sovereignty in Exile," *American Journal of International Law* 35 (1944): 667.

14. Krystyna Marek, *Identity and Continuity of States in Public International Law* (Geneva: Librairie Droz, 1968), 401.
15. Rogert N. Baldwin, "The Capital of the Men without a Country," *The Survey,* 1 August 1927, 462.
16. Myres McDougal and W. Michael Reisman, *International Law Essays: Supplement to International Law in Contemporary Perspective* (Mineola, N.Y.: Foundation Press, 1981), 529n.
17. Thomas Hovet, Jr., "Boundary Disputes and Tensions as a Cause of Refugees," in Hugh C. Brooks and Yassin El-Ayouty, eds., *Refugees South of the Sahara: An African Dilemma* (Westport, Conn.: Negro University Press, 1970), 26.
18. Hugh Thomas, *The Cuban Revolution* (New York: Harper & Row, 1977), 493.
19. Raymond L. Bull, "The Betrayal of Poland," *American Mercury,* January–June 1946, 337. For an exhaustive study of the Polish government-in-exile during World War II, see George Kacewicz, *Great Britain, the Soviet Union and the Polish Government in Exile (1939–1945),* (The Hague, The Netherlands: Martinus Nijhoff, 1979).
20. Irving Kaplan, ed., *Angola: A Country Study* (Washington, D.C.: Foreign Area Studies, American University, 1978), 124.
21. Alicja Iwańska, *Governments in Exile: Spanish and Polish* (Cambridge, Mass.: Schenkman Publishing Co., 1981), 86–89.
22. John Marcum, *The Angolan Revolution,* vol. 2, *Exile Politics and Guerrilla Warfare (1962–1976)* (Cambridge, Mass.: MIT Press, 1978), 38.
23. Marek, *Identity and Continuity of States,* 313.
24. Ibid., 312.
25. Cited in Oppenheimer, "Government and Authorities in Exile," 572.
26. Bernard Ledwidge, *De Gaulle* (London: Weidenfeld & Nicolson, 1982), 67.
27. Ibid., 71.
28. Cited in Charles de Gaulle, *War Memoirs,* vol. 1, *The Call to Honour, 1940–1942,* trans. Jonathan Griffin (New York: Viking Press, 1955), 94.
29. Oppenheimer, "Governments and Authorities in Exile," 576.
30. Roy C. Macridis, "France: From Vichy to the Fourth Republic," in John H. Herz, ed., *From Dictatorship to Democracy: Coping with the Legacies of Authoritarianism and Totalitarianism* (Westport, Conn.: Greenwood Press, 1982), 163.
31. Charles Maechling, Jr., "America's Nonrecognition Policy Is a Nonstarter," *New York Times,* editorial, 31 December 1983.
32. On the misuse of relief funds among rival factions of the exiled Spanish Republicans, see Nancy Macdonald, *Homage to the Spanish Exiles* (New York: Human Science Press, 1987), 71.
33. Aristide R. Zolberg, Astri Suhrke, and Sergio Aguayo, "International Factors in the Formation of Refugee Movement," *International Migration Review* 20 (1986): 166.
34. *Washington Post,* 30 November 1986, sec. 3.

35. Rowland Evans and Robert Novak, "Helping Out the Ayatollah," *New York Post*, 3 April 1987.

36. Robert D. Tomasek, "Caribbean Exile Invasions: A Special Regional Type of Conflict," *Orbis* 17 (1974): 1379.

37. See Mahnaz Ispahani, "The Perils of Pakistan," *The New Republic*, 16 March 1987, 19–25; "Contra Country" (transcript), CBS News, 60 Minutes 19 (29 March 1987).

38. John A. Marcum, "The Exile Condition and Revolutionary Effectiveness," 269.

39. Silvia Pedraza-Bailey, *Political and Economic Migrants in America: Cubans and Mexicans* (Austin: University of Texas Press, 1985), 160.

40. Cited in Lewis J. Edinger, *German Exile Politics: The Social Democratic Executive Committee in the Nazi Era* (Berkeley: University of California Press, 1956), 211.

41. J. Bower Bell, "Contemporary Revolutionary Organizations," in Robert O. Keohane and Joseph S. Nye, eds., *Transitional Relations and World Politics* (Cambridge, Mass.: Harvard University Press, 1973), 153–68.

42. Ibid., 165n.

43. Lois E. Smith, *Mexico and the Spanish Republicans* (Berkeley: University of California Press, 1955), 171–77.

44. Ibid., 171.

45. Anthony Glees, "The German Political Exile in London, 1939–1945," in Gerhard Hirschfeld, ed., *Exile in Great Britain: Refugees from Hitler's Germany* (Atlantic Highlands, N.J.: Humanities Press, 1984), 86.

46. Stephan M. Davis, *Apartheid's Rebels: Inside South Africa's Hidden War* (New Haven: Yale University Press, 1987), 37–44.

47. See Guy S. Goodwin-Gill, "International Law and the Detention of Refugees and Asylum-Seekers," *International Migration Review* 20 (1986): 204.

48. See Jack I. Garvey, "Repression of the Political Emigre—The Underground to International Law: A Proposal for Remedy," *Yale Law Journal* 90 (1980): 80.

49. Flora Lewis, "Mideast Shift for France," *New York Times*, 12 June 1986.

50. *Le Figaro*, 9 June 1986.

51. Louis Stein, *Beyond Death and Exile: The Spanish Republicans in France, 1939–1955* (Cambridge, Mass.: Harvard University Press, 1979), 39–125.

52. "Contra Country," 3.

53. Robert Jervis, *The Logic of Images in International Relations*, 14.

54. Ibid.   55. Ibid.

56. Nicholas Bethell, *The Great Betrayal: The Untold Story of Kim Philby's Biggest Coup* (London: Hodder and Stoughton, 1984), 3.

57. Ibid.

58. In a desperate attempt to regain the attention of the West during the Cold War, a representative of East European exiles declared: "[We] should be of particular interest, because [we] have every reason to take a resolute stand against Bolshevik imperialism; moreover [we] have knowledge of language and topography, as well as much more valuable information; many of [us] are experienced soldiers who fought in the last war. But what really matters

is the influence which [we] could exercise on public opinion in our own countries. It is in this sphere that [we] might render the greatest service to the West. [We] are listened to by [our] fellow countrymen at home much more than are any foreign quarters. . . . Here is a chance for the Western allies to establish co-operation with the men who are able to influence the feelings and attitudes of an important section of the public opinion in the European countries subjugated by the U.S.S.R." Francis Honti, "Atlantic Defence and Our Standpoint," *Eastern Quarterly* (July 1951), 7–8.

59. Kenneth J. Grieb, "The Myth of a Central American Dictators' League," *Journal of Latin American Studies* 10 (1978), 329–45.

60. See Robert L. Youngblood, "The Philippines in 1982: Marcos Gets Tough with Domestic Critics," *Asian Survey* 23 (February 1983): 213–14; Matthew K. Schatzman, "The New Democratic Party of South Korea and Their 'Embassy in Exile,'" unpublished paper, Yale University, January 1986.

61. *New York Times*, 5 March 1946.

62. This was particularly true in regard to the U.S.-Franco agreement on bases, although Spain was excluded from NATO and the Common Market.

63. Louis Stein, *Beyond Death and Exile*, 234.

64. A. Leroy Bennett, *International Organizations: Principles and Issues*, 3rd ed. (Englewood Cliffs, N.J.: Prentice-Hall, 1984), 265.

65. The U.N. resolutions are cited in Randoph Vigne, "SWAPO of Namibia: A Movement in Exile," *Third World Quarterly* 9 (January 1987): 89; and Shaul Mishal, *The PLO under Arafat; Between Gun and Olive Branch* (New Haven: Yale University Press, 1986), 19.

66. For example, the International Labour Organization, the United Nations Human Rights Commission, and the High Commission for Refugees.

67. For example, Amnesty International.

68. Antonio Cassese, "How Could Nongovernmental Organizations Use U.N. Bodies More Effectively?," *Universal Human Rights* 1 (October–December 1979): 73–80.

69. U.N. General Assembly Resolution 41/15 (1986) states that "the recognition by the General Assembly, the Security Countil and the United Nations organs of the legitimacy of the struggle of the colonial peoples to exercise their right to self-determination and independence entails, as a corollary, the extension by the specialized agencies and other organizations of the United Nations system of all the necessary moral and material assistance to those peoples and their national liberation movements." I am indebted to Mr. Kaiser Zamen, UNHCR Assistant Regional Representative, for informing me about this resolution.

70. Mansbach and Vasquez, *In Search of Theory*, 100.

CHAPTER SEVEN: *My Country Right or Wrong*

1. Lewis J. Edinger, *German Exile Politics: The Social Democratic Executive Committee in the Nazi Era* (Berkeley: University of California Press, 1956), 225.

2. *Los Angeles Times,* 5 August 1984.

3. *New York Times,* 7 February 1988.

4. See Nozar Alaolmolki, "Iranian Opposition to Khomaini and the Islamic Republic," *Australian Outlook* 38 (August 1984): 104; Claude van England, "Iran, France Gain from Iranian Exile's Exit," *Christian Science Monitor,* 10 June 1986.

5. John Somerville, "Patriotism and War," *Ethics* 91 (July 1981): 568–78.

6. Gustave Hervé, *My Country Right or Wrong,* trans. G. Bowman (London: J. Cape, 1921), 42–43.

7. A. H. Birch, "Economic Models in Political Science: The Case of Exit, Voice, and Loyalty," *British Journal of Political Science* 5 (1975): 74.

8. Cited in Olivia O'Leary, "The Peronist Mystique: The Falklands Crisis Quells a Populist Resurgence," *World Press Review,* June 1982, 48.

9. Andrew Graham-Yooll, "The Wild Oats They Sowed: Latin American Exiles in Europe," *Third World Quarterly* 9 (January 1987): 251.

10. "Inertness" is used by George Fischer to refer to citizens' "passive accommodation through apathy and evasion of political commitments." See George Fischer, *Soviet Opposition to Stalin: A Case Study in World War II* (Cambridge, Mass.: Harvard University Press, 1952), 128–29.

11. Harold D. Lasswell, *World Politics and Personal Insecurity* (New York: Free Press, 1965), 64.

12. Ibid.

13. Annabelle Sreberny-Mohammadi and Ali Mohammadi, "Post-Revolutionary Iranian Exiles: A Study in Impotence," *Third World Quarterly* 9 (January 1987): 125.

14. Internal opposition can often benefit from a war situation by "taking over the role of defenders of the country, when they are acting as nationalists fighting for their country in the first place, while also pursuing their long-term political, social, and ideological goals." Moreover, in case of military defeat, the opposition at home has better chances of provoking "disintegration of the army and the state's leadership," which eventually might pave their way to power. See Ekkart Zimmermann, *Political Violence, Crises and Revolutions: Theories and Research* (Boston: G. K. Hall & Co., 1983), 124, 323.

15. Margery Weiner, *The French Exiles, 1789–1815* (London: John Murray, 1960), 37.

16. Anthony Glees, "The German Political Exile in London, 1939–1945," in Gerhard Hirschfeld, ed., *Exile in Great Britain: Refugees from Hitler's Germany* (Atlantic Highlands, N.J.: Humanities Press, 1984), 83.

17. This was the predicament of Carlo Rosselli, the leader of Justice and Liberty, during the Fascist war in Ethiopia (see Chapter 5).

18. Rejani P. Dutt, *The Internationale* (London: Lawrence & Wishard, 1964), 43, 111.

19. Cited in Bertram D. Wolfe, *Three Who Made a Revolution,* 3rd ed. (New York: Dial Press, 1961), 278–79.

20. Cited in David Shub, *Lenin: A Biography* (London: Penguin Books, 1966), 162.

21. Louis Fischer, *The Life of Lenin* (New York: Harper & Row, 1964), 85.

22. Shub, *Lenin*, 170.

23. For more information about the resolutions in the Zimmerwald conference, see Alfred E. Senn, *The Russian Revolution in Switzerland, 1914–1917* (Madison: University of Wisconsin Press, 1971), 89–102.

24. Cited in Fischer, *The Life of Lenin*, 86.

25. Glees, "The German Political Exile in London, 1939–1945," 84.

26. Robert H. Johnston, "The Great Patriotic War and the Russian Exiles in France," *Russian Review* 35 (1976): 305–306.

27. Ibid., 307–13.

28. Cited in ibid., 305.

29. Cited in Fischer, *Soviet Opposition to Stalin*, 19.

30. Ibid.

31. John J. Stephan, *The Russian Fascists: Tragedy and Farce in Exile, 1925–1945* (New York: Harper & Row, 1978), 28.

32. Wilfried Strik-Strikfeldt, *Against Stalin and Hitler: Memoir of the Russian Liberation Movement, 1941–1945*, trans. David Footman (London: Macmillan, 1970), 69.

33. Ibid., 14.

34. Cited in ibid., 254.

35. George Fischer, "Vlasov and Hitler," in George Fischer, ed., *Russian Emigré Politics*, limited ed. (New York: Free Russia Fund, 1951), 58.

36. See Sven Steenberg, *Vlasov*, trans. Abe Farbstein (New York: Alfred A. Knopf, 1970), 110–11.

37. Frederick C. Barghoorn, "Factional, Sectoral, and Subversive Opposition in Soviet Politics," in Robert A. Dahl, ed., *Regimes and Oppositions* (New Haven: Yale University Press, 1973), 78–79.

38. Johnston, "The Great Patriotic War and the Russian Exiles in France," 307.

39. Fischer, *Soviet Opposition to Stalin*, 19.

40. Strik-Strikfeldt, *Against Stalin and Hitler*, 245.

41. Ibid., 14.

42. Anthony Glees, *Exile Politics during the Second World War: The German Social Democrats in Britain* (Oxford: Clarendon Press, 1982), 25.

43. Edinger, *German Exile Politics*, 44.

44. Cited in Glees, *Exile Politics during the Second World War*, 89.

45. Ibid., 24.

46. See Willy Brandt, *In Exile: Essays, Reflections and Letters, 1933–1947*, trans. R. W. Last (Philadelphia: University of Pennsylvania Press, 1971), 99–134.

47. Ibid., 124–44.

48. Edinger, *German Exile Politics*, 233.

49. Glees, *Exile Politics during the Second World War*, 88–89.

50. Ibid., 129.   51. Ibid., 147–48.

52. See below, on the German Communist exiles in Moscow.

53. Gordon Smith, *Democracy in West Germany: Parties and Politics in the Federal Republic* (New York: Holmes & Meier Publishers, 1979), 95.

54. Günther Nollau, *International Communism and World Revolution: History and Methods*, trans. Victor Anderson (Westport, Conn.: Greenwood Press, 1975), 200.
55. See Julius Braunthal, *History of the International, 1914–1943*, vol. 2, trans. Henry Collins and Kenneth Mitchell (New York: Praeger, 1967), 510.
56. Wolfgang Leonhard, *Child of the Revolution*, trans. C. M. Woodhouse (London: Ink Links, 1979), 113.
57. Glees, *Exile Politics during the Second World War*, 190.
58. Leonhard, *Child of the Revolution*, 67.
59. Ibid., 277, 279.
60. Nollau, *International Communism and World Revolution*, 189.
61. Leonhard, *Child of the Revolution*, 280.
62. William E. Griffith, *Communism in Europe: Continuity, Change, and the Sino-Soviet Dispute*, vol. 2 (Cambridge, Mass.: MIT Press, 1966), 63.
63. Glees, *Exile Politics during the Second World War*, 162.

CHAPTER EIGHT: *Counterexile Strategies by the Home Regime*

1. Howard C. Payne and Henry Grosshans, "The Exiled Revolutionaries and the French Political Police in the 1850s," *American Historical Review* 68 (July 1963): 966.
2. Martin A. Miller, *Russian Revolutionary Emigres, 1825–1870* (Baltimore: Johns Hopkins University Press, 1986), 199–212, 217.
3. See Gianfranco Cresciani, *Fascism, Anti-Fascism, and Italians in Australia: 1922–1945* (Canberra: Australia National University Press, 1980), 99.
4. On political exiles as information sources in exposing human rights abuses in their home countries, see Thomas Place and Andrea Darvi, *Secret Police: The Inside Story of a Network of Terror* (Garden City, N.Y.: Doubleday & Co., 1981), preface.
5. For an excellent study of the legal and political implications of agents of foreign against political exiles in the U.S., see Jack I. Garvey, "Repression of the Political Emigre—The Underground to International Law: A Proposal for Remedy," *Yale Law Journal* 90 (1980): 78–120.
6. See Fred Poole and Max Vanzi, "Hounding Philippine Exiles: Marcos's Secret War in America," *The Nation*, 12 May 1984, 577–78.
7. Raymond Aron, "Is Multinational Citizenship Possible?," *Social Research* 41 (Winter 1974): 649.
8. Harold R. Isaacs, "Nationality: 'End of the Road'?," *Foreign Affairs* 53 (April 1975): 438–39.
9. In multiethnic states "'citizenship' and 'national identity' are different and, at times, conflicting conceptions." See Myron Weiner, "Changing Conceptions of Citizenship in a Multi-Ethnic Society," in Sidney Verba and Lucian W. Pye, eds., *The Citizen and Politics: A Comparative Perspective* (Stamford, Conn.: Greylock Publishers, 1978), 107.

10. Michael Walzer, *Obligations: Essays on Disobedience, War, and Citizenship* (Cambridge, Mass.: Harvard University Press, 1970), 206–207.
11. In the case of *Kwakita* vs. *United States* 343 U.S. 717 (1952), Justice Douglas delivered the opinion of the Court: "An American citizen owes allegiance to the United States wherever he may reside." Cited in N. Bar-Yaacov, *Dual Nationality* (London: Stevens & Sons, 1961), 58.
12. John P. Fox, "Nazi Germany and German Emigration to Great Britain," in Gerhard Hirschfeld, ed., *Exile in Great Britain: Refugees from Hitler's Germany* (Atlantic Highlands, N.J.: Humanities Press, 1984), 41.
13. Michael R. Marrus, *The Unwanted: European Refugees in the Twentieth Century* (New York: Oxford University Press, 1985), 126.
14. Mark Vishniak, *The Legal Status of Stateless Persons* (New York: American Jewish Committee, 1945), 10.
15. Fredrick M. Barnard, "Patriotism and Citizenship in Rousseau: A Dual Theory of Public Willing?," *Review of Politics* 46 (April 1984): 253.
16. P. Weis, *Nationality and Statelessness in International Law* (London: Stevens & Sons, 1956), 124.
17. Ralf Dahrendorf, "Citizenship and Beyond: The Social Dynamics of an Idea," *Social Research* 41 (Winter 1974): 674.
18. Charles F. Delzell, "The Italian Anti-Fascist Emigration, 1922–1943," *Journal of Central Europe Affairs* 12 (1952): 21.
19. Charles D. Ameringer, *The Democratic Left in Exile: The Antidictatorial Struggle in the Caribbean, 1945–1959* (Coral Gables, Fla.: University of Miami Press, 1974), 58.
20. See Silvia Pedraza-Bailey, *Political and Economic Migrants in America: Cubans and Mexicans* (Austin: University of Texas Press, 1985), 148–50.
21. Anthony D. Smith, *Nationalism in the Twentieth Century* (New York: New York University Press, 1979), 148.
22. Benjamin R. Barber, *Strong Democracy: Participatory Politics for a New Age* (Berkeley: University of California Press, 1984), 226.
23. According to Soviet authorities, "appearing as a symbol and a means of consolidating the unity of a nation within the limits of society, [citizenship,] along with other legal institutions, is in fact more a perfect and flexible weapon of domination for the ruling class." See Viktor S. Shevtsov, *Citizenship of the USSR: A Legal Study,* trans. Lenina Ilitskaya (Moscow: Progress Publishers, 1979), 15.
24. Ibid.
25. Cited in Morton Grodzins, *Americans Betrayed: Politics and the Japanese Evacuation* (Chicago: University of Chicago Press, 1949), 159.
26. Under the Nuremberg Laws of September 15, 1935, Jews were classified as "state subjects." "They were defined as a separate race whose marriage or sexual contact with 'Aryans' was forbidden by law." See Sarah A. Gordon, *Hitler, Germans, and the "Jewish Question"* (Princeton: Princeton University Press, 1984), 121–22.
27. Hannah Arendt, *Totalitarianism,* part 3 (New York: Harcourt, Brace, and World, 1968), 121–23.

28. Fox, "Nazi Germany and the German Emigration in Great Britain," 41.

29. Morton Grodzins, *The Loyal and the Disloyal: Social Boundaries of Patriotism and Treason* (Chicago: University of Chicago Press, 1956), 233.

30. Charles F. Delzell, *Mussolini's Enemies: The Italian Anti-Fascist Resistance* (Princeton: Princeton University Press, 1961), 147.

31. Ryszard Wraga, "Russian Emigration after Thirty Years' Exile," in George Fischer, ed., *Russian Emigré Politics*, limited ed. (New York: Free Russia Fund, 1951), 25.

32. Ibid.

33. Paul Tabori, *The Anatomy of Exile: A Semantic and Historical Study* (London: Harrap, 1972), 204.

34. Pedraza-Bailey, *Political and Economic Migrants in America*, 29.

35. James F. Kirkham, Sheldon G. Levy, and William J. Crotty, *Assassination and Political Violence*, vol. 8 (Washington, D.C.: U.S. Government Printing Office, 1969), 541.

36. Herbert D'Souza, "Return Ticket to Brazil," *Third World Quarterly 9* (January 1987): 207.

37. Weis, *Nationality and Statelessness in International Law*, 222.

38. In these harsh words Arthur Koestler described French authorities' treatment of the stateless defeated army of the Spanish Republicans during World War II. Arthur Koestler, *Scum of the Earth* (New York: Macmillan, 1941).

39. Dr. Frijof Nansen, the Norwegian ambassador to the League of Nations, was behind the League's initiative to issue identity cards and travel documents to serve the massive Russian diaspora and other unassimilated refugees.

40. See Emil Lengyel, "Refugees from Many Lands Complicate Europe's International Relations," *New York Times*, 20 January 1935, sec. 9.

41. See John J. Stepan, *The Russian Fascists: Tragedy and Farce in Exile, 1925–1945* (New York: Harper & Row, 1978), 9.

42. Patricia W. Fagen, *Exiles and Citizens: Spanish Republicans in Mexico* (Austin: University of Texas Press, 1973), 59–60. For the effect of granting citizenship on the assimilation of the Spanish diaspora in Mexico, see also Lois R. Fishman, "Bittersweet Memories," and Sergio Sarmiento, "Starting Over," *Americas*, November–December 1984, 30–39.

43. Alicja Iwańska, *Exiled Governments: Spanish and Polish* (Cambridge, Mass.: Schenkman Publishing Co., 1981), 60.

44. See Houchang Chehabi, "Modernist Shi'ism and Politics: The Liberation Movement of Iran," Ph.D. diss., Yale University, 1986, vol. 1, 361.

45. Willy Brandt, *In Exile: Essays Reflections and Letters 1933–1947*, trans. R. W. Last (London: Oswald Wolff, 1971), 165.

46. Lewis J. Edinger, *German Exile Politics: The Social Democratic Executive Committee in the Nazi Era* (Berkeley: University of California Press, 1956), 210.

47. H. Hessell Tiltman, *The Terror in Europe* (New York: Fredrick A. Stokes, 1932), 306.

48. Ibid.
49. Bertram D. Wolfe, *Three Who Made a Revolution: A Biographical History,* 3rd ed. (New York: Dial Press, 1961), 518.
50. Louis Fischer, *The Life of Lenin* (New York: Harper & Row, 1964), 82.
51. Ibid.
52. Alan Dowty, *Closed Borders: The Contemporary Assault on Freedom of Movement* (New Haven: Yale University Press, 1987), 65.
53. See Wraga, "Russian Emigration after Thirty Years' Exile," 25.
54. Basil Shulgin, "How I Was Hoodwinked by the Bolsheviks," *The Slavonic Review* 6 (June 1927–March 1928): 509.
55. Dimitry V. Lehovich, *White Against Red: The Life of General Anton Denkin* (New York: W. W. Norton & Co., 1974), 428–29.
56. Roland Gaucher, *Opposition in the U.S.S.R., 1917–1967,* trans. Charles L. Markmann (New York: Funk & Wagnalls, 1969), 129.
57. Payne and Grosshans, "The Exiled Revolutionaries and the French Political Police in the 1850s," 955–56.
58. Fox, "Nazi Germany and German Emigration to Great Britain," 38.
59. Ibid., 51.
60. Anthony Glees, "The German Political Exile in London, 1939–1945," in Hirschfeld, ed., *Exile in Great Britain,* 86.
61. Cited in Tiltman, *Terror in Europe,* 313.
62. Ibid., 314.
63. See Lois E. Smith, *Mexico and the Spanish Republicans* (Berkeley: University of California Press, 1955), 209–10.
64. Ibid., 211. See also Louis Stein, *Beyond Death and Exile: The Spanish Republicans in France, 1939–1945* (Cambridge, Mass.: Harvard University Press, 1979), 125.
65. Iwańska, *Exiled Governments,* 35.
66. Ameringer, *The Democratic Left in Exile,* 64–72.
67. For reports on the fate of Libyan exiles in Morocco, see John Damis, "Morocco, Libya and the Treaty of Union," *American Arab Affairs* 13 (1985): 44–46.
68. Plate and Darvi, *Secret Police,* 273.
69. See "Ogpu Terror in London—The Truth," *The Saturday Review* (London) 19 September 1936, 378–80.
70. On the disappearances of Gen. Paul Alexander Kutepov and Gen. Evgenii Miller, the heads of the exiled monarchists, see Joseph Borenstein, *The Politics of Murder* (New York: William Sloane Associates, 1950), 74–94; Lehovich, *White Against Red,* 427–48.
71. See Karl Anders, *Murder to Order* (London: Ampersand, 1965).
72. Wraga, "Russian Emigration after Thirty Years' Exile," 26.
73. See *New York Times,* 21 April 1927.
74. Tiltman, *The Terror in Europe,* 157.
75. Isaac Deutscher, *The Prophet Outcast* (London: Oxford University Press, 1963), 362.
76. Ibid., 363.

77. For the story of Trotsky's assassination, see Nicholas Mosley, *The Assassination of Trotsky* (London: Michael Joseph, 1972).
78. See Tiltman, *The Terror in Europe*, 299–329.
79. See Borenstein, *Politics of Murder*, 22–26; Max Nomad, "Underground Europe," *Current History*, February 1938, 35–38.
80. See Tom Gallagher, *Portugal: A Twentieth-Century Interpretation* (Manchester: Manchester University Press, 1983), 159–60, 228.
81. Plate and Darvi, *Secret Police*, 274.
82. Lee Shin-Bom, "South Korea: Dissent from Abroad," *Third World Quarterly* 9 (January 1987): 140.
83. J. Bower Bell, *Assassin!* (New York: St. Martin's Press, 1979), 140.
84. Christine Moss Helms, *Iraq: Eastern Flank of the Arab World* (Washington, D.C.: Brookings Institute, 194), 79.
85. See Harold D. Nelson, ed., *Morocco: A Country Study* (Washington, D.C.: Foreign Area Studies, American University, 1979), 69–73.
86. Chehabi, "Modern Shi'ism and Politics," vol. 1, 365. On the SAVAK's suppression of exiles in the U.S., see Garvey, "Repression of the Political Emigre," 81, 84.
87. Stanley Meisler, "Thousands of Iranian Exiles Wait, Hope, Plot in Paris," *Los Angeles Times*, 5 August 1984.
88. See "Libya: Killings of 'Enemies of the Revolution,' " in *Political Killings by Governments* (London: Amnesty International, 1983), 69–77.
89. Ameringer, *The Democratic Left in Exile*, 167, 169.
90. See Salvatore Bizzaro, "Chile under the Jackboot," *Current History*, February 1976, 57–60; and Salvatore Bizzaro, "Rigidity and Restraint in Chile," *Current History*, February 1978, 66–69.
91. Juan J. Linz, "Totalitarian and Authoritarian Regimes," in Fred I. Greenstein and Nelson W. Polsby, eds., *Handbook of Political Science*, vol. 3 (Reading, Mass.: Addison-Wesley Publishing Co., 1975), 218.
92. Plate and Darvi, *Secret Police*, 273.

CONCLUSION

1. Ekkart Zimmermann, *Political Violence, Crises, and Revolutions: Theories and Research* (Boston: G. K. Hall & Co., 1983), 203.
2. See Joseph Bensman, "Max Weber's Concept of Legitimacy: An Evaluation," in Arthur J. Vidich and Ronald M. Glassman, eds., *Conflict and Control: Challenge to Legitimacy of Modern Governments* (London: Sage Publications, 1979), 23.
3. Ted Robert Gurr, *Why Men Rebel* (Princeton: Princeton University Press, 1971), 185.
4. Max Weber, *Economy and Society: An Outline of Interpretive Sociology*, vol. 3, Guenther Roth and Claus Wittich, eds., trans. Ephraim Fischoff, et al. (New York: Bedminster Press, 1968), 954.
5. Michael C. Hudson, *Arab Politics: The Search for Legitimacy* (New Haven: Yale University Press, 1977), 2.

6. See Adam Przeworski, "Some Problems in the Study of the Transition to Democracy," in Guillermo O'Donnell, Philippe C. Schmitter, and Laurence Whitehead, eds., *Transition from Authoritarian Rule: Comparative Perspective* (Baltimore: Johns Hopkins University Press, 1986), 51.

7. Max Weber, *Economy and Society,* vol. 1, 214.

8. For an excellent evaluation of social science as a "science of order," see Sheldon S. Wolin, "The Politics of the Study of Revolution," *Comparative Politics* 5 (April 1973): 349–52.

9. Ekkart Zimmermann, "Political Violence and Other Opposition Strategies: A Look at Some Recent Evidence," *Journal of International Affairs* 40 (1987): 339.

10. For a comprehensive story of the breakdown of the Colonels' regime and the arrival of Constantine Karamanlis, see Harry J. Psomiades, "Greece: From the Colonels' Rule to Democracy," in John H. Herz, ed., *From Dictatorship to Democracy: Coping with the Legacies of Authoritarianism and Totalitarianism* (Westport, Conn.: Greenwood Press, 1982), 251–73.

11. Anthony Glees, *Exile Politics during the Second World War: The German Social Democrats in Britain* (Oxford: Clarendon Press, 1982), 253.

Index

Acción Democrática (AD), 36, 60, 82, 85, 87–88, 168
Action Party (Italy), 109
Afghanistan, 120
Soviet invasion of, 83, 115
Afghan refugees, 58, 115
Africa, 5–6, 16
African governments-in-exile, 114–115
African National Congress (ANC), 34, 44, 80–81, 112, 122
African National Union, 44
African People's Union, 44
agents provocateurs, 35, 147, 154–155, 161
Albania, 125–126
Albanian exile organization, 125–126
Alexander, Grand Duke, 62
Alexander, Robert J., 78
Alexander III, Czar of Russia, 65
Algeria, 48
Algerian National Liberation Front (FLN), 114
Algerian war, 157
aliens, exiles as, 13
Allende Gossens, Salvador, 1, 32, 160
Allies, Western:
Free French and, 117
Polish government in exile and, 115
Soviet appraisals of, 138
Spain and, 150
SPD and, 139–140
World War II governments in exile and, 114
Almeyda, Clodomiro, 35, 92–93
Altamirano, Carlos, 35
Alvarez del Vayo, Julio, 80
American Revolution, 147
Ameringer, Charles D., 160

Amini, Ali, 38
amnesty, 93, 150–151
Amnesty International, 111
Amsterdam, 134
anarchism, 100
anarchosyndicalists, Spanish, 108
Anderson, Benedict, 5
Andreis, Mario, 101
Angola, 44, 47, 122
Angolan revolutionary government-in-exile, 115, 116
anti-Bolshevism, 48–49, 63–64, 135–138
anti-Castro exiles, 1, 29, 37, 57, 85, 115, 125, 150
anticolonialism, 5–6
anticommunism, 47, 64, 72–73, 156
anti-Fascism, 75
German, 1, 16, 51, 56, 81, 121, 122, 139–144, 154, 156
Italian, 1, 16, 42–43, 44, 51, 83, 94–109, 123, 146, 149, 150, 158–159
antimilitarism, 131
anti-Nazism, 1, 16, 51, 56, 81, 121, 122, 139–144, 154, 159
antipatriotism, 131
anti-Sandinistas, 55, 118, 120, 123–124
anti-Semitism, 64, 149–150
anti-Soviet exiles, 62, 73, 79–80
see also Bolsheviks; monarchists, Russian
antiwar campaigns, 15, 135
Aquino, Benigno, Jr., 90
Aquino, Corazón, 16
Arendt, Hannah, 11
Argentina, 33, 51, 78, 131–132, 168
aristocrats, exiled, 3–4
Aristotle, 2
Arocena, Eduardo, 85

Aryans, 56
Ascoli, Max, 101
assassination, 20, 147
  of key leaders, 157–160
  of Rosselli, 36, 109, 159
  assignation à residence, 122
assimilation, language problems and, 10
asylum, political, 3–4, 10, 71, 120–121
  definition of, 120
  eligibility for, 13, 120
  limitations of, 121, 122–123
  temporary, 13
  violation of, 13
Athens, 2, 16, 55
attachés, 158
Austin, John L., 112
Austria, 3, 96, 98
  Milanese insurrection against, 100
Azaña, Manuel, 33, 70–71, 73
Aziz, Tariq, 130

Badajoz, 159
Baha'i faith, 55
Bakhash, Shaul, 22
Bakthiar, Shahpour, 38, 160
Bakunin, Mikhail A., 95
Balkan states, 66, 114
Baltic states, 17, 114
Banderivtsi, 46
Bani-Sadr, Abolhassan, 131, 160
Bank of Spain, 123
Barry, Brian, 24
Basque Nationalist Party, 73
Basque Provinces, 16
Bassanesi, Giovanni, 101
Ba'th, Syrian, 159
Bauer, Riccardo, 98, 100
Bavaria, 67
Bay of Pigs invasion, 29, 37, 125
BBC, 117
Belgium, 114
Bell, J. Bower, 121
Ben Barka, Mahdi, 159
Benelux government-in-exile, 29–30
Beneš, Edvard, 122, 156
Berlin, 64
Bern, 107
Betancourt, Rómulo, 36, 88
Birch, A. H., 24
Black Guelphs, 2

blackmail, 154
Black Shirts, 104
Blum, Léon, 120–121
boat people, 13
Bolshevik Central Committee, 154
Bolsheviks, 5, 39–40, 63, 65, 69, 89, 93,
  134–138, 149, 154–155
Bonaparte family, 64, 145–146
Botkin, Gleb, 67
Botswana, 122
Bourbon family, 3–4, 28, 64, 133
bourgeois republicanism, 5
Brandt, Willy, 139, 153
Brazil, 47, 151, 159
  coup d'état in, 91, 93
  democratization of, 90–91
  government's repression of exiles, 151
  Labor Party of, 91
  Liberal Constitutional Party of, 91
  Social Democratic Party of, 91
broadcasts, television and radio, 84–85,
  108–109, 117, 142
Buenos Aires, 51, 91, 160

Cain, 151–152
Calvin, John, 3
Calvinism, 3
Caracas, 35
Cárdenas, Lázaro, 121
Cardona, José Miro, 29
Caribbean exile organizations, 1, 119,
  149
Carter, Jimmy, 160
Casal, Lourdes, 37
Castro, Fidel, 9, 25, 29, 37, 54, 57, 115,
  120, 149, 150
Catalonia, 108
caudillos, 126
Central Intelligence Agency (CIA), 125,
  147
Chile, 33, 54, 77–78, 82, 92–93, 151
  Communist Party of, 82, 83
  secret police of, 160
  Socialist Party of, 35
Chilean Popular Unity, 78
China, People's Republic of, 17, 52
China, Republic of, 52
Chorley, Katherine, 19
Chun Doo Hwan, 1, 53, 79, 92, 127
Churchill, Winston, 117, 138

citizenship, 145–153
  acquiring of, 152–153
  as bourgeois fiction, 149, 196n23
  manipulation of, 150–151
  modern concept of, 147–148, 149
  racist concept of, 149–150
  restoration of, 150
  withdrawal of, 146–153, 164
city-states, 2, 148
clandestine operations, 77–78, 79, 81, 84, 99
Coburg, 65
collective guilt, 140, 142
Comite, 29
Comité de Libération, 72
Committee of 75, 57
communism, 36, 47, 82, 83, 100, 103, 105, 141, 142
communist exiles, 133, 134, 141
Communist International (Comintern), 105, 141, 142
Concentrazione antifascista, 42–43, 103
Constitutional Democrats, 63
"Contemporary Revolutionary Organizations" (Bell), 121–122
Contrary Commonwealth (Starn), 163
Contras, 118, 120, 123–124
Coolidge, Calvin, 67
Copenhagen, 67
Coppedge, Michael J., 82
Cortes, Spanish, 71, 72, 73–74
Coser, Lewis A., 9, 11
Cossacks, 67
Costa Rica, Communist Party of, 36
Council of National Resistance, 160
Council of Russian Ambassadors, 35, 64, 65, 179n53
Council of Scientific Unions (CSU), 111
counterrevolutionaries, 10, 25, 149, 158
coups d'état, 21, 35, 91, 93, 159, 167
CPSU, 5
Cranston, Alan, 53
Crito (Plato), 2
Cuba, 9, 150, 157
  Castro revolution in, 9, 120
  exiles' invasion of, 29, 37, 125
  U.S. relations with, 57, 115
  war for independence of, 4
Cuban exile organizations, 1, 29, 37, 115, 125, 150

Cuban Revolutionary Council, 29
cultural organizations, 111, 118
Cyprus, 167
Cyril, Grand Duke, 64–69, 136
Czechoslovakia, 114, 122, 156, 159

Dahl, Robert, 84, 86, 183n27
Daladier, Édouard, 123
Dalai Lama, 17, 33
Dante Alighieri, 2
David, King of Israel, 1–2
Decatur, Stephen, 131
Declaration of Pillnitz (1791), 3
decolonization, 5–6, 16, 17, 114, 163
Decree on Public Safety, 148
de Gaulle, Charles, 17, 32, 72, 116–117, 124, 168
Delgado, Humberto, 47, 48, 159
Delzell, Charles F., 83, 103, 106
democracy, 16, 138, 139, 167
demonstrations, 85, 92
denationalization, 147–153
departees, exiles as, 13
diálogo Cuban (dialogue), 57, 150
diaspora:
  Chinese, 52
  demographic aspects of, 54
  Filipino, 52–53, 127
  German, 51
  Italian, 51
  Iwańska's analysis of, 52
  political definition of, 51–52
  Russian, 56, 62–70
  South Korean, 127
  Spanish, 70–76
  support of exile organizations by, 50–76, 127, 163
  Tibetan, 33
"Dictators' League," 126
diplomatic immunity, 113
diplomatic status, 114, 118
Dirección de Inteligencia Nacional (DINA), 160
Direzione Generale degli Italiani all'Estero, 51
displaced persons, exiles as, 13
Dni, 61, 63
Dolci, Gioacchino, 99
Dominican Republic, 84, 157, 160

Dominican Revolutionary Party (PRD), 157

Don Juan, King of Spain, 89–90

Dowty, Alan, 155

Duma, Russian, 89, 134–135, 154

Dutra, Eurico, 91

Eden, Anthony, 116

Edict of Nantes, 4

Edinger, Lewis J., 10, 23–24, 81–82

Egypt, 2

Eichenbaum, Jacob, 8

Eisenhower, Dwight D., 115

El Salvador, 126

emigrants, émigrés, 10–11, 15, 51, 53

"pushed" vs. "pulled," 8–9

England, see Great Britain

Eritreans, 58

Esclamado, Alex, 53

Estado Nôvo (Brazil), 91

Estonia, 114

état c'est moi, L', 3

Ethiopian war, 36, 103–107, 108, 133, 150

Etzioni, Amitai, 56–57

Exiled Governments (Iwańska), 52

exile organizations, 27–37

  accomplishments exaggerated by, 61, 112

  avoidance of collaboration by, 88

  charismatic leaders and, 36, 78–79, 108, 116–117

  civil organizations in support of, 111, 118, 122

  coalitions of, 28–29, 41–43, 47, 48–49, 62–63, 64, 95, 103

  competition of, 165

  counterexile strategies against, 145–162

  criteria of success in, 167–168

  decolonization, 16

  discrediting of, 146–147, 151, 153–155, 157, 158

  domestic communication with, 93–94, 97, 99, 146

  domestic opposition and, 77–109, 162

  financial support of, 63–64, 67, 118

  foreign intervention and, 46–49

  foreign support of, 85, 86, 110–129, 164–165

  fund-raising campaigns of, 30, 63–64, 67

  governmental, 40–41

  host governments and, 119–129

  ideology and, 36–37, 43–45, 77, 100, 162

  incentives for support of, 56–62, 118–119

  infiltration of, 147, 154–155

  insider-outsider relations in, 45–46, 77–109, 132, 163

  internal divisions in, 34–35, 38–41, 44–46, 78, 118, 153–154

  international recognition of, 110–129

  legitimacy of, 83–84, 116–117

  myths generated by, 126–129

  national memorial days proclaimed by, 60

  neutralization of, 90–91

  nongovernmental, 90

  political image and, 124–127, 132

  prestate self-determination, 16

  recognition of, see recognition, international

  reform, 15

  revolutionary, 15–16, 115, 118

  structure of, 77–78, 116

  symbolic activities of, 116

  territorial bases established by, 120, 123–124

  welfare and social agendas of, 31

  see also governments-in-exile; national exile committees; national fronts; national liberation movements; underground organizations

exiles:

  classifications of, 15, 52

  definitions of, 7–13, 15, 120

  foreign alliances and, 3–4, 46–49, 110–129

  groups vs. individual, 15

  homecoming of, 93–94, 146, 167–168

  honorable, 2

  ideal types of, 14

  legalistic vs. pragmatic, 41

  new citizenships acquired by, 152–153

  political activists as, 13–17

  range of commitment in, 15

  refugees vs., 10–11

  reprisals against, 122, 146, 157

revolutionary activities by, 1, 45–46, 71
revolutionary vs. reform, 15–16
symbolic definitions of, 14
as traitors, 138, 148–149, 150, 151, 165
wartime dilemmas of, 130–144
Exit, Voice, and Loyalty (Hirschman), 24
interpretation of, 173n32
expatriates, 10–11, 15

Fagen, Patricia W., 152
Fairchild, Henry P., 8
Falklands/Malvinas War, 131–132
Fascism:
  Central American "Dictators' League" and, 126
  in German invasion of Soviet Union, 142
  in Italy, 101–109, 149
  Rosselli on, 101, 102
Fascist Grand Council, 105
Federal Bureau of Investigation (FBI), 53
Ferdinand, King of Bulgaria, 65
feudal system, 3
Filipino exile organization, 1, 82, 90, 126–127, 147
Finland Station, 93
First Savoy Expedition, 107
Fischer, Louis, 38, 40, 154
five days of Milan, 100
Florence, 2, 98
France, 3–4, 68, 127, 159
  exiles in, 31, 35, 36, 42, 63, 65, 66, 91, 99, 100, 104, 109, 114, 121, 122–123
  Fourth Republic of, 168
  Iran and, 122–123, 131
  National Assembly of, 3
  Nazi occupation of, 17, 117, 139
  see also Vichy France
Franco, Francisco, 76, 107, 156–157
  coup d'état of, 107, 108
  opposition to, 42, 46, 70, 72, 73, 75, 79, 88, 89–90, 107–109, 121, 150
  support of, 107, 108, 121, 123, 127
freedom fighters, 13
Free French, 17, 116–117
French army, Revolutionary, 3

French Committee on National Liberation, 17, 116–117
French Political Police, 145
French Revolution, 3–4, 133, 147, 148
Frente Antitotalitária dos Portugueses Livres Exilados (FAPLE), 47
Frente Patriótica de Libertação Nacional (FPLN), 48
fuorusciti, 51, 149

Galtieri, Leopoldo, 131
Galvão, Henrique, 47
Garibaldi, Giuseppe, 4
Garibaldi Battalion, 108
Garosci, Aldo, 101
Geisel, Ernesto, 151
Gellner, Ernest, 20
General Bureau of Italians Abroad, 51
General Confederation of the Spanish Workers, 73
Geneva, 3, 34, 96, 148
Georgia, Soviet, 114
Georgian government-in-exile, 114
German Communist Party (KPD), 141–143
German Democratic Republic (East Germany), 78, 141, 143
German Federal Republic (West Germany), 141, 167
Germany, Nazi, 11, 34, 148
  allies of, 59, 136–138
  attempts to overthrow government of, 18, 75, 139, 142–143, 167
  governments deposed by, 114
  Propaganda Ministry of, 51
  Soviet campaign of, 41, 133, 136–138
  Soviet nonaggression pact with, 141, 158
Gestapo, 159
Gillies, William, 35, 140
Giovine Italia, La, see Young Italy
Giral, José, 75
Giustizia e Libertà, 101, 106, 107, 108
Glees, Anthony, 135, 167
Gobetti, Piero, 97–98
Goebbels, Joseph, 51
Goodwin-Gill, Guy S., 13
Göring, Hermann, 18
governments-in-exile, 60
  anti-Fascist, 16–17, 30

governments-in-exile *(continued)*
  dependence on patrons by, 115, 116, 129
  deposed governments as, 113–114
  diplomatic recognition of, 41, 57, 113–116
  exile organizations as, 114–116
  historical origins of, 30–31
  institutional structures of, 28, 31, 32, 116
  jurisdiction and authority of, 57, 116
  legitimacy of, 31–33, 75–76, 113, 114
  passports issued by, 152
  pre-exile authority of, 116
  taxes paid to, 30
  see also specific exile organizations
Govêrno Revolucionário de Angola no Exílio (GRAE), 115, 116
G.P.U., 69, 79, 155, 158
Graham-Yooll, Andrew, 23
Grau San Martín, Ramón, 157
Great Britain, 10, 125–126, 127
  diplomatic recognition by, 115, 116–117
  exiles in, 3–4, 10, 57, 71, 116–117, 134, 156, 159
  Falklands/Malvinas War of, 131–132
  French relations with, 156
  governments-in-exile in, 114, 116–117, 139–140
  Labour Party of, 35, 140
  restoration of monarchy in, 64
  Tory government in, 140
  War Office of, 117
Greece, 55, 114, 167
Greece (ancient), 1–2, 16
Grodzins, Morton, 60
Guatemala, 126, 157
Guelphs, 2
guerrilla warfare, 20, 155, 167
gusanos, 149

Hansen, Art, 8
Hassan II, King of Morocco, 157, 159
Hawaii, 16
Heidelberg, 53
hegemonic regimes, 83–88
Henry VIII, King of England, 3
Hervé, Gustave, 131
Herzen, Alexander, 50, 53, 96–97, 146

hijacking, 47
Hirschman, Albert O., 20–21, 24, 164
Hitler, Adolf, 51, 67, 95, 105, 121–122, 133, 138, 140
  attempted overthrow of, 18, 75, 139, 142–143, 167
Hoffman, Eva, 30
home nations:
  foreign occupation of, 17, 117, 139, 163
  home regimes vs., 25, 139–144
  sentimental vs. instrumental attachment for, 13–14
home regimes:
  confiscation of property by, 146
  countercampaigns by, 145–162
  demonstrations against, 85, 92
  dependence on international support by, 162
  hegemonic, 83–88
  home nations vs., 25, 139–144
  host governments relations with, 120–129, 133
  international criticism of, 146, 160, 162, 167
  legitimate vs. illegitimate, 166
  likelihood of counter-exile measures by, 161–162
  loyalty as seen by, 164–165
  mixed, 86–88
  nonrecognition of, 118
  persecution of exiles' families by, 146, 157
  repression by, 84, 94
  reprisals against exiles by, 122, 146, 157
  strife among exiles engendered by, 153–155, 164
  tolerated opposition in, 86–88, 162
  wars against, 130–144, 167
Honduras, 126
  Contra base in, 120, 123–124
honor, concepts of, 3
host governments:
  attacks by home regimes on, 120
  diplomatic pressure on, 155–157
  exile organizations and, 119–129
  home regimes at war with, 133
  home regimes relations with, 120–129
  impartiality of, 122

motives of, 118–119, 121–124
patterns of exile relations with, 121–124
rejection of exile organizations by, 123–124
states within states established in, 123–124
Hoxha, Enver, 125
Huguenots, 4
humanitarian organizations, 111, 118
human rights, 152, 157
Huntington, Samuel P., 27

identification papers, 152
ideology, 43–44
Idi Amin Dada, 111
illegal immigrants, 13
In Defense of Anarchism (Wolff), 1
India, 17
Indicatore Genovese, 95
In Exile (Brandt), 139
International Conference for the Defense of the Ethiopian People, 104
internationalism, radical, 20, 135
international recognition, *see* recognition, international
International Socialist Congress (1904), 134
Iran, 22, 168
    French relations with, 122–123, 131
    Islamic regime in, 38, 60, 85, 119, 122, 153
    opposition in, 84–85
Iranian Cultural Center (Paris), 160
Iranian exile organizations, 1, 38, 60, 84–85, 119, 122–123, 130–131, 160, 168
Iranian Revolutionary Guards, 85
Iranian secret police (SAVAK), 159–160
Iran-Iraq War, 130–131
Iraq, 54, 130–131
irredentists, 20
Iskra, 39
Islamic revolution, 1, 28, 153, 160
Israel (ancient), 2
    tribes of, 2
Italian exile organizations, 4, 16, 30, 36, 42–43, 94–109, 149
    see also anti-Fascism, Italian
Italy, 2, 42, 94–109, 114

Austrian rule of, 96, 98, 100
Communist Party (PCI) of, 83, 100, 103, 188n145
Republican Party of, 43
revolution of 1847–48 in, 96, 100
Socialist Party (PSI) of, 103, 105
Iwańska, Alicja, 52, 55, 152
izgnanie, 63

Jakson, Frank, 158
Japan, 133, 134–136
Jeroboam, King of Israel, 2
Jervis, Robert, 112, 124
Jews, German, 150
Johnston, Robert H., 136
Junta de Auxilio a los Refugiados Españoles (JARE), 58, 71
Junta Española de Liberación, 72–73, 74–75
Junta Suprema de Liberación Nacional, 73
Justice and Liberty, 30, 36, 42–43, 94, 95, 97–98, 99–104, 106–109, 187n116

Kadets, 63, 64, 69, 89
Karamanlis, Constantine, 167
Kashag, 33
Katayama, Sen, 134
Kelman, Herbert C., 13–14
Kerensky, Alexander, 61, 63–64, 65, 68, 69, 136
Khomeini, Ayatollah Ruhollah, 22, 28, 38, 153, 160, 168
    exile of, 54
    opposition to, 38, 60, 85, 119, 122, 130–131
kidnapping, 147, 157, 159, 160
Kim Dae Jung, 53, 79, 159
Kim Hyung Wook, 159
Koblenz, 3
Koestler, Arthur, 197n38
Kohn, Hans, 97
Korean Central Intelligence Agency (KCIA), 159
Korean Embassy-in-Exile, 79
Kremlin, 5
Krupskaya, N. K., 34
Kunz, Egon F., 8–9, 10, 11–12, 14
Kutepov, Paul Alexander, 69

labor unions, 118
Latvia, 114
Laval, Pierre, 104
law, international, 113, 114, 117–118
leaders, exile:
  assassination of, 20, 36, 85, 109, 147,
    157–160
  betrayal of, 156, 157
  charismatic, 36, 78–79, 108, 116–117
  execution of, 138, 156, 157
  kidnapping of, 147, 157, 159, 160
League of Nations, 104, 105–106, 152
Ledeen, Michael A., 21
Ledwidge, Bernard, 117
legitimacy, 22
  concept of, 165–166
  loyalty vs., 166
  Max Weber's sociology of, 28
Lehovich, Dimitry V., 66
Leighton, Bernardo, 160
Lenin, V. I., 5, 21–22, 34, 39–40, 134,
    142, 154–155
  on Duma, 89
  homecoming of, 93, 146
  political exile of, 64, 133–135
  Russo-Japanese conflict and, 134–136
Leonhard, Wolfgang, 142, 143
Lesotho, 122
Letelier, Orlando, 160
Lewis, Flora, 122
Lewis, Paul H., 44, 45, 82
liberalism, 100, 103
Liberation Front of Mozambique
    (FRELIMO), 44
libertà, 2
Libya, 85–86, 157, 160
  Foreign Liaison Bureau of, 160
Libyan exile organization, 85–86, 119,
    157, 160
Libyan General People's Congress (GPC),
    160
Life of Lenin, The (Fischer), 38
Liga de Instruccíon, La, 4
Linz, Juan J., 25, 86, 87, 88, 161
Lipari, 98–99
Lithuania, 114
Lodge, Tom, 110
London, 35, 44, 114, 115, 116–117, 156
López, Walter, 124
Los Angeles Times, 160

Louis XIV, King of France, 4
loyalty, 1–3
  building of, 18–19, 163
  exploitation of, 164, 165, 166
  home regimes' views of, 164–165
  legitimacy vs., 166
  national loyalty vs., 22
  national vs. international, 5
  pre-exile, 77–79
  recognition vs., 18, 163–164, 166
  state vs. factional, 3
  in war time, 130–144
Lublin Committee, 115
Lusaka, 80
Lussu, Emilio, 99, 108
Luxembourg, 114

McFarlane, Robert, 123–124
Machajski, Waclaw, 35
Madrid, 4
Magna Carta, 115
Malinovsky, Roman, 154–155
Malvinas, 131–132
Malyshkin, V. F., 138
Managua, 118
Manglapus, Raúl, 90
Marcondes Filho, Alexandre, 91
Marcos, Ferdinand, 1, 16, 53, 82, 90,
    127, 147
Marcum, John A., 46
Marian exiles, 3
Marie, Empress of Russia, 66–67
Marseilles, 96
Martí, José, 4
Martínez Barrio, Diego, 71, 73, 74, 75
Marx, Karl, 5
Marxism, 12, 100, 103, 149, 158
Mary, Queen of England, 3
Mazzini, Giuseppe, 4, 5, 16, 29, 43, 94–
    99
  imprisonment and exile of, 95–96
  leadership of, 96–97, 107
  principles of, 94–96, 98, 99, 107
Mazzinian Society, 101
Mensheviks, 40, 63, 89, 134, 136, 154–
    155
*Messenger of the Russian Monarchists'
    Union*, 67–68
Mexico, 156

Spanish refugees in, 30, 31, 32–33, 42, 56
Spanish Republicans recognized by, 35, 71, 113, 121, 152
Mexico City, 74, 75
Michael, Grand Duke, 66
Michels, Robert, 130
Milan, 100, 101
military juntas, 58, 71, 72–73, 74–75, 82, 167
Miliukov, Paul N., 63, 64, 69
Miller, Evgenii K., 69
Miller, Martin A., 15
mixed regimes, 86–88
monarchists:
　factionalism among, 64–76
　French, 3–4, 64
　Iranian, 38, 84–85, 160
　Russian, 16, 59, 64–70, 80, 137, 167
　Spanish, 70–76, 89–90
Morocco, 114, 157, 159
Moscow, 5, 133, 134, 141, 143
Movimento Nacional Independente (MNI), 47
Movimento Popular de Libertação de Angola (MPLA), 44, 47, 115
Mozambique, 44, 122
Mujahedeen National Council of Resistance (NCR), 38, 60, 119, 130–131
Münchener Neueste Nachrichten, 67
Munich agreement, 158
Mussolini, Benito, 51, 95, 100, 101, 123, 148, 154, 156
　Ethiopian campaign of, 36, 103–107, 108, 133
　fall of, 109
　Franco backed by, 107–108
　opposition to, 42, 44, 75, 83, 146
My Past and Thoughts (Herzen), 50

Nabokov, Vladimir, 11, 152
Nansen passports, 152
Napoleon III, Emperor of France, 145–146, 156
National Committee for Free Germany, 140, 142
national councils, 28–29, 60
national exile committees, 28–29, 60, 64, 116–118

National Front of the Salvation of Libya (NFSL), 157
national fronts, 28–29, 157
national interest, 20, 25, 172nn7, 10
nationalism, 5, 6, 20, 64, 131, 145
Nationalist China, 52
national liberation movements, 114–115
　collaboration of, 95
National Socialist Party, 67
National Union of Popular Forces, 159
nation-states, 1, 12, 20–23
　consolidation of power in, 3
　self-sufficiency of, 151
　symbolic nature of, 132
naturalization, 150, 152–153
Negrín, Juan, 58, 70–75, 80
Nenni, Pietro, 103
Netherlands, 114
New Beginning, 81
New Korea Democratic Party, 79
New Republic, 74
New York, N.Y., 4, 67
New York Times, 65, 67–68, 69, 70
Nicaragua, 55, 118, 120, 126, 151
Nicaraguan exile organizations, 118, 120, 123–124, 151
Nicholas, Grand Duke, 65–69
Nicholas I, Czar of Russia, 65
Nicholas II, Czar of Russia, 40, 56, 65, 66–67
Nitti, Francesco Fausto, 99
Noli me tangere (Rizal), 4–5
Nollau, Günther, 141
Nolte, Ernst, 187n116
Nomad, Max, 35
Non Mollare!, 98, 100
Norway, 114, 153
Norwegian government-in-exile, 29–30, 114
Nyerere, Julius, 111

October Revolution, 39, 46, 62
O'Donnell, Guillermo, 90
Okhrana, 154
Oliveira, Armando de Salles, 91
Oliver-Smith, Anthony, 8
Ollenhauer, Erich, 140
Omega 7, 57, 85
opposition:
　above ground vs. underground, 87

opposition (*continued*)
  exile vs. inside, 88–94
  under hegemonic systems, 84
  Linz on, 86
  under "mixed regimes," 86
  in wartime, 131–132, 143, 193n14
Organization of African Unity (OAU),
  111, 114, 115, 116
Organization of American States (OAS),
  111
Organization of Volunteers of the
  Repression of Anti-Fascism (OVRA),
  158–159
Ortega Saavedra, Daniel, 118
ostracism, 2, 63
Oufkir, Mohammed, 159

Pact of Punto Fijo, 87
Pahlavi, Mohammed Reza (Shah of Iran),
  22, 54, 159–160, 168
Pahlavi, Reza II, 38, 84–85
Pakistan, 58, 115, 120
Palencia, Isabel de, 70, 73–74
Palestine Liberation Organization (PLO),
  16, 128
Pan-Africanist Congress, 44, 81
Pandraud, Robert, 122–123
Papadopoulos, George, 55
Paraguay, 33, 82
Paraguayan Febrerista Revolutionary
  Party (PFR), 33, 60
Parini, Piero, 51
Paris, 35, 36, 42, 63, 91, 99, 100, 104,
  109, 121, 122–123
Parri, Ferruccio, 98, 100, 109
Partido Social Democrático (PSD), 91
Partido Trabalhista Brasileiro (PTB), 91
passports, 116, 149, 151–152
patriotism, 3, 130–144
Paulus, Friedrich von, 142–143
Peking, 52
people, concept of, 3
Pérez Jiménez, Marcos, 82, 85
Perez v. Brownell, 145
Perón, Juan, 78, 168
Peronistas, 131–132
personalismo, 70
Pétain, Henri Philippe, 117, 123, 156
Petersen, William, 8
Petrograd, 5

Philby, Kim, 125–126
Philippine News, 53
Piedmont, 97
Piedmontese Army, 96
Pinochet, Augusto, 35, 54, 93, 160
Plekhanov, Georgi, 134
pluralistic hegemony, 86–88
Poland, 33, 83, 114, 139
Policia Internacional de Defesa de Estado
  (PIDE), 48, 159
polis, 2, 3
Polish government-in-exile, 28, 29–30,
  33, 41, 81, 115, 116
Politburo, 138
political asylum, *see* asylum political
political image, 124–129
*Political Organizations in Changing So-
  cieties* (Huntington), 27
political parties, 118
Political Parties (Michels), 130
Popolo d'Italia, Il, 107
Popular Front, 120–121
Popular Movement for the Liberation of
  Angola (MPLA), 44, 47, 115
Populist Socialists, 63
Port Arthur, 134
Portugal, 47, 48
  Communist Party (PCP) of, 47
  1974 coup d'état in, 159
  secret police (PIDE) of, 48, 159
power, political:
  "God-ordained," 2
  secularization of, 3
Prague, 81
Prats Gonzáles, Carlos, 160
Pravda, 69
pre-exile organizations, 30–35
  loyalty at home and, 77–79
press, suspension of, 123
pretenders-to-the-throne:
  French, 3–4, 28, 64
  Iranian, 38, 84–85
  Russian, 28, 64–70, 136
Prieto, Indalecio, 58, 70–75, 89–90
prisoners of war, 137, 138
propaganda, 51, 53, 63, 67–68, 101, 105,
  122, 139, 146, 150
Propaganda Movement, 4
Protestantism, 3
Provisional Government, Milanese, 100

Prussia, 3, 133
Przeworsky, Adam, 166
Psinakis, Steve, 53

Qaddafi, Muammar al-, 85–86, 119, 157, 160
Qotbzadeh, Sadeq, 159
Quaderni di Giustizia e Libertà, 103
quasi-refugees, exiles as, 13

Rabat, 47
racism, 149–150
Raczynski, Edward, 30
radicalism, 3, 53
Radio Barcelona, 108–109
Rajavi, Masood, 38, 60, 122, 130–131, 160
Rechtsgemeinschaft, 148
recognition, international, 35, 110–129
    conditional nature of, 115
    de jure, 116
    of deposed governments, 113–114, 117
    of governments-in-exile, 41, 57, 113–116
    of national exile committees, 116–118
    limiting factors of, 117–118, 122
    withdrawal of, 115–116
    withholding of, 113, 115, 116–117
refoulement, 13
refugees, 9
    displaced, 12
    event alienated, 11
    exiles vs., 10–11
    integration realist, 11
    majority identified, 12
    passive hurt, 11–12
    political nomenclature for, 13
    political non-status of, 13, 152
    political vs. economic, 55–56
    psychiatric symptoms of, 12, 31
    self alienated, 11
    status of, 12–13
    statutory, 12
Refugee Scholars in America (Coser), 11
Rehoboam, King of Israel, 2
relief agencies, refugee, 118
religious organizations, 111, 118
revolution:
    American, 147
    Cuban, 9, 120

French, 3–4, 133, 147, 148
    Islamic, 1, 28, 153, 160
    religion-inspired, 3, 54
    Russian, 39, 46, 62
Rhineland, 3
Risorgimento, 16, 95, 97, 98, 99, 103
Rivoluzione Liberale, 97–98
Rizal, José, 4–5
Rodrigues, Félix García, 85
Rodríguez, Amiceto, 35
Roman Catholic Church, 3, 121
    monarchies and, 4
    Venezuelan, 88
Roman Empire, 148
Romanov family, 28, 64–70
Rome Agreement (1935), 104
Roosevelt, Franklin D., 138
Rose, Peter I., 11
Rosengarten, Frank, 95
Rosselli, Carlo, 30, 42–43, 95, 97–104, 107–109
    assassination of, 36, 109, 159
    imprisonment and escape of, 98–99
    political philosophy of, 94–95, 99–100, 103
    Spanish Civil War and, 107–109
    Swiss trial of, 101–102
Rosselli, Nello, 94, 95, 109, 159
Rosselli, Pellegrino, 94
Rossi, Ernesto, 100–101
Rousseau, Jean-Jacques, 148
Ruggiero, Guido de, 98
Russia, Imperial, 62–70, 154
    see also Soviet Union
Russian Armed Services Union (ROVS), 49, 66, 69
Russian Army of Liberation, 59, 136, 137–138
Russian exile organizations, 6, 59, 64–70, 80, 134–138, 167
    see also Bolsheviks
Russian Orthodox Church, 64
Russian Provisional Government, 35, 63, 65, 113–114
Russian Revolution, 39, 46, 62
Russian Social Democratic Labor Organization, 39–40, 63
Russo-Japanese conflict, 133, 134–136

Said, Edward W., 10

Salazar, Antonio de Oliveira, 1, 47, 48, 159
Salvemini, Gaetano, 98, 104, 109
Sandinistas, 118
San Francisco, Calif., 75
Santa Maria, 47
São Paulo, 47
Saragat, Giuseppe, 103
Savona, 95, 98
Schaar, John H., 22
Schmitter, Philippe C., 90
secessionists, 20
Second International, 5
Second Italian Risorgimento, 99
Second Savoy Expedition, 107
self-determination, national, 16, 114, 117, 163
Senate Committee on Governmental Affairs, U.S., 147
Servicio de Emigración para Repúblicanos Españoles (SERE), 58, 71
Seven Theses on the War (Lenin), 134
Shishak, King of Egypt, 2
Shishakli, Adib, 159
Shultz, George, 112
signoria, 2
Smouldering Freedom (Palencia), 70
Social Democratic Party, German (SPD), 18, 34, 81, 121, 122, 133, 139–141, 143, 167
social fascism, 105
Social Revolutionary Party, 61, 63, 69, 89
Socrates, 2, 98
Solidarity (Poland), 33, 83
Solomon, King of Israel, 2
Somoza García, Anastasio, 151
South Africa, 34, 44, 55, 80–81, 122
South Korea, 1, 53, 79, 92, 159
South Korean exile organizations, 1, 53, 79, 92, 126–127
South West Africa People's Organization (SWAPO), 128
Soviet Union, 5, 127
 annexations of states by, 114, 115
 Chinese relations with, 46
 counterrevolutionaries in, 10, 158
 exiles in, 10, 77–78, 133, 134
 Military Administration (SMA) of, 143

Nazi invasion of, 41, 133, 136–138, 142
Nazi nonaggression pact with, 141, 158
 repression in, 84, 158
 secret police of, 69, 79, 155, 158
 western governments relations with, 59, 68, 73, 115, 127
Soweto uprising, 80
Spain, 25, 46, 48, 79, 107–109, 123, 150
 authoritarian rule in, 86
 colonial rule by, 4
 coup d'état of 1936 in, 107, 108
 Socialist Party of, 35, 58
 strategic importance of, 127
Spanish Civil War, 56, 71, 95, 107–109
Spanish government-in-exile, 75–76, 81, 113, 157
Spanish Nationalists, 127
Spanish Republicans, 1, 16, 30, 31, 35, 42, 58, 62, 70–76, 80, 89–90, 123, 150, 167
 foreign support of, 95, 107–109, 113, 121, 127
SPD, *see* Social Democratic Party, German
Speier, Hans, 9
spies, 35, 125–126, 146, 154, 160, 161
Stalin, Joseph, 1, 10, 79, 105, 126, 133, 138, 142, 143, 158
Stalingrad, 142
Starn, Randolph, 14, 163
statelessness, 147–153, 164
Stein, Barry N., 9, 11
Stein, Louis, 71, 75–76, 127
Stepan, Alfred, 77
stowaways, exiles as, 13
Strik-Strikfeldt, Wilfried, 137
Stuart family, 64
students, foreign:
 Iranian, 54
 opposition activities by, 53–54, 111
 Russian, 53
 support of exiles by, 118
Sudan, 58
Sulzberger, C. L., 70
Supreme Monarchist Council, 64, 65
Swaziland, 122
Switzerland, 3, 53, 101–102, 135
symbols, 20, 60

of home regime vs. exiles, 61–62
Syria, 159

Tabori, Paul, 14
Taipei, 52
Taiwan, 52
Tambo, Oliver, 112
Tanzania, 122
Tanzanian army, 111
Teheran, 160
terrorism, 20, 57, 85, 119, 157, 160
Thayer, William Roscoe, 97
third-world countries, 114–115
Third World Quarterly, 110
Tibet, 17
    Chinese occupation of, 33
    General Assembly of, 33
Tiltman, Hugh Hessell, 158
Tito, Marshal (Josip Broz), 159
Tomasek, Robert D., 59
Toronto, 15
"Totalitarian and Authoritarian Re-
    gimes" (Linz), 161
travel, restrictions on, 54–55, 86, 123,
    151–152
treason, 138, 148–149, 150, 151, 165
Trotsky, Leon, 5, 158
Trotsky, Lyova, 158
Trotsky, Sergei, 158
Trotskyites, 158
Trujillo Molina, Rafael Leónidas, 84,
    157, 160
Trust, 79–80, 155
Tshokdhu Gyezom, 33
Turati, Filippo, 98
Turin, 97, 101, 103

Uganda, 111
Ugandan exile organizations, 111
Ukrainian government-in-exile, 46
Ukrainian National Council, 46
Ulam, Adam B., 93
Ulbricht, Walter, 143
Unamuno, Miguel, 132
underground organizations, 82–83, 84,
    97, 100
    above-ground opposition vs., 86–88
Union Nationale des Forces Populaires
    (UNFP), 159
Union of American Exiles (UAE), 15

Union of Soviet Socialist Republics, *see*
    Soviet Union
United Arab Republic, 114
United Nationalist Democratic Organi-
    zation (UNIDO), 90
United Nations (UN), 75, 85
    diplomatic recognition by, 73, 111, 128
    formation of, 73, 128
    General Assembly of, 128
    Security Council of, 128
United Nations High Commission for
    Refugees (UNHCR), 12–13
United States, 36, 52
    Congress of, 127
    Cuban exiles in, 1, 4, 9, 29, 37, 46,
        57, 115, 120, 125
    diplomatic recognition by, 114, 115,
        118
    Filipino exiles in, 82
    foreign interests of, 118, 119
    foreign intervention by, 29, 37, 125,
        157
    selective nonrecognition policy of, 118
    State Department of, 119, 126
Universal Declaration of Human Rights,
    12
Uruguay, 4

Vansittartism, 35
Vargas, Getúlio, 90–91
Venezuela, 35, 36, 47, 60, 85, 157
    redemocratization of, 82, 87–88, 168
Ver, Fabian, 147
Vichy France, 17, 117, 123, 156
Victor Emmanuel III, King of Italy, 95,
    98
Victoria Melita, Grand Duchess, 65, 67
Vietnam War, 15, 25
Vita, 30
Vladimir Kirillovitch, Prince, 65
Vlasov, Andrei Andreyevitch, 137–138
Vlasov Army, 59, 136, 137–138
Voci d'officina, 101
Vogel, Hans, 34, 139, 140, 141
Volk, 148, 149–150
Vperyodist Bolsheviks, 89

Walzer, Michael, 3
War Memoirs (de Gaulle), 124
Warsaw, 17, 115

wars of liberation, 5–6
Washington, D.C., 79
Weber, Max, 19, 28, 106–107, 108, 166
Wehrmacht, 137, 142
Weiner, Margery, 133
White Guelphs, 2
White Russian armies, 31, 65, 66, 67, 68
White Russians, 158
"Why I Took Up Arms against Bolshe-
    vism" (Vlasov), 137–138
Wilson, James Q., 39, 57
Wolff, Robert Paul, 1
work camps, 12
workers:
    emancipation of, 20
    solidarity of, 33, 83, 135–136
Workingmen's Association, 5
World Council of Churches, 111
World War I, 5, 53, 65, 131, 133, 148
World War II, 5, 10, 34, 35, 42, 59, 72,
    80, 91, 109, 158

governments-in-exile during, 16, 30,
    57, 114, 116–117, 139–140
Wrangel, Baron Peter N., 18, 49, 59, 66,
    68, 69
Wyden, Peter, 29

Yalta Conference (1945), 115
Yazdi, Ebrahim, 153
Young Europe, 5, 95, 107
Young Italy, 4, 16, 94, 96, 97, 99, 107
Young Poland, 4
Young Switzerland, 95, 107
Yugoslavia, 66, 114, 159
    secret police (UDBA) of, 159

Zaire, 115
Zambia, 112
Zimbabwe, 44, 122
Zimmermann, Ekkart, 165
Zimmerwald conference (1915), 135
Zinoviev, Gregory E., 40
Zolberg, Aristide R., 58

About the Author

YOSSI SHAIN is Professor of Government and Diaspora Politics at Georgetown University and Head of the School of Government at Tel Aviv University. He earned his B.A. and M.A degrees from Tel Aviv University and his Ph.D. from Yale University. He was previously Head of the Department of Political Science at Tel Aviv University, and held visiting appointments at Yale University, Wesleyan University, the Fletcher School of Law and Diplomacy, and Middlebury College. He was a Senior Fellow at St. Antony's College, Oxford, and a research fellow at the Woodrow Wilson Center of International Studies at Princeton University. Dr. Shain received many scholarly awards for his work on nationalism, ethnicity, and diaspora politics, including the American Political Science Association's Helen Dwight Reed Award for *The Frontier of Loyalty*. In addition to his many books, Dr. Shain is also the author of numerous articles in leading academic journals and other essays. He has given speeches throughout the world on ethnic and diaspora politics as well as on Middle Eastern affairs and has made frequent appearances in the media.

Printed and bound by CPI Group (UK) Ltd, Croydon, CR0 4YY

09/06/2025